Power and Politeness in the Workplace

A Sociolinguistic Analysis of Talk at Work

REAL LANGUAGE SERIES

General Editors:
JENNIFER COATES, University of Surrey, Roehampton

JENNY CHESHIRE, Queen Mary and Westfield College, University of London, and

EUAN REID, Institute of Education, University of London

Titles published in the series:

Norman Fairclough (Editor) Critical Language Awareness

James Milroy and Lesley Milroy (Editors) Real English: The Grammar of English Dialects in the British Isles

Mark Sebba London Jamaican: Language Systems in Interaction

Janet Holmes Women, Men and Politeness

Ben Rampton Crossing: Language and Ethnicity Among Adolescents

Brian V. Street Social Literacies: Critical Approaches to Literacy in Development, Ethnography and Education

Srikant Sarangi and Stefaan Slembrouck Language, Bureaucracy and Social Control

Ruth Wodak Disorders of Discourse

Victoria L. Bergvall, Janet M. Bing and Alice F. Freed (Editors) Rethinking Language and Gender Research: Theory and Practice

Anne Pauwels Women Changing Language

Monica Heller Linguistic Minorities and Modernity: A Sociolinguistic Ethnography

Alison Sealey Childly Language: Children, Language and the Social World

Power and Politeness in the Workplace

A Sociolinguistic Analysis of Talk at Work

Janet Holmes and Maria Stubbe

An imprint of **Pearson Education**

London · New York · Toronto · Sydney · Tokyo · Singapore · Hong Kong · Cape Town
Madrid · Paris · Amsterdam · Munich · Milan

Pearson Education Limited

Head Office:
Edinburgh Gate
Harlow CM20 2JE
Tel: +44 (0)1279 623623
Fax: +44 (0)1279 431059

London Office:
128 Long Acre
London WC2E 9AN
Tel: +44 (0)20 7447 2000
Fax: +44 (0)20 7447 2170
Website: www.pearsoneduc.com

First published in Great Britain in 2003

© Pearson Education Limited 2003

The rights of Janet Holmes and Maria Stubbe to be identified as Authors
of this Work has been asserted by them in accordance
with the Copyright, Designs and Patents Act 1988.

ISBN 0 582 36877 4

British Library Cataloguing in Publication Data
A CIP catalogue record for this book can be obtained from the British Library

Library of Congress Cataloging in Publication Data
A CIP catalog record for this book can be obtained from the Library of Congress

10   9   8   7   6   5   4   3   2   1

Typeset in 10/12pt Janson by Graphicraft Limited, Hong Kong
Printed and bound in Malaysia

The Publishers' policy is to use paper manufactured from sustainable forests.

Contents

Acknowledgements   vii

1 Power, Politeness and the Workplace Context   1
   Power, politeness and context   1
   Power   3
   Politeness   5
   Context   8
   The Wellington Language in the Workplace Project   12
   Brief outline of content of the book   14
   Notes   17

2 From Office to Production Line: Constructing a Corpus of
      Workplace Data   18
   Designing a method of collecting workplace data   19
   Collecting the data   20
   Conclusion   28
   Notes   30

3 Getting Things Done at Work   31
   Being direct downwards   33
   Mitigation and management between equals   40
   Getting the boss to cooperate – requests and indirectives   43
   Hints   50
   Conclusion   53
   Notes   54

4 Workplace Meetings   56
   Introduction   56
   Types of meetings   59
   How are meetings structured?   65

Managing interaction in meetings   71
Doing power and politeness in meetings: two case studies   78
Conclusion   85
Notes   86

5   Small Talk and Social Chat at Work   87
    The distribution of social talk in the workplace   89
    Social functions of non-task-oriented talk at work   96
    Conclusion   106
    Notes   107

6   Humour in the Workplace   109
    Functions of humour in the workplace   110
    Humour and workplace culture   122
    Conclusion   134
    Notes   135

7   Miscommunication and Problematic Talk at Work   137
    Miscommunication   139
    Negotiating with the boss   144
    Negotiating 'downwards'   148
    Problems, power and partnership   154
    Conclusion   162
    Notes   163

8   Conclusion: Some Implications and Applications   164
    Introduction   164
    Getting integrated at work   165
    Reflection as a learning strategy for the workplace   172
    Conclusion   176
    Notes   180

    Appendix: Transcription Conventions   181
    References   182
    Index   192

Acknowledgements

While this book is based primarily on research done by the authors in their roles as Director and Research Fellow in the Wellington Language in the Workplace (LWP) Project, it also draws on the published and, in some cases, as yet unpublished research of several other members of the LWP team. This work is specifically acknowledged in the text and in the references, but the LWP Project's collaborative approach means our debt to others in the research team remains a large one. Any errors or infelicities are on the other hand entirely our responsibility.

We would particularly like to thank the two other members of the core research team for their invaluable contribution to the production of this book and the research on which it is based. Bernadette Vine, in her role as corpus manager, has been closely involved in the processing, transcription and archiving of the project data from the earliest stages of the Project, and helped research some of the topics covered in this book, especially Chapter 3. Meredith Marra, a research officer with the Project, was a co-researcher for several of the topics covered in this book, especially Chapters 4 and 6, and also competently gathered together the reference list and formatted the many examples and excerpts from transcripts we have included.

We also wish to acknowledge the important contributions of the many other individuals who participated in the construction of the unique LWP data set, critiqued our analyses, or debated the various theoretical frameworks on which the research presented in this book is based.

First and foremost, we would like to express our appreciation to the workplace volunteers who did the actual recording, or allowed their workplace interactions to be recorded, and who gave so generously of their time to provide us with ethnographic information and feedback on our analyses.

Thanks are due next to several Research Associates of the LWP Project. They include Harima Fraser and Frances Austin who facilitated our entrée into the two workplaces where we first piloted our research methodology, and have continued to provide us with feedback on our analyses from their perspectives as workplace practitioners. Rose Fillary collected and helped analyse data from the small businesses employing students with intellectual disability, and Pascal Brown collected and analysed the data from an Auckland factory.

Deborah Jones has contributed her expertise in organisational communication to the design and piloting of a communication evaluation and development model which provides a way of helping people in workplaces to apply the research findings presented here. We have also had valuable input from our other colleagues in the School of Linguistics and Applied Language Studies, especially Chris Lane who provided useful methodological advice, and has helped supervise three doctoral projects using LWP data, Mary Roberts who collected data on the ESL provisions at one of the factories, and Derek Wallace who has challenged us to explore the relationship between spoken interaction and electronic and written modes of workplace communication.

Over the past seven years, we have also been fortunate to have on board a number of very enthusiastic and competent research assistants, who have helped us to collect, catalogue, transcribe and analyse the data. They include Megan Ingle, our fieldworker in the government workplaces and the Wellington factory, who often went beyond the call of duty in collecting the data recorded at these sites, and Louise Burns who, as well as being a skilled transcriber and proofreader, also helped analyse several of the data subsets referred to in this book. Thanks are also due to the many other research assistants who have persevered with the often tedious task of transcription and provided various kinds of administrative support: Melanee Beatson, Katie Brannan, Tim Brown, Jacqui Burnett, Sasha Calhoun, Fleur Findlay, Robert Holmes, Kate Kilkenny, Diane McConnell, Emily Major, George Major, Antonia Mann, Fiona Mann, Shannon Marra, Martin Paviour-Smith, Bobby Semau, Rowan Shoemark, Clare Solon, Michaela Stirling, Ben Taylor.

The Project has also had outstanding technical support from Mark Chadwick, who helped set up and streamline our computerised databases, and Richard Keenan from the Language Learning Centre who offers his skills with audio and video equipment.

Finally, we express a huge debt of appreciation to our families who provided support and encouragement throughout this project: to Tony, Rob and David Holmes, and Mike, Johanna and Lindsay Freeman, a sincere and heartfelt 'thank you'.

The research for this book has been supported by grants from the New Zealand Foundation for Research, Science and Technology since the Project commenced in 1996, as well as by internal research grants from Victoria University.

Sources

To reduce the amount of repetition in the text, we here identify contributing sources of material in different chapters where it has been previously published by the authors.

Chapter 1 draws on Holmes, Stubbe and Vine (1999); Holmes (2000a); Holmes and Stubbe (2001); Holmes and Stubbe (2003).

Chapter 2 draws on Stubbe (1998a, 2000, 2001); Holmes (2000a).

Chapter 3 draws on Stubbe (1998b, 1999a, 2000); Holmes, Stubbe and Vine (1999); Holmes (2000b); Stubbe and Holmes (2000).

Chapter 4 draws on Holmes (2000b); Holmes and Stubbe (2001); Stubbe (2003).

Chapter 5 draws on Holmes (1997); Holmes, Stubbe and Vine (1999); Holmes (2000c).

Chapter 6 draws on Stubbe (1999a, 1999b, 2000); Holmes (2000d); Holmes, Marra and Burns (2001); Holmes and Stubbe (2001); Holmes and Marra (2002); Holmes and Marra (ip); Holmes and Stubbe (2003).

Chapter 7 draws on Stubbe (1998b, 1999a, (fc)); Holmes, Stubbe and Vine (1999); Stubbe and Holmes (2000); Holmes and Stubbe (2001).

Chapter 8 draws on Holmes (1999); Stubbe (1999a, 2000); Holmes and Fillary (2000); Holmes, Fillary, McLeod and Stubbe (2000); Jones and Stubbe (fc).

1

Power, Politeness and the Workplace Context

Power, politeness and context

This book explores the complex and fascinating relationship between power and politeness in the workplace. Our focus is workplace discourse and we examine how people 'do' power and politeness throughout the day in their talk at work. A good starting point for our exploration is the following brief excerpt taken from a meeting of a project team in a multinational organisation (Example 1.1).

Example 1.1
Context: Regular weekly meeting of project team in white-collar, commercial organisation.[1]

```
1  HAR:   look's like there's been actually a request for screendumps
2         I know it was outside of the scope
3         but people will be pretty worried about it
4  CLA:   no screendumps
5  MATT:  we-
6  CLA:   no screendumps
7  PEG:   [sarcastically] thank you Clara
8  CLA:   /no screendumps\
9  MATT:  /we know\we know you didn't want them and we um er/we've\
10 CLA:   /that does not\ meet the criteria
          [several reasons provided why screendumps should be allowed]
11 CLA:   thanks for looking at that though
12 SAN:   so that's a clear well maybe no
13 CLA:   it's a no
14 SAN:   it's a no a royal no
15 CLA:   did people feel disempowered by that decision
16 PEG:   [sarcastically] no
```

This excerpt, taken from the middle of the team's meeting, provides a useful means of introducing some of the main themes of this book. First, it is very difficult to understand without substantial glossing. Second, it illustrates a very blunt and explicit exercise of power and authority, and an apparent disregard of the norms of conventional politeness. Third, it demonstrates the kinds of things people achieve with words at work: giving instructions, disagreeing with and challenging each other, avoiding miscommunication, amusing their colleagues, maintaining good collegial relations, and so on. We will briefly discuss these points in this chapter, but they will also recur regularly throughout the book.

In the meeting from which Example 1.1 is taken, a project team is discussing how best to provide instructions to other members of their organisation about a specialised computer process. The group has been meeting for several weeks and has developed very good rapport and a sparky style of interaction. Example 1.1 revolves around a request to allow people to print off material from the computer screen (i.e. to 'screendump'). Clara is the overall manager of the section from which most of this project team has been selected; Sandy is the project manager. With this background it is easier to understand the referential content of the excerpt: Clara is giving a very clear directive that under no circumstances will people be allowed to print material from their screens.

A great deal of workplace talk is firmly embedded in its social and organisational context in this way. Co-workers typically take a great deal for granted; they share common assumptions, a common reference system, and use the same jargon or system of verbal shortcuts. They often share extensive background knowledge and experiences and may have similar values and attitudes towards work and the objectives of their organisation. Together these constitute a common workplace culture. Indeed, many workplace groups, such as those interacting in Example 1.1, could be described as 'communities of practice' – groups who regularly engage with each other in the service of a joint enterprise, and who share a repertoire of resources which enables them to communicate in a kind of verbal shorthand which is often difficult for outsiders to penetrate (Wenger 1998). The community of practice is a concept which illuminates a number of aspects of workplace interaction.

Example 1.1 is also a very clear instance of 'doing power' at work. Clara is the most senior person at the meeting and her uncompromising, explicit and repeated directive *no screendumps* (lines 4, 6, 8) reflects her status in the organisational hierarchy. No one else in this meeting, not even Sandy, the project manager, could acceptably express themselves in such an uncompromisingly direct manner, except perhaps with humorous intent (see Chapter 6). Clara is here doing power very explicitly and baldly, apparently disregarding conventionally polite ways of disagreeing with her colleagues.

On the other hand, the team's well-established rapport and its in-group solidarity mechanisms enable them to 'manage' Clara's peremptory veto in a way that preserves good working relations. Peggy's sarcastic *thank you Clara* (line 7) provides an initial tension-breaker. Members of the team then provide reasons for allowing screendumps, and Clara responds (line 11) with a more conventionally polite dismissal of their suggestions *thanks for looking at that though*. Sandy's internally contradictory suggestion that Clara may be wavering *so that's a clear well maybe no* (line 12) is deliberately humorous, but it leads Clara to restate her position quite explicitly *it's a no* (line 13). Again Sandy defuses the tension with a humorous hyperbolic comment *it's a no a royal no* (line 14), echoing a reference to an earlier episode in which Clara's status had been satirised as *queen*. Finally, Clara too contributes to the defusing of the tension with a tongue-in-cheek comment which draws explicit attention to feelings which people usually conceal in a business context *did people feel disempowered by that decision* (line 15). The team's firmly established good relationships thus enable them to ride out Clara's 'bald-on-record' directives, without irreparable damage to the 'face needs' of team members.[2]

This short excerpt illustrates nicely the ongoing negotiations between power and politeness which are typical of interactions in many workplaces. Effective management of workplace relationships takes account of the face needs of colleagues, as well as the objectives of the organisation and the individuals involved. Before describing the database used in the analyses of workplace interaction in this book, we will briefly discuss the concepts of power, politeness and context which underpin the analyses, and in the process introduce the theoretical frameworks we have found useful.

Power

There are many ways of defining power. From a sociological or psychological perspective, power is treated as a relative concept which includes both the ability to control others and the ability to accomplish one's goals. This is manifest in the degree to which one person or group can impose their plans and evaluations at the expense of others.[3] A more anthropological and social constructionist perspective extends this potential influence to embrace definitions of social reality (Gal 1995). Language is clearly a crucial means of enacting power, and equally a very important component in the construction of social reality. A social constructionist approach analyses every interaction as involving people enacting, reproducing and sometimes resisting institutional power relationships in their use of discourse by means of a range of coercive and collaborative strategies (e.g. Crawford 1995; Davies 1991; Dwyer 1993; Fairclough 1989; Ianello 1992).

Power in the workplace may be manifested in a number of ways. In Example 1.1, Clara's authoritative position enabled her to define the rules which others were obliged to follow. But the linguistic manifestation of power need not be so blatant. In Example 1.2, a government organisation is discussing an issue which is a current hot topic in many New Zealand workplaces, namely the extent to which employees' access to the internet should be monitored and, in particular, the organisation's responsibilities and liability in cases where employees gain access to pornography through their workplace internet connections.

Example 1.2

Context: Regular meeting of senior management team in white collar organisation.

```
 1 SAL:  it's all too woolly I think in regards values violations
 2       I'm more likely to come down on someone strongly and thumpingly
 3       for a personal values violation than a minor rules valuation
 4 GEO:  what I said in the beginning was it all depends where you sit
 5       in other words whether you think that's a values violation /and =
 6 SAL:  /well I guess that depends on what they are\
 7 GEO:  = that's I mean\ as I said you know
 8 SAL:  but if it's the bestiality issue
 9 ROB:  oh yeah
10 SAL:  something which is at the edge of the law there's the legal side
11 ROB:  bestiality is not at the edge of the law it's absolutely black and white
12       illegal
```

The excerpt illustrates Sally and Georgia exploring the issue of what the legislation means and how it should or could be interpreted (lines 1–7). Sally then introduces a specific issue, *the bestiality issue* (line 8) at which point Robin enters the discussion, following up her sceptical *oh yeah* (line 9), with an assertive and decisive pronouncement (lines 11–12) which effectively ends that particular line of discussion. Robin's words are influential not because she has higher status or authority than others involved in the discussion (she does not), but rather because this issue involves her area of expertise and responsibility. Robin's contribution makes it clear that the discussion (lines 1–7) between Sally and Georgia about whether or not personal values are involved, is irrelevant, and the chair brings the whole discussion to a conclusion shortly afterwards. This is 'expert' power in operation (Spencer-Oatey 1992, 2000; Thomas 1995). Although Sally and Georgia are superior to Robin in the organisation's status hierarchy, in this area she has the power to define the situation and influence the decision reached. The example illustrates clearly that status is not the only source of power. Relative power needs to be assessed not only in the particular social context in which an interaction takes place, but more particularly in the specific discourse context of any contribution. As Example 1.2 illustrates, the particular topic of discussion may be relevant in identifying where power or authority lies in a particular section of talk, as well as how it is enacted.

Another dimension of power in the workplace is brought into focus by a Critical Discourse Analysis (CDA) approach (e.g. Fairclough 1995; van Dijk 1998). A CDA framework characterises the power of those in authority as 'oppressive' or 'repressive' (Pateman 1980; Fairclough 1995), and focuses on ways in which it is, often subtly, exerted in discourse, both spoken and written (e.g. see Lee 1992; Talbot 1998). Critical Discourse analysts demonstrate that the definitions, values, and attitudes assumed by most speakers and writers are typically those of the group in power; hence the dominant ideology in a society generally underpins apparently 'objective' descriptions. Taken for granted assumptions tend to go unquestioned, but they are often a means of repressing challenges and inhibiting change, and language clearly plays an important part in encoding (or masking) such assumptions. It is easy to see how Examples 1.1 and 1.2 could be analysed in these terms, i.e. as examples of 'coercive discourse' (Fairclough 1995). In both cases, the enactment of power through talk is relatively explicit, and there is no doubt about whose 'rules' and 'values' are assumed to be relevant. Moreover, in both cases the effect of the contributions of those with the relevant power is to bring the discussion to an end. Because a CDA approach typically adopts the perspective of those 'out of power', it provides interesting insights into what is taken for granted by those in positions of power.

Politeness

While power may license the use of relatively overt 'coercive' discourse strategies, our analyses indicate that most workplace interactions provide evidence of mutual respect and concern for the feelings or face needs of others, that is, of politeness. Politeness is one important reason for modifying the blatant imposition of one's wishes on others (Goffman 1967; Brown and Levinson 1987). Example 1.3 illustrates some of the ways in which this may be linguistically manifested. The extract is taken from a team meeting devoted to allocating responsibilities for a range of tasks, including departmental filing which has got severely behind. One solution, proposed by the manager, Leila, is to bring in external filers, 'the flying filers'. However, a relatively senior team member, Zoe, is not happy with this suggestion, and she raises a variety of objections. Leila could simply insist on her solution, but she does not. Rather, as illustrated in Example 1.3, she explicitly responds to each of Zoe's reservations, and she phrases her responses in ways which pay attention to Zoe's face needs.

Example 1.3

Context: Planning meeting of policy unit team in white-collar, commercial organisation.

1 LEI: I think that Kerry and Zoe could do with having a little sit down
2   and just talking through about the fly-
3   whether or not to get the flying filers in to replace Kerry or not
4   and if you got the flying filers in Kerry could come and help with the
5   information but I think you need to work that through it's gonna be +
6   you know what will work +++
7   cos I mean I think you've got a wee bit of a difference here
8   in that you're obviously a little bit uncomfortable about a new set of
9   people and I can understand that because you're thinking consistency

While Leila restates the advantages of her suggestion (line 4), she clearly does not intend to force Zoe to agree to it (lines 1–3). Rather, she indicates that she understands Zoe's reservations by restating them in a sympathetic way (lines 8–9). Concern for Zoe's feelings is also evident in the extensive use of linguistic hedging devices throughout this excerpt.[4] These include pragmatic particles such as *I think* (lines 1, 5, 7), *you know* (line 6), and *I mean* (7), which tone down the strength of Leila's directive, and attenuators such as *little* (line 1), *a wee bit of* (line 7) and *a little bit* (line 8) which minimise the problematic aspects of the disagreement.

Politeness towards a subordinate can be interpreted as an indication that the more powerful protagonist is concerned with constructing good workplace relations, and in developing rapport and maintaining collegiality (Spencer-Oatey 2000): that is, the expression of collaborative power vs coercive power or, in Ng and Bradac's terms 'power to' vs 'power over' (1993: 4).

Communication Accommodation theory provides a useful framework to account for linguistic and non-linguistic adjustments between participants in an interaction in order to maintain good social relations (Giles, Coupland and Coupland 1991). As the theory suggests, however, politeness may also be politic, since treating others with consideration is more likely to result in the cooperation which will assist in achieving workplace goals (see also Watts 1992; Eelen 2001).

By contrast, it is self-evidently in the interests of a subordinate to express themselves politely or with deference to a superior. Our data provides a multitude of examples illustrating deferential politeness.[5] Example 1.4 is a particularly clear example of the contrast between the pressures on superior and subordinate, especially when the subordinate is the supplicant. Kerry has obtained a position with a different organisation. Before she leaves her current job, however, she wishes to attend a conference without having her pay docked. This information very gradually emerges in the course of an interview with her acting manager, Ruth. The excerpt in Example 1.4 illustrates Kerry's extensive use of deferential politeness and hesitation devices (in bold) to hedge her request, which contrast with Ruth's very direct and unmitigated demands for information (lines 1, 6, 8, 16).

Example 1.4
Context: Manager in government organisation discussing leave application with employee.

```
 1 RUTH:  when do you finish here
 2 KER:   well I'm not sure- [voc] well my contract goes till April but
 3        [the new organisation] rung me today and they're trying to negotiate
 4        sort of me to go over there and Jamie to come over here
 5        and just do a swap while we change over to train each . . .
 6 RUTH:  okay when do you need to make a decision
 7 KER:   well um /Re- + Re-\
 8 RUTH:  /you need to confirm\ today do you
 9 KER:   well Rene's sort of um + doing some negotiations
10        with some people this afternoon about our funding . . .
11        and it's just that I'd I said to them not to worry about it
12        cos it + you know I was changing over and it was gonna be quite
13        difficult time off and da da da da things like this
14        but she said oh no you should go if you can get it
15        so she /said just ask\
16 RUTH:  /mm\ . . . okay so you need to know today
```

Ruth, in the position of authority, uses direct questions to elicit the information she needs to reach a decision. In this context, she does not need to be polite. Kerry is clearly aware that her request could be regarded as unreasonable; she uses a wide range of strategies to minimise its apparent cost and reduce its force, including, finally, even shifting responsibility for making it (lines 14–15). Deference is the mirror image or underside of power.

Not all workplace colleagues are respectful and cooperative, however; there are many alternative responses to authority. Critical Discourse analysts draw attention to ways in which people may challenge, contest, undermine or subvert power and authority. In the data we examined, we found that challenges to authority were typically expressed not with direct and confrontational strategies, but rather in socially acceptable or 'polite' ways, such as through the use of humour, including irony and sarcasm. Humour functions as a particularly effective politeness strategy, especially in a hierarchical context, as demonstrated in Chapter 6. It is very difficult for a superior to react negatively to a criticism or challenge that is expressed as a humorous comment without losing face. Humour provides a 'cover' for a remark which might otherwise be considered unacceptable in the work context. Example 1.5 illustrates a subordinate, Ivan, using humour to negotiate the complexities of contesting a superior in a polite and cooperative way.

Example 1.5
Context: Meeting between three policy advisors in a government organisation.

1 EST: you were supposed to bring coffee and he was bringing croissants
2 IVAN: was he
3 EST: yeah we had this discussion last week
4 IVAN: ah you should have got it in writing
         [laughter]

Ivan's remark is an example of good-humoured sarcasm. At the most global level, he is sending up bureaucratic procedures generally. At the local level, he is also parodying Esther, in particular, who is inclined to want everything well documented. In other words, using a CDA approach, this could be analysed as contestive discourse from a subordinate to a superior. From another perspective, however, Ivan's remark could be analysed as a good-tempered response to a criticism: i.e. a cooperative attempt to amuse, to keep the tone light and maintain good collegial relations. This analysis is typical in its complexity – almost every example of authentic discourse has several layers of meaning and yields different insights depending on the analytical framework adopted.

Context

The examples discussed so far have illustrated that analysing ways in which power and politeness are played out in the workplace requires careful attention to context. Moreover, the term 'context' applies at a number of different levels of analysis. The most local context of any utterance is the immediate discourse context. The precise location of an utterance in relation to preceding and following utterances may be crucial to interpreting its precise meaning. So, for example, an agreeing *yes* at the end of a long discussion in which one participant is trying to persuade another to approve a particular course of action, has very different significance from a quick *yes* in a series indicating routine approval. The interpretation of Clara's directive *no screendumps* in Example 1.1 required attention to its position in the discourse: her utterance gathers weight with each reiteration, as reflected in the efforts of other participants to defuse the tension by ameliorating Clara's message with humour. Attention to the discourse context underpins all discourse analysis, but it is developed to a very high level of specificity by conversation analysts (e.g. Psathas 1995; Pomerantz and Fehr 1997; Hutchby and Wooffitt 1998), and we draw on such techniques where appropriate in the analyses in this book.

A second relevant level of contextual analysis requires attention to the relationships between those contributing to the interaction: what are their relative roles, where do they fit in the organisational hierarchy, how long have they worked together, and so on. While such relationships often appear 'given', a social constructionist approach emphasises the extent to which participants are constantly constructing their social roles as they interact with others. Clara is 'doing power' in Example 1.1, and in the process reaffirming her role as manager. In different social contexts, people tend to emphasise different aspects of their social identity. In Example 1.2, Robin's influence depends on the fact that her specialised role in the organisation becomes relevant at that particular point in the discussion. In Example 1.3, Leila uses linguistic features and discourse devices which understate her power, and emphasise collegiality and even femininity. In other contexts, with different colleagues, she highlights different aspects of her complex social identity.[6] Similarly, the deferent Kerry in Example 1.4 is likely to be considerably more assertive in describing this interaction to a friend over lunch. Attention to the social relationships between participants is a fundamental aspect of the sociolinguistic analysis of social interaction, and is a crucial element in the analysis of workplace interaction throughout this book.

Taking account of context also involves considering factors such as the physical setting in which interactions take place, and the background knowledge participants bring to the interaction. Talk in the boardroom of a large commercial organisation has interesting similarities and differences to talk between factory team members on the factory floor. The social banter which precedes meetings in each of these settings, for instance, has much the same range of functions (see Chapter 6), while the ways in which the team leader conveys instructions contrasts markedly in the different settings (see Chapter 3). Typically, in order to comprehend the succinct shorthand and often technical jargon used by those who habitually work together, detailed background information must be gathered, using the kinds of ethnographic techniques advocated both by interactionist sociolinguists (e.g. Gumperz 1982, 1999; Roberts, Davies and Jupp 1992) and by those adopting a community of practice framework (e.g. Eckert and McConnell-Ginet 1995; Eckert 2000). Such information is crucial in helping the analyst to unpack the layers of meaning and interpret the significance of work-place talk. Reading Example 1.6 with minimal background information helps illustrate this point.

Example 1.6
Context: Early morning team briefing meeting on factory floor. Ginette is team manager.

```
 1 GIN:  they put [product] twelve point five on the running sheet
 2       we do two sizes at twelve point five boxes and bags
 3       when youse do these sheets do them properly [sighs]
 4 MAR:  obviously those people who are no good at cheating [voc]
 5 GIN:  fill them out properly
 6       I spent two hours yesterday with Isabelle going through the sheets
 7       over the last um month and a half
 8       and the ones that we did were bloody shocking all bullshit
 9       we managed to pack nearly six thousand cases on this line here
10       in three and a half hours
         [laughter]
11 SAM:  do the do the temps know how to fill them out
12 GIN:  I don't know no they don't
13 SAM:  no ( )
14 GIN:  the temps weren't here at three o clock four o clock
15 SAM:  yeah I know I'm j- I'm just saying it could be
16 GIN:  that's our people
```

Some of the interactional complexities of the issue referred to in this example will be discussed in Chapter 7. Here we simply draw attention to the extent to which meaning is embedded in context, and the crucial status of shared background knowledge in comprehending what is going on. Detailed ethnographic information is essential to any meaningful analysis. Understanding Ginette's message involves, at the minimum, knowing what should be recorded on the sheets she refers to and what would be an expected number of cases. The fact that *line* refers to the factory line on which the team work, and that *temps* refer to people brought in to assist in physical handling of the cases, is also useful information. It helps to know the significance of the difference between *boxes*, *bags* and *crates*, and the significance of the different sizes referred to, as well as the relative status of different contributers. This brief illustration indicates that rich ethnographic description is clearly an essential analytical tool for providing the contextual information required to understand much workplace talk.

Finally, it is also important to consider the social meaning of discourse in an even wider social context. Any interaction can be regarded as a particular instance of more general sociolinguistic patterns. So, at the institutional level, the range of appropriate strategies for instantiating power relations will be constrained by the dominant ideology and the values it encodes. The interaction between Ruth and Kerry, for instance, from which the excerpt in Example 1.4 was taken, represents one means of negotiating a potentially contentious work issue in a New Zealand organisation. The interaction as a whole provides an instance of how institutional power is exercised and deference expressed in such contexts. The long discussion from which Example 1.3 is taken (to which we return in Chapter 4), illustrates an alternative strategy: Leila gives collegial relations high priority and adopts a more consensual approach to decision making. Example 1.6 exemplifies yet another approach. Ginette, the factory manager is direct and explicit in her instructions (lines 3, 5) and reprimands (line 8), leavened only by some dry humour (lines 9, 10). Her language is forthright and she directly challenges attempts to provide excuses with counter-evidence (lines 14, 16). To what extent are these different ways of doing power influenced by the institutional or wider societal context within which they occur? To what extent are they instantiations of a particular ideological framework which encodes particular attitudes to authority and specific values regarding workplace activity? These broader contextual issues raised by a CDA framework can be regarded as underpinning any sociolinguistic analysis.

Clearly, it is possible to analyse workplace interaction at many levels, each of which highlights different aspects of the many kinds of meaning constructed by workplace participants. The starting point for the exploration of workplace interaction in this book is a broadly social constructionist model of communication which rests on two broad assumptions, now generally accepted in discourse and interactional sociolinguistics. The first, as we have outlined above, is that an understanding of the wider context is crucial, both for interpreting the discourse at a local level, and for defining social identity or 'who we are' in any particular encounter. Workplace interactions in particular tend to be strongly intertextual in nature, and are embedded in the business and social context of a particular work group, as well as in a wider social or institutional order.

Our second assumption is that interaction and identity construction are dynamic interactional processes where meanings and intentions are jointly and progressively negotiated between the individuals involved in a given interaction. In the words of Linell:

> What is apparent when we take a close analytic look at the practice of actual interaction among real persons is that both the persons and the situations in which they interact are never fully determined. They are continually in production, under construction, through the boot-strapping processes of contextualisation, shifts in footing, and adaptation by interlocutors to each other's actions.
>
> (Linell 2001: 160)

A social constructionist approach, then, frames communication as a process which is instrumental in the creation of our social worlds, rather than simply as an activity that we do within them. It emphasises the dynamic aspects of interaction and the constantly changing and developing nature of social identities, social categories and group boundaries (Weedon 1987; Unger 1989; Butler 1990), a process in which talk clearly plays an essential part. Social constructionism is also basic to the notion of the 'community of practice' (Wenger 1998), a model which we have found particularly valuable in comparing and contrasting how power and politeness are played out in different organisations or work teams.

By taking a 'bottom-up' approach and looking closely at the micro-level of individual workplace interactions, it is possible to see how what Goffman (1974) terms the 'interaction order' intersects with institutionally ordered social relationships (Cook-Gumperz 2001: 119–20), including those traditionally analysed by sociolinguists in terms of social categories such as gender, ethnicity and status.

The rest of this chapter describes the broader project from which the material analysed in this book is drawn, and then briefly outlines the structure of the book.

The Wellington Language in the Workplace Project

The data used to illustrate the analyses in this book was collected as part of the Language in the Workplace (LWP) Project, based at Victoria University of Wellington in New Zealand.[7] The broad objectives of the project are to identify characteristics of effective communication in New Zealand workplaces, to identify causes of miscommunication, and to disseminate the results of the analysis for the benefit of workplace practitioners. Despite the recent growth of interest in workplace interaction,[8] there has been remarkably little New Zealand research focused on how people actually communicate verbally with their colleagues at work on a daily basis, and how they use language to manage the inevitable tensions between their various professional and social roles. At the time of writing, our database comprises approximately 2000 interactions recorded in a wide range of New Zealand workplaces, including government departments, factories, small businesses, semi-public or non-government organisations (NGOs), and private, commercial organisations (see Figure 1.1). This corpus deliberately includes interactions from some workplaces with a relatively high proportion of women, some with a relatively high proportion of Maori workers, and a number with an ethnic and gender balance more closely reflecting the New Zealand norm.[9] The interactions include both business talk and social talk, informal talk and meetings of many different sizes and kinds, with participants from a wide range of different levels in the workplace hierarchy.

Much of the data recorded in government departments, for instance, comprises small, relatively informal work-related meetings and discussions,

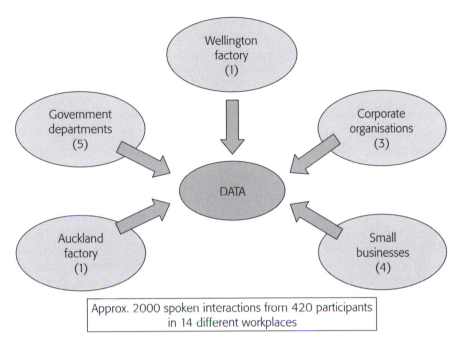

Fig 1.1 Components of the Language in the Workplace database (1996–2001)

some on the phone, but most face to face, and varying in length between 20 seconds and 2 hours. Such interactions fulfil a wide variety of purposes: to plan, to convey instructions, to seek advice, to check reports, to solve a problem or do a task, to provide feedback, to evaluate proposals, and so on. A number of larger and generally longer meetings were also tape recorded and video taped. For instance, from large commercial and semi-public organ-isations, we recorded sets of more formal meetings, typically involving project teams who met regularly over a period of time, and sometimes for several months. In the factories, we recorded team meetings, briefing sessions, one-to-one interactions between individuals on the factory floor and in the administrative offices, communications over the factory intercom system and conversations in a control room. In small businesses, in addition to typical work-related interactions, more social conversations at tea breaks and lunch-time were a particular focus.

For all workplaces, a rich fund of ethnographic information was gathered by means of meetings, interviews and observations to assist with interpreting the data. In some cases, more systematic structured observations of work patterns were undertaken before recording commenced. Wherever relevant, written documentation was also collected to provide background for the spoken com-munication, including agendas and minutes of meetings, reports, notices, manuals, production documents, and so on. Chapter 2 provides a detailed de-scription of the methodology used to collect the material in the LWP database, a methodology which was ground-breaking and innovative in a number of respects. In all the data collection sites, for instance, the methodology was designed to give participants the maximum control possible over the data collection process. The LWP corpus thus provides a rich resource for investigating how power and politeness are played out in workplace interaction.

Brief outline of content of the book

Following Chapter 2, which describes the way our data was collected, each chapter focuses on a specific aspect of workplace talk. Chapter 3 examines the many different strategies people use for getting things done at work, and in particular the different ways in which power relations and politeness interact in the achievement of workplace goals. Workplace goals include social and affective objectives, such as team building and being supportive of others, as well as more obvious task-oriented objectives, such as completing a project or reaching a decision. The interaction of power and politeness is worked out within the wider contextual constraints outlined above, including such factors as the physical setting, the length of the relationship between people working together, and the kind of relationship and understandings they have developed. The difficulty of the task, and whether it is routine or not, are also relevant factors. The examples analysed in Chapter 3 demonstrate that in many workplaces getting things done is not simply a matter of explicitly telling people what to do, but often involves subtle and complex negotiations extending over sometimes lengthy sections of discourse. It is the latter which throw most light on the nature of the interaction of power and politeness at work.

Workplace meetings are the focus of Chapter 4. Meetings take many different forms and serve a wide variety of functions from providing feedback on a draft report, discussing problems and negotiating a period of leave, through to extensive strategic planning. Interestingly, however, at a general level, there appears to be a relatively small range of structural patterns among the meetings we have analysed. They tend to involve some combination of linear and spiral patterning, often reflecting the function of the talk, as Chapter 4 illustrates. Problem solving is also characterised by surprisingly regular patterns, consisting of identifiable phases which go through successive iterations in a meeting. The interaction of power and politeness in meetings is most evident in the management of the agenda, whether formal or informal, and in decision making, and this inevitably interacts with the basic structural patterns identified. Chapter 4 identifies some of the strategies used by those in positions of power to take and keep control of talk in meetings, to keep participants on track and to reach decisions efficiently. We also consider ways in which less powerful participants contribute to meetings, whether cooperatively or subversively. Meeting talk typically builds on, exploits, constructs and maintains collegiality, and this is often especially apparent in the way decisions are reached, or the way problems are explored. Not all meetings are smooth sailing, however, and subtly subversive strategies are one means by which less powerful participants can undermine or derail progress in a 'polite' manner. Two contrasting case studies are used to illustrate the ways in which managers in meetings from different communities of practice make use of diverse discourse strategies to assert power and reduce or maintain social distance, in relation to their colleagues.

The crucial role of small talk and social talk at work has become increasingly apparent with the recent growth of research in this area (e.g. Coupland 2000). Chapter 5 illustrates how small talk assists the transitions between interpersonal or social talk and work or task-oriented talk in the workplace. Small talk is flexible, adaptable, compressible and expandable. While its primary function is to express social affect, these characteristics also make it an attractive strategy for managing workplace relationships. Our analyses of the various functions of small talk at work clearly demonstrate that, in addition to its obvious contribution, as 'positive facework',[10] to constructing solidarity, it also makes a contribution to expressing and maintaining power relationships. So, for example, high status managers often use small talk to 'do collegiality' in contexts where they interact as equals. In unequal encounters, on the other hand, small talk may be used not only to establish and maintain good relations with subordinates, but sometimes as an expression of 'repressive discourse' (Pateman 1980), with superiors manipulating small talk to achieve organisational goals.

Humour is another flexible and adaptable discourse strategy which serves a wide range of functions in workplace talk. Chapter 6 illustrates how humour can be used to hedge or attenuate face-threatening acts such as directives and negatively affective speech acts such as criticisms, thus contributing to social cohesion in the workplace. Humour can be very sensitively oriented to participants' face needs, and serve as a dynamic means of expressing and constructing solidarity, and is an effective strategy for reducing potential offence. Our data suggests, however, that in interactions where relative power is particularly salient, the way humour functions in constructing and negotiating relationships is often complex. It may serve as a management strategy – a way of attenuating or reinforcing power relationships. Using a humorous key, for instance, a risky or unacceptable proposition may be skilfully packaged in a superficially innocuous utterance. Or humour may license a challenge which subverts overt control, or serve as a 'polite' strategy for undermining authority. So, while humour appears superficially friendly and positive, it also has a dark side, as Chapter 6 illustrates.

Humour can also be considered a distinctive feature of workplace culture, with considerable variation in the amount and type of humour which characterises workplace interaction in different organisations. Looking more closely at the humour of three specific work teams or communities of practice revealed interesting differences in the detailed interactional practices of each team. In one team, humour was predominantly supportive and positive in pragmatic effect, and typically collaborative in style. A much more robust style of humour characterised the interaction of the second team; jocular abuse was frequent and the boundaries between power and solidarity were very fluid, with humour an interesting indication of this. The third community of practice paid much more attention to status and power distinctions. This group specialised in subversive humour, typically conveyed in pithy, ironic one-liners. Indeed members of this team seemed to thrive in a competitive and contestive context and, not surprisingly, this extended to their use of humour. Chapter 6 illustrates how humour can provide an interesting clue to the distinctive culture of different communities of practice.

While ways in which people manage challenging situations at work are illustrated throughout the book, Chapter 7 turns the spotlight quite explicitly on more problematic aspects of workplace interaction. Analysing the skilful ways in which people manage problematic talk at work helps tease out the complex threads of power and politeness in such interactions, and provides useful insights into the nature of problematic discourse. Communicating successfully with colleagues and clients is obviously crucial for the well-being of working people, as well as for the efficiency of their organisations and institutions. The discussion focuses first on examples where the referential or information content of the message is the source of the problem. We then turn to consider much more typical and pervasive types of problematic talk, namely encounters where considerations of power and politeness are relevant in the management of different people's often competing face needs in workplace interaction. The analysis explores the ways in which participants manage the complexities of the dynamics of power and politeness in problematic workplace relationships, and the many and diverse strategies which they use to skilfully avoid negative outcomes in potentially destructive, explosive or corrosive workplace interactions.

The final chapter addresses the issue of the relevance of socio-pragmatic research, such as that described in this book, for practitioners involved with training and professional development programmes, especially those concerned with workplace communication. We discuss some practical implications of the analyses of workplace communication covered in the preceding chapters, and describe some areas of potential application of research on workplace talk. Accurately interpreting and effectively conveying directive intent, for instance, is central to workplace effectiveness. The crucial importance of social talk in the workplace and the ability to manage such talk at tea breaks and around the edges of the day is very apparent from our analyses. Skilful management of workplace humour is another area of obvious relevance. In fact, learning to manage the affective and social aspects of workplace interaction – the 'polite' talk – emerges as one of the most important priorities for communication development programmes and transition to work programmes of all kinds. Competence in these areas is at least as important as developing abilities in managing power relations at work, or the management skills on which many current programmes tend to focus. A specific action-reflection model which has been trialled with our participant workplaces is briefly outlined as one illustration of ways in which our research can be applied.

In concluding this chapter, we return to the importance of context in every aspect of our analyses. The following chapters provide extensive evidence of the very 'situated' nature of workplace interaction. While some messages can be communicated relatively directly, the precise choice of linguistic form is always influenced by the relationship between those talking, and the context of their talk. Getting things done at work is a very dynamic process. People typically negotiate their way through the working day using complex and sophisticated discourse strategies. Power and politeness provide a volatile and exciting mix at work as we will demonstrate.

Notes

1. Transcription conventions are provided in the Appendix at the end of the book. Examples have been edited to protect the anonymity of the contributing organisations and sometimes for ease of reading where the edited features are irrelevant to the point being made.
2. These terms are components of Brown and Levinson's (1987) politeness theory, which incorporates Goffman's (1967) notion of 'face'.
3. This definition reflects the influence of Weber (1947). See, for example, Leech (1983); Brown and Levinson (1987); Ng and Bradac (1993); Ianello (1992).
4. See Holmes (1995: Chapter 3), for a discussion of relevant hedging devices.
5. Deferential politeness is one aspect of what Brown and Levinson (1987) call 'negative politeness', a term that is less transparent and confuses many readers.
6. See Holmes (1997) for a discussion of the variety of features speakers may draw on in constructing a particular social identity.
7. See www.vuw.ac.nz/lals/lwp for further information.
8. See, for example, Drew and Heritage (1992); Roberts, Davies and Jupp (1992); Boden (1994); Tannen (1994); Sarangi and Slembrouck (1996); Bargiela-Chiappini and Harris (1997); Hunston (1998); Sarangi and Roberts (1999); Candlin and Sarangi (fc).
9. Maori are the indigenous people of New Zealand and comprise about 15 per cent of the population.
10. Brown and Levinson designate the addressee's 'positive face' as their need to be liked and to have their interests, wants and goods appreciated by others (1987: 101–2), i.e. an orientation to solidarity with others.

2

From Office to Production Line: Constructing a Corpus of Workplace Data

Interview excerpt 2.1[1]

Context: Manager in government department.

. . . the power thing I think is a really interesting one in workplaces . . . having been a staff member and then moving to be a manager . . . it's been one of the the hardest learnings . . . um where um you think because you've worked here forever that you get on with people pretty well and so they must understand where you're coming from and you're just being your ordinary friendly self and you're just walking round the other side to someone else's room to ask them what you think's a quite minor question but because you're not just who you were before but you're actually- you have the capital M manager + title people get into a complete tizzy and you don't see that that's happening? . . .

People spend a good deal of their lives at work, and the workplace is a very obvious site for exploring the ways in which power and politeness are played out in spoken interaction. Until recently, however, sociolinguists and discourse analysts have paid relatively little attention to this important social context. One reason for this may be the complexity of the workplace as a social setting. Gathering good data in the wide diversity of places where people spend their working day poses a formidable range of methodological challenges. In this chapter, we describe some of the ways that we addressed these challenges in our research.

In the last ten years, a considerable body of linguistic research has developed which focuses on institutional discourse, but, with some exceptions (e.g. Clyne 1994; Neill 1996), this has tended to concentrate on rather specialised 'frontstage' contexts such as classrooms, courtrooms and doctor–patient interactions (Sarangi and Roberts 1999). Moreover, the material which has been recorded in these contexts has typically involved interactions in which the participants keep relatively still, and the background noise levels are relatively low. Data from offices, where people move around to talk to different colleagues, or from factories where many jobs entail continuous movement and considerable machinery noise, is relatively rare. In the management field, most reported studies on organisational communication use material derived from indirect sources such as self-report data, interviews with significant personnel and anecdotal observations. There is thus a surprising dearth of research based on genuine, 'real-life' data, drawn from actual interactions in workplace contexts, which is where people conduct the day-to-day business of organisations.

In this context, the Language in the Workplace Project team took up the challenge of devising ways of collecting data which provided a more realistic picture of the ways in which people talk in a variety of different workplace contexts. This decision raised a number of interesting methodological and ethical issues of a kind which do not usually face researchers engaged in more traditional types of sociolinguistic research. In what follows, we first outline the various factors which needed to be built into the project design and describe the participatory research model developed as a way of addressing these. We then illustrate how the approach was adapted to cope with the distinctly different challenges posed by the 'talking conditions' in different workplaces.

Designing a method of collecting workplace data[2]

In designing the project methodology, the team had to consider and weigh up a number of factors. In the first instance we needed a practical method of collecting a reasonably large and representative database comprising high quality, natural interaction data from everyday workplace contexts. This data had to provide a suitable basis for detailed discourse and pragmatic analysis, and allow us to take explicit account of sociocultural factors such as gender, culture, and relative status and power relationships. The data collection process could not be too intrusive, both in order to avoid 'tape shyness' and to minimise disruption to the normal flow of work and interaction. It also had to meet certain logistical and technical requirements: it could not be overly time consuming for either the individuals or organisations involved; it had to be achievable within a limited time frame; the technical quality of the recordings had to meet a minimum standard so that analysis was possible; and each recording had to be accompanied by a certain amount of demographic and contextual information.

Second, we needed to establish an ongoing relationship with our participants, in part because we wanted our analysis to be as accurate as possible, but also because we aimed eventually to feed the results into practical applications for the benefit of the participating and other workplaces. It was difficult to predict at the beginning exactly what form this collaboration might take in a given organisation, and so the methodology had to be sufficiently flexible and adaptable to evolve with the project. The process of data collection and analysis also had to be managed in such a way that at least some applications addressing issues of concern to the participating organisations (as well as other potential users of the research results), could be developed within a reasonably short time frame. In other words, we had to build in some short-term outcomes as well as the longer term results more typical of the research process. Even though the participating organisations were convinced that the research had the potential to be useful in the longer term, most still expected a more immediate, concrete benefit in return for their investment of staff time and goodwill.

Third, the research design had to meet a number of stringent ethical requirements, the most immediate of which were ensuring that genuine informed consent was obtained from everyone who was recorded, and guaranteeing confidentiality to the individual informants and organisations involved in the project. These are of course quite usual considerations in any sociolinguistic research, but they acquired an extra edge in the workplace context, where people are very aware of the need to protect sensitive information, and to protect their relationships with their clients and colleagues. Even though they knew that the content of their interactions would not be the focus of the research, our participants were initially very wary of losing control over any data that could potentially identify and compromise either individuals, or the organisations concerned. Finally, we wished the research process to be as open and empowering as possible, and to avoid any exploitation or misrepresentation of our informants. We thus based our design as far as possible on the action research principle of 'research on, for and with' our participants (Cameron et al. 1992: 22).

In order to accommodate both the various design constraints outlined above and the project's objectives, the research team devised a flexible and innovative research methodology. Essentially this involved establishing and maintaining an ongoing dialogue with the organisations involved, and giving participants maximum control over the collection and subsequent uses of the data. Consequently, the research team and the participants collaborated in setting the research agenda and exchanging relevant information. This approach took account of the particular needs identified by each party to be addressed, as well as meeting the overall goals of the project, which were briefly described in Chapter 1.

Collecting the data

Our main goal in collecting data has always been to record good quality everyday talk in a range of different workplace contexts. To achieve this, we have used a variety of strategies to obtain both audio and video recordings of naturally occurring workplace interaction, along with important associated contextual and ethnographic information. As mentioned in Chapter 1, the LWP corpus includes workplace talk recorded in a number of large and medium-sized government and commercial white-collar organisations, as well as in small businesses and in blue-collar factory environments. We have recordings of social talk as well as task-oriented talk, of formal and informal meetings, and a variety of more casual interactions, together ranging in length from short telephone calls and brief interactions of less than a minute to long meetings which last more than four hours. In what follows, we describe the three main strategies adopted to obtain this rich and diverse data set.

Collecting data from office workers

The approach we have used most often to collect workplace talk is a participatory approach which entails the use of volunteers. This approach was developed in the collection of our very first data set from four white-collar government agencies. Within these agencies we focused on policy and advisory units, environments where talk was integral to the core business of the workplace. These were contexts with which we were familiar and where we had strong network links. Hence they provided an appropriate and practical context in which to develop our participatory methodology. The basic methodological principles of the approach were:

- to give participants as much control as possible over the research process, and especially the data collection process
- to reduce the researchers' involvement in the physical collection of data to the absolute minimum
- to provide speedy and relevant feedback, as a basis for working with organisations to develop useful applications of our findings.

In outline, this model entailed four distinct stages, from making contact, through recording talk and collecting ethnographic information, to finally providing feedback.

Making contact

We first identified a number of potential organisations with whom we wished to work and then used personal contacts (i.e. someone to vouch for us as people to be trusted) to gain an entree to the chief executive, from whom we sought permission to put our research proposal to the senior management group. This initial meeting was crucial in establishing a common area of interest and identifying what we could offer to the organisation, as well as what we wanted from them. This was followed by an open presentation to all interested parties in the organisation in which we provided background information on related research, outlined the aims, methods and expected outcomes of our project, and gave people the opportunity for questions and comments.

Recording the talk

The next step involved asking for volunteers to record data for us. In each organisation, a group of volunteers representing a range of roles and levels within the organisation agreed to identify and record a representative range of their everyday interactions at work over a period of two to three weeks. They were asked to record samples of all the different kinds of interaction they engaged in at work, including social chat and telephone calls, as well as more obvious kinds of 'work-oriented' talk. We provided pocket-book-sized tape recorders and lapel microphones, and a training session on their use. We made sure all those involved were aware of the relevant ethical issues, and especially the need to gain permission in advance from anyone who was likely to be recorded (Interview excerpt 2.2).

> **Interview excerpt 2.2**
> *Context*: Policy analyst in government department.
>
> . . . in our staff meeting . . . we actually discussed that whole issue about consent . . . yeah well they had questions and one of them was it had political overtones which was + well who benefits from this research and how does it benefit Maori so we had a long discussion about that . . .

Some people kept the tape recorders and microphones on their desks, or took them along to meetings, and switched them on to record a range of interactions throughout the data collection period. Others carried the equipment round with them in belt bags designed for the purpose. Throughout the data collection process participants were free to edit and delete material as they wished. Even after they had completed recording and handed over the tapes, they could ask us to edit out material which they felt in retrospect they did not wish us to analyse or use in any published material.

As people became more accustomed to the recording process, the amount of material they edited, or which they asked us to edit, decreased dramatically. One striking example of this occurred when an informant with an employment-related grievance recorded a full and frank discussion about it with a friend over lunch, and also a subsequent lengthy meeting with a senior manager about the same issue. Moreover, because people were recording a large number of their interactions within a short space of time, we regularly obtained a series of such linked interactions which were particularly valuable from the point of view of undertaking 'thick' description and qualitative analysis (Sarangi and Roberts 1999).

Collecting contextual information

Every person recorded (i.e. not just those collecting the data) was asked to fill in a sheet providing demographic information, as well as explicitly agreeing that the data could be used for linguistic analysis by the project team. In each workplace, a fieldworker was available either on site or by telephone to assist unobtrusively with any problems that arose, and to collect background data which would help in the interpretation of the material. Ethnographic data was also collected by means of contextual notes provided by the participants at the time of recording, notes made by the fieldworker, and formal briefing and debriefing sessions with volunteers, as well as general background information provided by the management of each organisation. During the intensive data analysis phase of the project, we also undertook follow-up interviews with selected informants involving the reflexive analysis of data extracts and summaries. This follow-up functioned as a way of

- supplementing the contextual information
- checking that our interpretations were on track
- trialling some of the ways the project data and our analysis of it might be applied
- providing further opportunities for feedback in both directions.

Providing feedback

Once the initial data collection and some preliminary analysis had been completed, formal feedback sessions were held at each workplace. These took the form of open forums, including a report on progress and findings to date, discussion of any issues arising and an exploration of possible future directions and applications for the research. In fact, liaison with most workplaces has continued well beyond the stage of data collection, principally through continued contact with people in each organisation who developed a particular interest in our project, some of whom agreed to become research associates of the LWP team. These people were especially valuable in providing guidance on potential applications of our research, and in identifying directions which would be most useful to their organisations in terms of practical outcomes. Members of the LWP team also ran a range of workshops and seminars at participating workplaces, based on analyses of 'in-house' data. These sessions targeted the evaluation and development of selected aspects of workplace communication, focusing particularly on areas which had been identified as relevant by participants, such as meeting processes, the communication styles of managers and the relationship between gender or ethnicity and workplace language.[3]

Collecting data from larger meetings

Although the basic principles of the methodological design remained the same (i.e. to minimise our involvement and maximise that of the participants), the data collection methods needed some adjustments to enable us to collect good quality recordings of larger and longer meetings in a range of workplaces. When more than three people were involved in a meeting, it was impossible to accurately identify and distinguish the voices of participants solely from audio recordings alone. A second data collection strategy was therefore developed to collect both audio and video recordings of larger workplace meetings. This had the advantage of providing additional information on aspects of the interaction, such as the intended addressee, gestures, facial expression, gaze direction, body language, and so on. This strategy was piloted in the government policy units, but was used most extensively to collect material from private sector organisations, where we focused on the discourse processes which characterised the interactions of specific project teams (see Marra fc). Using this approach we recorded the regular meetings of a number of workplace teams over a period of several months. Again the data collection involved a number of steps.

Preparatory observation and choice of equipment

Initial observation of the range of contexts in which we aimed to record larger meetings indicated that we needed to be able to cope with anywhere from 6 to 14 people around a meeting table, as well as considerable variability in the size and shape of both the tables and the rooms where the meetings were held. Even one team might hold meetings in different rooms on different occasions and we often had very short notice of where a meeting was to be held. It was therefore essential to use portable recording equipment which could be quickly set up in a range of venues, and which could capture the non-verbal and verbal behaviour of a large number of participants.

To ensure good quality visual and oral coverage we used both video and audio recording. To capture all participants on the video recording, two cameras were set up on tripods in different corners of the meeting room. Because they were fixed, participants adjusted to the cameras remarkably quickly and by the second meeting they were treated as simply part of the furniture. For the audio recordings, a Sony Professional recorder, which is small, discreet and effective, was used, together with a flat inconspicuous soundgrabber microphone.

Recording the talk

Because we needed to set up two video cameras in meeting rooms, it was not possible to leave the responsibility for collecting the recorded data entirely to the participants in this case. Project team members needed to be on site for this purpose. Nevertheless, we wanted to maintain our practice of minimal intrusion and disruption to the participants' normal discourse practices in order to minimise the participant observer effect. Often, meeting rooms were booked for back-to-back meetings so that the amount of time available to set up the equipment and withdraw from view was very short. As a result team members developed the skills of a pit crew team, moving in and setting up the equipment with remarkable speed and efficiency and withdrawing before any of the meeting participants arrived.[4] This had obvious benefits for collecting the kind of 'face attention' data, including small talk and humour, which typically characterises the beginning of meetings but which is often edited out or omitted completely when participants control the point when recording commences.

While the video tapes ran for up to four hours without needing attention, audio tapes needed to be changed more frequently. Portable digital minidisk recorders solved this problem in the longer term, but in the early stages of the project it was necessary to ask one of the participants (usually the minute taker) to take responsibility for changing the audio tapes as necessary. To make this process as easy as possible, the tapes were sequentially labelled in advance.

Collecting additional information

One of the advantages of collecting data from larger meetings was the fact that a range of written material was often available to supplement the recorded data. Most meetings had a written agenda and typically a set of minutes was provided after the meetings. Often there were background reports or profiles which related to the issues under discussion. These were made available to us to assist with the interpretation of the data. In addition, as with all our recordings, we were able to consult participants to obtain clarification where necessary, and we conducted interviews with some contributers to gain additional perspectives on the data.

Collecting data from factories and small businesses

The data collection methodology was developed in a third direction in order to meet the challenges of recording in busy environments where participants were engaged in physical activities entailing lots of movement and often a good deal of noise. Small businesses such as recycling companies and plant nurseries fell into this category, as well as sites such as an Auckland tanning plant and the Wellington soap factory where we collected a wide range of recorded data on the shop floor, especially from one particular production team. By contrast with the white-collar environments where talk was typically the main work activity of those recorded, in these blue-collar workplaces talk was generally regarded as a means to an end and tended to be more sporadic and intermittent. We describe the process adopted in the soap factory to exemplify the distinctive features of this adaptation of the methodology. Several stages were again necessary to collect good quality data which could be accurately transcribed and interpreted.

Participant observation

Because the factory floor was such a different workplace from any we had worked in previously, we decided to use a participant observer in the first stage of the data collection process. A fieldworker donned overalls and spent several days in the factory just mixing with factory workers in one production team, observing the factory layout, and noting the range of activities in which workers engaged, including their communication patterns. Following the advice of an experienced and able team leader, she approached each team member individually during this period to talk to them about the planned research, to discuss their work roles and practices and generally to establish a rapport that would provide a sound basis for the data collection process which would follow.

Later, when people were used to her presence around the place, the fieldworker began discreetly testing out recording equipment in different contexts within the factory environment. She identified a number of factors which needed to be taken into account in order to successfully record talk in the factory environment. In addition to the obvious problem of obtaining good quality recording in a noisy environment, there were physical challenges such as the issue of a safe place to locate equipment and the problems of changing and storing tapes in a context where informants moved around constantly. It was also crucial that we obtained essential contextual information about each interaction. Most interactions were very brief and remarkably context dependent; workers were concise and did not waste words in a context where the focus was on the production activity. Without someone to take written or oral notes, much of the data was likely to be incomprehensible to anyone not involved. This in turn highlighted the ethical problems of obtaining informed consent from all those involved to all aspects of the recording process. The fieldworker carefully negotiated this with each person individually to ensure that as far as possible no pressure (managerial or peer) was experienced. In this context, one of the fieldworker's tasks involved explaining to potential contributors that other factory staff, including management, would not be allowed to listen to the recordings without the express permission of those involved.

Recording the talk

It quickly became clear that it was not possible to hand over the task of selecting and recording interactions to workplace volunteers, as this sort of activity is simply not compatible with the nature of work in a factory. The data collection process had to be much more 'hands on' in this context which entailed a range of logistical problems. The production team worked in two separate areas. One was a manufacturing area, where operations were monitored from a computerised control room. People were constantly moving in and out of this room and a radio intercom to the factory floor was in regular use. The second area was the packing line where talk tended to be intermittent to impart specific information or instructions, and workers moved around as they monitored machinery. The staff from these two areas did not typically interact physically during the course of the day. Different methods of recording were required in each context. Adding to the complexity, the team coordinator moved between both of these areas and management offices in a separate location, and other workers such as engineers and stores staff also moved in and out of the area and engaged in interactions with the team on which we were focusing.

In the control room, we found the best quality of recording was obtained using a portable digital minidisk recorder and a soundgrabber microphone. For particular individuals or for static and less noisy situations, such as the morning briefing sessions, the fieldworker set up a minidisk recorder, together with a high quality omni-directional lapel microphone. In this context, agreement to record was obtained on every occasion before the recorders were switched on. For workers who moved about the factory floor, one or two 'key' individuals carried radio microphones for two to three hours at a time, transmitting to a minidisk in a suitable location and monitored by the fieldworker. The latter produced good results, especially in situations with a lot of background noise, and had the added advantage that the person 'wired up' was not constantly reminded that they were being recorded by the need to change disks. In fact, minidisks provided an extended recording time of 148 minutes, together with a full random access editing capability, which proved invaluable in a situation where there were often long intervals between interactions. The changing over of microphones provided a natural point at which the fieldworker gathered background information, with people generally reporting that they had quickly forgotten about the fact they were being recorded. As in all previous recording, participants had the right to ask for material to be deleted or to veto the use of any talk they did not want used for analysis.

For a variety of reasons, including the fact that they were identified as an outstandingly productive team, we focused on one particular factory production team. Recording and observation of this team was undertaken over two separate periods. In the first stage, the fieldworker was present at the factory for a rolling three to four hours a day over successive shifts, in order to obtain samples from each part of a typical day and each day of a four-day shift, and to gather baseline data for a collaborative action research project. The second stage of this project, three months later, involved more intensive data collection for six full 12-hour days. (This included recording and ob-serving a complete four-day shift, plus a day at the end of the previous shift and one at the beginning of the following shift.) The fieldworker remained on site throughout each recording period to change disks and batteries, write up interaction notes, obtain ethnographic information and begin data processing. She eventually developed considerable skill in balancing the prac-tical requirements of data collection (e.g. servicing equipment, recording contextual information) with being as unobtrusive as possible in order not to interfere with the team's usual patterns of work and communication. This multicomponent method of data collection, which was developed initially for use in the factory environment, has subsequently provided a useful model for other busy, noisy and complex workplaces, such as hospital wards and small business contexts. It has also produced very rich and multiplex data sets, with excellent potential for triangulation and intertextual analysis.

Providing feedback

Because the kinds of data collection undertaken in factories and small busi-nesses were generally framed very explicitly right from the start as action research, feedback to the participants and other interested parties (such as human resources and supported employment personnel) was an integral part of the process. Thus at the soap factory, the fieldworker and principal re-searcher from the LWP team had regular meetings with the team coordina-tor and with training and human resources staff to explore how the results of the research could most usefully contribute to team development programmes at the factory. The team members themselves also had a number of oppor-tunities to interact informally with members of the research team and were invited to two feedback sessions where they were able to hear samples of the recordings and discuss how the material might be used. [5]

Conclusion

We have outlined in this chapter the essential features of the innovative and adaptable methodology which enabled us to collect a wide range of workplace data in very disparate contexts. Initially, when we handed over control of exactly what data was to be collected, and from whom, we were aware of taking the risk that the range and quality of data would be less than optimal. But because the recording process was typically spread over several weeks (a 'drip-feed' method), we were able to monitor the data as it came in. We were thus able to achieve a representative mix of informants and data types over the total period of data collection. Extending the data collection to encompass larger meetings led to the incorporation of video tape into the recording process. Even so, we managed to minimise the intrusion of the research team by setting up and removing equipment before participants arrived and after they had left the meeting room. Although not appropriate in less formal contexts, video recording provided valuable non-verbal data for large meetings, which obviously enhanced our ability to accurately interpret what was going on between participants, as well as providing material we could easily discuss with people from the relevant workplaces after the event. Even in the factory environment, where the logistics of obtaining good quality recording were most challenging, the basic principle of a participatory methodology was maintained. Indeed, the participant observer/ fieldworker integrated so successfully into the soap factory that at the end of the period of data collection she was offered a full-time job there!

By consulting extensively at every stage of the research process and ensuring everyone involved was fully informed of our goals and methods, we developed very successful collaborative relationships with the various workplaces with whom we cooperated. This approach also allowed us to develop a relationship of mutual trust with our informants, so that we were able to go back later to ask more questions, get feedback on our interpretations and obtain permission to use extracts for presentations, workshops and publications. In the course of this process, we received a great deal of positive feedback from informants about the benefits of the data collection approach to them personally and professionally. Many reported that they had gained useful insights into actual patterns of workplace communication, as compared to their perceptions, e.g. the amount of gossip, small talk or swearing which occurred; who they tended to interact with, for what purposes, and where (Interview excerpt 2.3).

Interview excerpt 2.3

. . . but what was interesting was that because of this project I realised how often that happened? it's just constant you're working on something and your boss is there talking about something completely different and um ++ yeah . . . like when Leila say like today she had a management meeting and she's not in there AT ALL you actually get all this work done [laughter] . . . it wasn't till I started doing this and had to turn the tape on and off that I realised the interruptions?

Participants found it particularly illuminating to have the opportunity to look in detail at some of their own interactions during the feedback and follow-up sessions, and the research team found it equally valuable to collect suggestions from participants to guide the next stage of analysis (Interview excerpt 2.4).

Interview excerpt 2.4

. . . it was really interesting when you came and did that feedback session with us . . . it was um kind of like you know lightbulbs go on when you do the explanations you suddenly realise- ++ what's going on here some of it was not unfamiliar + to me but to others I think it really was quite a revelation . . . yeah and the step beyond that which is how you could- what you could do to change the situation if you like if you can identify that something's going on what strategies could you use to to get a good outcome . . .

The participatory research model described in this chapter initially evolved in response to the particular challenges inherent in collecting a large amount of natural interaction data in a workplace setting. However, this methodology clearly has a number of significant advantages over more traditional sociolinguistic methods, and as such has the potential to apply well beyond this particular project. The model has also produced ongoing benefits for the participating workplaces in terms of a range of practical outcomes. Finally, and of direct relevance to this book, the resulting diverse database, comprising both recorded interactions of naturally occurring spontaneous workplace talk and a large amount of ethnographic information, obviously provided an ideal corpus for analysing and illustrating the complex ways in which people do power and politeness in workplace interaction.

Notes

1. The examples in this chapter are quotations from interviews, debriefing meetings and practical workshops which we held with participating workplaces after the data had been collected.
2. See Stubbe (1998a, 2001) for a fuller discussion of the development of the LWP research design.
3. See Chapter 8 (also Jones and Stubbe fc) for a discussion of how this action research partnership subsequently developed into a more comprehensive communication evaluation and development (CED) model.
4. See Marra (fc) for a more detailed description of this process.
5. Subsequently, members of this team were involved in the filming of a video produced by the LWP team as part of a training resource kit, aimed at the development of effective communication in multicultural factory teams.

3

Getting Things Done at Work

Example 3.1[1]

- give it to Peter
- go right through this
- send them back to us
- get rid of them now
- check it with Gordon
- throw them straight in the water
- seal off the corners
- salt them
- get a printout
- get him to make the changes

These utterances were taken from recordings made in a New Zealand factory (Brown 2000). They are instructions given by a factory manager to members of his staff and can be labelled 'directives', or 'control acts', speech acts intended to get someone to do something.[2] They are all imperative in structure, the canonical form of a directive, and they are direct and explicit. Despite this, the actions they prescribe are largely opaque to a reader, since the utterances include exophoric and anaphoric references to people and things that are clear only in the context in which they were produced (e.g. *them*, *it*, *him*). The absence of contextual information also prevents an outsider knowing how 'normal' such direct instructions are, whether they reflect familiarity between the participants, or whether they are instantiations of explicit managerial authority.

For rather different reasons, Example 3.2 is equally opaque in the absence of contextual information and interpretive comment. The directives are in bold.

Example 3.2
Context: A large meeting in a government organisation focusing on evaluation.

```
 1 LEN: how do we- can we capture some of these things that we want to um
 2 BAR: do you want me to write them down
 3 LEN: can you
 4       I mean I just think where we've we've identified something
 5       we want to carry that through
 6       cos later on we may want to come back to it . . .
 7 CHR: one that I'm am surprised at is [institution] engineering
 8 LEN: hang on can we can we stay in the- do this block first
 9 CHR: oh okay you want to /do service\ first
10 LEN: /all right\
11       um + do service first otherwise we'll we'll we'll dart a bit
12       I just want to try and deal with the a-
13       do the scores make sense with people's perceptions
14       or if there's a difference big difference in the scores
15       that we've got some comment that covers that big difference
```

This excerpt is taken from an evaluation meeting in a government organisation. Len is the unit manager and his role is to facilitate a wide-ranging
discussion. In this excerpt he negotiates the group's approach to the issues
they have to discuss. In line 3 he uses a modalised interrogative *can you*, to
accept an offer from Barbara, and follows this with a justification for getting
her to keep a written record of the group's ideas (lines 4–6). The justification is also modalised using a range of devices including pragmatic particles
(*I mean, I just think*), a modal verb (*may*), and hesitation phenomena (*we've
we've*). At line 8, he uses an imperative *hang on*, followed by another modalised
interrogative to prevent Chris taking items in a different order from that on
the agenda. Again he provides a justification *otherwise we'll we'll we'll dart a
bit* (line 11). This is followed by a complex and mitigated (*just, try and*)
declarative (lines 12–15), with a question embedded within it, to indicate
what he wants to address first.

This example illustrates the range of structures that can be used to express directive intent (imperative, interrogative, declarative), as well as
some of the epistemic devices which may be used to mitigate a directive,
for example, modalised forms, rationalisations or justifications, hesitation,
and so on. It also exemplifies the *negotiation* of directive intent which is
very typical in interactions between professionals in white-collar workplaces
and in contexts where power differences are played down and politeness is
paramount.

This chapter explores some of the complexities of the ways people get
things done at work. Giving directives and making requests are the most

obvious means by which one person can get another to do as they wish; but, as these examples illustrate, there are many different ways of giving direct-ives. While, as we will see, they are not the only relevant factors, power and politeness are certainly among the more obvious reasons why people adopt different strategies for conveying directive intent.

Being direct downwards

The imperatives in Example 3.1 were collected in a factory where the tasks were very familiar and routine and the power relationships clear and uncon-tested. Our analyses suggest that imperatives are more frequent than other forms in such contexts (Brown 2000), a finding supported by earlier work-place research.[3] Indeed, Bernsten (1998) discusses forms other than imper-atives as 'marked choices' on the factory floor in an American car factory. Example 3.3 provides a more extended example from a different New Zea-land factory. After an initial *I want* declarative, Ginette uses a spate of imperative directives, most of which are 'bald' and unmitigated.[4]

Example 3.3
Context: Ginette, a production team manager, giving her team instructions at the early morning meeting.

```
1 GIN:  the very last twenty-five cases that you take off that line I want them put
2       aside the very last twenty-five cases put them on a pallet
3       get them stretch wrapped
4       they're going to be a memento for everybody
5       so make sure you er remember that . . .
6       so just remember the last the very last twenty-five cases put them on a
7       pallet get them stretch wrapped
8       put them aside for er [name] . . .
9       send them through with no glue
```

Imperative directives recorded in the white-collar workplaces were also frequently delivered to subordinates, and typically concerned routine tasks. Example 3.4 provides instances of directives addressed by a policy manager to her administrative assistant.

Example 3.4
Context: Meeting between policy unit manager and administrative assistant in government organisation.

1 MAN: check that out . . .
2   ring the applicants and say they've been shortlisted . . .
3   ring them today . . .
4   make sure that's booked

Another direct and explicit form of directive is a 'want' or 'need' declarative, as illustrated in line 1 of Example 3.3, and in the utterances in Example 3.5.

Example 3.5
Context: Policy unit manager to administrative assistant in government organisation.

- I need these by ten . . .
- I need to see that file . . .
- you need to get that to me soon
- that needs to be couriered today

People typically use explicit and direct forms, then, when they hold a higher position in the institutional hierarchy than their addressee(s), and the addressee's obligations are clear; i.e. the required action is a routine part of their responsibilities, or when the degree of imposition is low (Brown and Levinson 1987). These patterns are unsurprising and confirm those reported in earlier research.[5]

More illuminating is an analysis of variations from this pattern and an exploration of the contextual factors which account for modifications to such generalisations. First, it is interesting to consider in what contexts and in what ways people in authority *intensify* routine directives to subordinates. When and how do speakers boost the strength of a directive? And what can be stronger, more explicit and direct than an imperative? Second, in what circumstances, and using what strategies, do those in authority select less direct or more mitigated means of conveying directive intent to subordinates?

Turning up the heat

Speakers exploit a variety of linguistic and pragmatic devices to intensify their directives: increasing the volume of their utterance, using contrastive stress, incorporating intensifiers such as *very, definitely, just*, making use of deontic modals such as *must* and *have to* and strategies such as repetition, and so on.[6] Example 3.6 illustrates some of these strategies being used by the team leader during the early morning factory team briefing referred to in Chapter 1.

Example 3.6

Context: Regular 6am team briefing meeting. Ginette is telling the packers that there have been serious delays caused by their mistakes with documenting the packing codes.

1 GIN: you must fill them out properly
2   the purpose of these sheets is to give information for people up there
3   on how these the efficiencies of these lines
4   when we fill out a sheet that says we nearly packed six thousand cases
5   in three- three and a half hours that's a load of shit
6   that's running the machine at five hundred packets a minute . . .
7   fill them out properly . . .
8   so make sure you check them properly . . .
9   cos like I said it's just one person's stupid mistake
10   makes the whole lot of us look like eggs (5)
11   check them properly [laughs]
12   we shouldn't blame Lesia cos he's got a good memory
13   and that was the end of the run
      [general laughter]
14   please fill them out properly fuck youse

The problem that Ginette is addressing is serious and potentially very costly for the factory. It is important that she gets her message over and that the team understands it and responds to it. She is angry and direct because she has raised the issue of mistakes on the packing code slips before, and yet forms are still being wrongly filled out. Though she suspects the problem lies with just one or two 'slack' individuals, she wants the team as a whole to take responsibility for getting things right.

Ginette uses a variety of means to intensify the force of her basic message 'fill out the forms properly'. The opening declarative in line 1 is strengthened by deontic *must*, and uses the direct address form *you*. The whole message is delivered with declamatory force. But perhaps the most obvious intensifying devices are the regular repetitions of her message (lines 1, 7, 8, 11, 14), and the use of swear words (lines 5, 14), and especially the finale of this tirade with the very direct and challenging address form *fuck youse* (line 14). This is high energy (but good-humoured) abuse, of a kind regularly used by members of this team, aimed here at getting the team to follow procedures.

Ginette also supplies logical reasons why the sheets need to be filled out (lines 2–3), and reasons why filling them out wrongly has negative consequences, not only for the company but also for the team's image (lines 4–6, 9–10). In other words, she conveys her message by skilfully combining pragmatic intensifying devices, logical arguments and appeals to team solidarity, a point discussed further below. This example thus nicely illustrates the kinds of factors which lead those in authority to turn up the heat, as well as some of the pragmatic strategies available for doing so.

Lowering the heat

If direct and explicit forms typify routine directives from superiors to subordinates, in what ways and in what circumstances do those in authority *mitigate* directives to those working for them? Again speakers draw on a variety of linguistic and pragmatic devices to decrease or attenuate the force of directives: modal verbs, modal particles, tag questions, pragmatic particle hedges, rising intonation, and so on. Example 3.7 is an excerpt from an interaction following up the team meeting from which Example 3.6 was taken.

Example 3.7
Context: Ginette, the production team leader, is talking to Sam, a team member who has made an error of the kind she had been warning about at the morning team meeting.

```
 1 SAM:  no er well yeah I did I know it was my- that was my mistake
 2 GIN:  yeah
 3 SAM:  yeah
 4 GIN:  no the way you did it this morning is good
 5        that's what we're supposed to do (9)
 6        see how important important the checks a- are
 7        you know if you do them properly
 8 SAM:  well I yeah I'm usually pretty good on on that sort of thing now so-
 9 GIN:  yeah
10 SAM:  if you go by the book you can't go wrong
11 GIN:  that's right just remember that when you're doing the check list
12        you put down what YOU find not what it should be
13        so you're checking against what it should be
14        if it don't match then there's something wrong
```

Ginette is giving the same message as in Example 3.6, 'fill in the forms properly', but in this one-to-one interaction she greatly modifies the directness of the instruction and her delivery is quite different. The message is attenuated in a variety of ways: it is preceded by praise (lines 4–5) and it is hedged with phrases which reduce its force, e.g. *just remember that* (line 11). Moreover, the message is delivered over several turns with positive reinforcement (*that's right* line 11) when Sam provides evidence (line 10) that he has got the message. Finally, Ginette summarises (lines 11–14), spelling out very clearly for Sam what 'fill in the forms properly' means for him in his particular job. In this one-to-one interaction with a cooperative employee who hasn't quite got the message, we see a very different style of delivering directives from the declamatory in-your-face presentation illustrated in Example 3.6. There would be little to gain from engaging in such directly face-threatening behaviour in a one-to-one encounter, and much to lose, both in terms of Sam's goodwill and in terms of persuading him to do the task in the required way.

Context and dynamics

As indicated by this analysis, we repeatedly found that it was very important to take account of the relevance of the surrounding discourse context in interpreting the force of a directive. At the end of a long discussion of the best strategy for dealing with a problem, for instance, one manager said to a colleague *right you send those out today*. Out of context this looks like a very peremptory directive which could cause offence between status equals. However, it was evident from the preceding discussion that this line of action had been agreed between them. Indeed, the following utterance *and I'll prepare the agenda*, indicated clearly that the imperative simply confirmed their understanding of the division of responsibilities. It was quite common for explicit directive forms to be softened in this way, not by any specific and identifiable linguistic device, but rather by virtue of their position in relation to preceding or following 'supporting moves'.[7]

In another white-collar organisation, an interaction, illustrated in Example 3.8, between a section manager, Hera, and her administrative assistant, Ana, highlights further reasons why even routine instructions from a superior to a subordinate might be mitigated or hedged, as well as indicating the importance of taking account of the dynamic nature of any interaction. Ana is a newly arrived and temporary appointment, and hence a peripheral member of the tightly integrated community of practice in which Hera works. The directives in Example 3.8 are from the first section of their interaction.

Example 3.8
Context: Hera is giving instructions to Ana about organising job interviews for the following week.

1 HERA: I wondered if you wouldn't mind spending some of that time in
2   contacting + while no one else is around contacting the people for their
3   interviews what we might need to do is send down a confirmation note . . .
4   if we just tell them exactly where it is . . .
5   what I suggest you do is read through . . .

In this initial encounter with her new assistant, Hera uses a range of devices to soften her directives. The choice of the pronoun *we* rather than *you*, for instance, functions as a softening device (cf Jones 1992). The use of modal verbs (*would, might*) and hedged syntactic structures, as in *I wondered if you wouldn't mind, what we might need*, and the use of an illocutionary force-indicating device *what I suggest you do*, all function to reduce the strength of the directive. Hera's use of these softening devices reflects both the lack of familiarity between the two women and the fact that, as a 'temp', Ana's responsibilities are not as clearly defined as they would be if she had been in the job longer.

As the interaction progresses, however, the directives become gradually more direct, with Hera using more imperatives and fewer hedging devices. In the directives in Example 3.9, for example, *you* rather than *we* is the explicit pronoun in line 2, and the implicit pronoun in lines 1, 2, 3, 4 is also *you*.

Example 3.9
Context: Later in the same interaction.

1 HERA: ring the applicants and say that . . .
2   see if you can ring her first . . .
3   check to see what time the plane actually lands . . .
4   just write down the list of their names . . .

This change in the pattern of directive strategies may be attributed to at least two dynamic aspects of the interaction. First, the participants are obviously becoming more comfortable with one another as the interaction proceeds. Second, some urgency develops as the interaction progresses and the time for Hera's next meeting approaches. This is a nice illustration of how the forms of directives can reflect and indicate participants' sensitivity to changes in alignment or 'footing' (Goffman 1981), and the increasing ease of the relationship as the interaction develops.

Our data set allowed us to contrast Hera's directives to Ana with the way she interacted with her usual executive assistant, Kay, on her return from leave (Example 3.10). In this interaction Hera used very explicit directives, reflecting the fact that these two women had worked closely together for a long time and could afford to dispense with elaborate politeness strategies. Instructions were frequently expressed with very direct strategies such as 'want' and 'need' statements and deontic modals such as *should* and *must*.

Example 3.10
Context: Hera sorts out tasks with Kay, her usual executive assistant.

1 HERA: all the other letters should go on the file . . .
2   that needs to be couriered up to X today . . .

3   I need a master sheet ...
4   you need to just check the travel booking ...
5   will you let me know what the story is ...

Nevertheless, it is interesting to note that even these relatively direct instructions are realised by a range of linguistic forms other than simple imperatives, including declaratives (lines 1, 2, 3, 4), personal and impersonal 'need' statements (lines 2, 3, 4) and modalised interrogatives (line 5).

However, as illustrated in Example 3.11, at times Hera uses indirect rather than direct strategies for giving instructions to Kay (e.g. line 15, *you might need to check*). This is not a case where indirectness reflects social distance (i.e. lack of familiarity) as in the previous example with Ana. Rather Hera's use of indirect strategies in Example 3.11 illustrates the ability of Kay, the well-established administrative assistant, to infer what is required without Hera always needing to be explicit either about the tasks themselves, or the fact that she is in the position of control. The mix of direct and indirect strategies, together with the informality of their style in this inter-action, illustrates the close and relaxed relationship between Hera and Kay, which allows them to make reliable inferences about each other's intended meanings. The same point is evident from the fact that Kay is confidently proactive in working out what needs to be done (e.g. lines 4, 9, 11, 13).

Example 3.11
Context: Hera sorts out tasks with Kay, her usual executive assistant.

1 HERA: yeah somehow I have to try and get the the scholarships done
2 KAY: oh that's right
3 HERA: I don't know how the hell I'm gonna do that
4 KAY: um is this one oh yeah it is you too + the briefing
5 HERA: which briefing oh yeah no I'm not going to be going to that
6   you can cross me off for that
7 KAY: oh okay
8 HERA: so that's there it's in it what's this five thirty to seven thirty ++ oh
9 KAY: yours is five fifteen to five thirty
10 HERA: yeah and then there's five thirty to seven thirty David Hooper
11 KAY: no not on yours that's um Marcie's that one there
12 HERA: oh oh just- good [clears throat] (8) [sighs]
13 KAY: and the election briefing
14 HERA: [clears throat] yeah oh (7) I think we've cancelled that ++
15   you might need to check I'm fairly sure that's been cancelled
16 KAYE: yeah

In response to Hera's statements that she faces a problem organising her time (lines 1, 3), Kay states clearly how events need to be reorganised in order to facilitate and support Hera's activities, e.g. *yours is five fifteen to five thirty* (line 9), *and the election briefing* (line 13). This is a good example of two professionals working together to get things done. Kay's role is to support Hera and she takes the lead at various points in suggesting how this can be achieved. The success of the various indirect strategies and the frequent elliptical forms used by both participants reflect the close and effective working relationship that these two women have developed. This interaction nicely exemplifies the complexity of the ways in which people get things done at work. Although Hera is technically 'in charge' and has the right to tell Kay what to do, the reality is clearly much more complex.

The examples analysed so far have suggested a number of reasons why those with power and authority in an organisation do not always give instructions in direct and explicit ways when they want something done. Considerations of setting and context, the nature and length of their relationship with the person they are talking to and the nature of the required task are all relevant in interpreting the complexities of how people get things done at work. Underlying every interaction, and accounting for the form in which directives are expressed or dynamically negotiated, is the delicate balance between the pressure to get the job done well and efficiently on the one hand and *affective* considerations of collegiality and concern for people's feelings, i.e. politeness, on the other. Managers turn the heat up or down as a result of their assessment of the relative weight of such factors in the wider context of the ongoing relationships between people who work together. The sophisticated skills involved in achieving this balance are even more apparent when we turn to a consideration of interactions involving status equals or near equals.

Mitigation and management between equals

Getting a fellow worker to do something when you are both at the same level of the institutional hierarchy clearly requires attention to considerations of politeness. Overtly direct forms do occur on occasions between equals: when there is a recognised emergency or unexpected deadline, for instance or, as mentioned above, at the end of a discussion where the next steps have been negotiated and agreed. In such contexts, one manager might say to another, *so you write that up and I'll arrange the follow-up*. But generally imperatives are not frequent in this kind of situation. Much more typical, even at the end of a discussion, is a declarative such as *so you will write that up then*. The simple phrase *you will* indicates that the speaker is checking an agreed next step, rather than issuing a directive. Example 3.12 illustrates the strategy that Jocelyn uses to tell her fellow manager, Kim, to add a late application to their short list.

Example 3.12

Context: Jocelyn and Kim, senior managers in a white-collar organisation, are discussing job applications.

1 JOC: there's one more late application
2 KIM: okay
3 JOC: so we might as well put that in mightn't we

Instead of saying directly *put that in*, Jocelyn uses three different means of hedging or mitigating the force of her directive. She uses the epistemic modal verb *might*, she invites Kim to agree with a tag question *mightn't we*, and she uses the pronoun *we* emphasising this is a joint decision, rather than simply Jocelyn's decision. Jocelyn is certainly paying attention here to the need to avoid causing offence to a status equal.

In general, then, attention to politeness concerns tends to increase as the 'right' of one person to give directives to another decreases. In Example 3.13, the same two managers negotiate their respective responsibilities around the interviewing process.

Example 3.13

Context: Jocelyn and Kim are discussing the interview process for appointing someone to a position in Kim's section.

1 JOC: okay + and what role do you want me to play
2   do you want me to play do you want me to play just a recorder role +
3   do you want me to ask some questions
4   what do you want me to do
5 KIM: well how do you want to play it?
6   /I mean\
7 JOC: /oh I'm easy I'm easy\
8   I mean I'm happy to ask some questions
9   but you know it depends how you you and the rest of the panel
10   view my role there I'm happy to play either role
11 KIM: well I'll think about it
12 JOC: yeah
13 KIM: I did see you as a as as a recorder and a d- and an advisor type
14 JOC: yeah
15 KIM: in a more independent advisor in between the
16 JOC: that's probably I probably could
17 KIM: when we're when we're doing the discussion in between
18   when we need to
19 JOC: mm I'll probably feel more comfortable about that
20 KIM: okay

Because of her position as human resources manager, Jocelyn could, in principle, take a prominent role in the appointment process. However, this is an appointment to a position in Kim's section, and Jocelyn makes it clear that she is willing to play a supportive role, taking a back seat and simply recording, or alternatively taking a more active role asking questions (lines 1–4). Her offer makes it much easier for Kim to tell her what she wants her to do, but even so Kim first offers Jocelyn the opportunity to select her role, *well how do you want to play it?* (line 5). It emerges that Kim actually does already have an idea of what role she wants Jocelyn to play (lines 13–15, 17–18). She clearly does not want Jocelyn to ask questions. She would prefer her to take a back seat during the interviews and act as recorder, so that she can be available as a more independent advisor at a later stage in the process. Since Jocelyn twice asserts her willingness to ask questions (lines 3, 8), Kim faces a somewhat tricky task. Asking Jocelyn to take a more subordinate role as recorder involves some facework. This is apparent from a number of mitigating devices in Kim's discourse. First she says she will *think about it* (line 11), although it is apparent from her later utterances that she already has a preference. Then when she indicates her preference, she verbally hesitates *as a as as a* (line 13) before producing the word *recorder*, and then quickly adds a more responsible role *and a d- and an advisor type*. Jocelyn's rather muted and unenthusiastic responses *yeah* (lines 12, 14) lead Kim to elaborate this second role further (lines 15, 17–18), eliciting a hedged agreement from Jocelyn to the proposed role *that's probably I probably could. . . mm I'll probably feel more comfortable about that* (lines 16, 19). This interaction continues with further evidence at several points that, despite her offer (lines 1–4), Kim feels the need to 'mollify' Jocelyn for suggesting she take a back seat in the interview process. Clearly, trying to get an equal to do something when the required action is not consistent with her status requires considerable attention to politeness considerations.

This interaction is typical of many, many others in our data, where equals or near equals carefully manage the interaction in order to reach agreement on their respective responsibilities in relation to a course of action. Politeness considerations or concern to protect their addressee's face are evident throughout such negotiations. Example 3.14, a short excerpt from a long interaction in another organisation, illustrates the range of strategies used by one manager to a slightly lower level manager, to indicate the direction she thinks he should take in managing his staff who have not been performing well. Heke, the lower level manager, has indicated he intends to ask his team to work harder, including evenings and weekends. Jan wants to convey to him that he should not go overboard. She therefore opposes his suggestion, while simultaneously indicating that she appreciates his good intentions. She achieves this by expressing her instructions in a form that are themselves an illustration of linguistic soft-pedalling.

Example 3.14

Context: Jan, the branch manager, and Heke, a policy manager in a government organisation, are in Jan's office discussing how to improve the performance of his team.

1 JAN: although I mean I can appreciate the that sort of message but on the
2   other hand um + don't sort of + sort of say that as something
3   that sh- that should be the norm like that's
4 HEKE: mm
5 JAN: really you know when things are really
6 HEKE: from time to time
7 JAN: from time to time that it's not a good way of them expecting to
8   organise their work all the time
9 HEKE: ae yeah
10 JAN: that they need you know it's the old work smarter sort of stuff
11 HEKE: yeah
12 JAN: and we need to- to sort of be aware of we being a (friend-) family
13   friendly workplace

Jan negotiates the directive meaning very carefully. She is clearly taking account of Heke's face needs as a manager himself, but in addition her message is a complex and subtle one. On the one hand, she does not want to undermine her earlier message that the team needs to work harder, but on the other she does not want Heke to go too far in making unreasonable demands on his team. Her directive to Heke, to manage the situation with moderation, is skilfully conveyed using a range of linguistic devices which serve as softeners, such as the pragmatic particles *you know*, *sort of*, *I mean* (lines 1, 2, 5, 10, 12), repetition (lines 2–3, 7–8), and echoing devices, e.g. *from time to time* (lines 6–7). At the same time, Jan makes an appeal to the organisation's policy of being a family friendly workplace (lines 12–13), and a strategic assumption that Heke understands the concept of 'working smarter' rather than harder, to reinforce her message indirectly.

Getting the boss to cooperate – requests and indirectives

The preceding discussion has drawn attention to the crucial importance of contextual considerations in accounting for the complexities of the way people get things done at work. While routine tasks are typically realised in the form of relatively direct instructions, non-routine tasks and special requests require more mitigated and less direct forms. Asking someone to perform a task which is not part of their defined duties requires commensurate attenu-ation of the strength of the directive. This often involves a finely balanced assessment of relative rights and duties in relation to work objectives, as well as politeness considerations or attention to both parties' face needs.

Not surprisingly, the same range of factors is relevant in considering how subordinates 'manage' their bosses. But politeness considerations typically weigh even more heavily when directives are targeted upwards. The research literature uses many different labels to identify what people are doing when they use language to 'get someone to do something'. Recognising the delic-ate nature of directives 'upwards', some analysts label such utterances as 'requests', underlining the fact that generally subordinates have no formal right to direct a superior.[8] However, there are situations where the work responsibilities of subordinates do entail their having to give instructions to a superior. In organisations where we recorded, for instance, administrative assistants were typically expected to look after their managers' appointments diaries. This meant that at times they needed to indicate to their managers in explicit and clear terms what they should do next: *don't forget that lunch engagement with John Taylor; you need to be at the Ministry of X by 2pm remem-ber.* Similarly, an assistant's responsibilities often included getting their manager to sign papers or plan meetings. Example 3.15 illustrates directives uttered at different times by a pay clerk, Leola, to her manager, Phil.[9]

Example 3.15
Context: Factory pay clerk to accountant.

- can you sign these for me
- have a look at this for me please
- can you scribble here for M W wages paid cash
- can you sign this cheque for V for last week's wages
- can you authorise the wages please Phil

Even though her job requires her to get her superior to cooperate, Leola very rarely uses bald imperatives for this purpose. Softeners such as *please*, or the use of the manager's name, typically accompanied her directives. The most frequently selected form for these task-oriented directives was the *can* interrogative, as illustrated in Example 3.15.

More interesting and more complex are transactions where a subordinate has an objective which involves getting a superior to do something which is not self-evidently part of their obligations. There are many such interactions in our data set and in some cases achieving the objective takes most of the interaction. Example 3.16 is taken from an interaction between two policy analysts from different sections within a government organisation. The more junior analyst, Nicola, has asked Claire for a meeting to discuss a particular

Parliamentary Bill, and Claire has agreed, expecting to provide information and advice. During the course of the interaction, however, it emerges that Nicola wants to persuade Claire to take responsibility for briefing the Minister on the Bill. This problem of sorting out who should take responsibility for particular tasks is a common challenge for staff working in large organisations.

Nicola begins with some general questions about the dates of the reading of the Bill and its current progress which Claire answers. Nicola then moves to her real purpose.

Example 3.16

Context: Nicola is junior to Claire and they are from different departments. The discussion takes place in Claire's office.

```
 1 NIC:  well + um + the thing is that the minister needs to be briefed
 2       remember we talked about that
 3 CLA:  yeah
 4 NIC:  and that you did the original brief
 5       and Tom's not wanting me to do the brief because it's not our work
 6 CLA:  OH and you want to bring it over /here\
 7 NIC:  /yeah\ and so we were wondering if you could do the brief
 8       because + we're not going to +
 9       and because /you've got the first\ one
10 CLA:  /[drawls] oh\
11 NIC:  and we were just hoping you could whittle down
12       what you wrote last year and just [inhales]
13 CLA:  problem I've got is that um that um . . .
```

This is Nicola's first attempt to get Claire to agree to write the briefing paper. Her main strategies are first to minimise the task and second to appeal to a higher authority. She reminds Claire that they have already agreed that a briefing paper is needed (lines 1–2) and that Claire has written *the original brief* (line 4), implying that this could serve as a basis for the task. She then indicates that her manager, Tom, has told her that she, Nicola, should not be writing the brief (line 5). Only at this point (after more than two minutes of talk) does Claire realise that Nicola has not come simply for advice and information, but has another objective. Claire's surprise is signalled by the stressed *OH* which introduces an explicit statement of what she has inferred (line 6). Nicola quickly confirms the inference, overlapping Claire's final word, and then makes her request explicit (line 7), constructing the task as a minimal imposition on Claire (lines 9, 11–12). Claire gradually takes in the import of Nicola's words (line 10) and begins to outline why it will not be possible for her to take on this task (line 13).

The main mitigating strategy Nicola uses throughout this attempt to get Claire to cooperate is to minimise what is being asked. This is reinforced by many features of her discourse. She introduces her main point with three discourse markers, each of which signals her awareness that what follows may not be welcome: a qualifier *well*, a hesitation marker *um* surrounded by brief pauses, and an introductory tag *the thing is*. The statement of the directive itself is introduced with the attenuating phrase *and so we were wondering if*, and it includes the epistemic modal *could* (line 7). After a clear restatement of the reasons (lines 8–9) in reverse order (cf lines 4–5), Nicola restates the directive, again phrased in ways which minimise the task: *we were just hoping you could whittle down what you wrote last year and just [inhales]* (lines 11–12). The pronoun *we* strengthens the directive by associating it with her manager, but the words *hope, just* and *could* are attenuators or hedges, and reduce its force. Claire's response (line 13) indicates the ploy has not worked, however, and in fact, the remainder of this seven-minute meeting consists of variations on these themes, with Claire firmly resisting what Nicola wants her to do.

There are many similar interactions, though with different agendas, where a subordinate tries to get a superior to cooperate in doing something to the subordinate's advantage. They are routinely characterised by deferent discourse, involving a wide range of hedging devices and attenuation strategies and, in general, deferential politeness becomes increasingly important, as status differences increase.[10]

These interactions also illustrate the fact that the multifunctionality of discourse permits participants considerable flexibility in simultaneously pursuing a number of objectives, some more overt than others and some more 'acceptable' than others. So, for example, in relation to the interaction between Claire and Nicola, seeking advice was an 'acceptable' objective for Nicola from the perspective of her superior. In another interaction, in which this time it is Claire who is the subordinate, Claire uses the same strategy of presenting one 'acceptable' objective, while simultaneously pursuing others. Examples 3.17–3.19 are excerpts from a 40-minute interaction between Claire and her superior, Tom, in which Claire successfully achieves a number of interactional objectives.[11] Like Nicola she has sought the interview and, like Nicola, her ostensible goal is to obtain advice on various issues, and especially individual staff development. She is concerned that she is not being given opportunities to gain experience which will enhance her promotability. Quite specifically, she has not been appointed as joint acting manager of her section while her immediate boss is away, despite a promise that she would be, and she is very annoyed about this (as we know from ethnographic information and from interactions she recorded with others). The decision to appoint someone else was Tom's. Example 3.17 is an extract from the beginning of the interview where she presents her ostensible reason for seeking the meeting.[12]

Example 3.17

Context: Claire has sought a meeting with Tom, the overall manager of the area in which Claire's section is located in a government organisation.

```
1 CLA:  well I've been overlooked quite a few times
2       but I wanted to find out specifically how
3       what I could do to help myself be considered next time . . .
4       well I just want to talk to you about it
5       and I suppose I just want to get some ideas on what I could do
6       to actually be considered favourably next time . . .
```

Rather than confronting Tom with accusations that his decision was unfair, Claire presents the issue as a personal staff development matter. She is seeking advice and she phrases her request in very deferential language, including minimisers such as *well* (lines 1, 4), *just* (lines 4, 5), and *I suppose* (line 5).

After exploring the issue thoroughly, and eliciting a statement from Tom that the reason for appointing someone else was not that he had any doubt about her capabilities, but was rather based on logistics and simplicity (*what was practically easy that would create the least amount of hassles at that point in time*), Claire pursues her goal of getting Tom to promise she will not be overlooked again. First she restates her ostensible objective in terms very similar to those with which she opened.

Example 3.18

Context: Later in same interaction as Example 3.17.

```
 1 CLA:  I suppose that I just + I suppose I wanted you to sort of
 2        look more closely at it from the point of view
 3        of opportunities for me as well
 4 TOM:  yeah
 5 CLA:  because I mean if you go on precedent
 6        and if I don't get any any opportunities
 7        then I don't get considered next time
 8 TOM:  mm
 9 CLA:  and basically otherwise I don't see myself moving much
10        if I don't get any experience myself
11 TOM:  mm
12 CLA:  so that's that's really what I wanted to sort of talk to you about
13        and if there was anything I could do just to- just to
14        um [tut] develop my own ability to be able to like that
```

The deferential attenuators and minimisers that characterised Claire's first approach to the issue are again evident in the opening and closing lines of this excerpt: *I suppose* (twice in line 1), *just* (lines 1, 13), *sort of* (lines 1, 12),

I mean (line 5), together with a hesitant style evident in the repetition of *just to* followed by a voiced hesitation *um* (lines 13–14). But enclosed within the deferential packaging, there is a core of rational logic in the form of an explicit and direct proposition, which is clearly stated (lines 5–7), namely, if precedent is relevant, as Tom has already stated, Claire cannot possibly qualify unless she is given opportunities to gain relevant experience. In other words, she is in a Catch-22 situation. Claire follows this succinct summary of her argument with a statement of its promotion implications (lines 9–10). This argument is the platform for her complaint and the lever for eliciting a promise from Tom with respect to future decisions.

Example 3.19 is taken from the final section of the discussion of this issue. After eight minutes, the discussion has reached the point where Claire can, without causing offence, give her boss a directive.

Example 3.19
Context: Later in same interaction as Examples 3.17 and 3.18.

```
1 CLA:  so next time if a you would you'll consider me as /the same as X\
2 TOM:  /oh yeah I mean I\ think what you're raising is quite valid . . .
3       you know and I um well as I say
4       I didn't er qualify my decision other than look at the precedent
5 CLA:  oh
6 TOM:  so now- I mean + next time it happens and if it does happen again
7       then yeah sure no difficulties
8 CLA:  all right then oh good
```

Between lines 2 and 3, for reasons of length, we have omitted 22 lines in which Tom recycles yet again the points he has made and Claire politely acknowledges them. At the end of this complex argument, she has (on tape!) a commitment from Tom that next time she will be seriously considered for the position of acting manager, together with a statement that she has the necessary abilities and an acknowledgement that precedent is an inadequate basis for such a decision. This is a nice example of the construction of the discourse of power and politeness by skilled participants. Getting one's superiors to do something may require the skilful employment of indirect strategies and sophisticated discourse devices.

Getting the boss to do something that is in one's interests is more of a challenge when one's interests do not obviously coincide with those of the organisation. In Chapter 1, Example 1.4, we discussed an example where an employee, Kerry, was attempting to persuade her acting manager, Ruth, to approve leave with pay for a conference, despite the fact that Kerry was about to leave the organisation. Kerry made extensive use of deferential politeness to hedge her request, indicating her awareness that it was not a straightforward one. Another feature of Kerry's request was the aura of imprecision and vagueness around the work activities in which she was currently involved, and the precise timing of the conference in relation to the date when she would be leaving the organisation. In response to Kerry's stream of repetitious, imprecise discourse, full of unfinished phrases and changes of grammatical direction, Ruth put a series of precise questions to Kerry which required a simple *yes* or *no* answer: e.g. *so you haven't got that much longer here?*, *so you basically need to have Thursday and Friday off?*, *you need to confirm today do you?* However, Ruth's strategy for keeping Kerry on track and eliciting the precise information she needed was repeatedly subverted by Kerry.

Example 3.20 provides one illustration of how Kerry managed in this interaction to reframe her request in a way that constructed her, not as a devious young woman attempting to obtain funding to which she was not entitled, but rather as a cooperative young professional assistant making a reasonable request.

Example 3.20
Context: Meeting between library assistant, Kerry, and her acting manager, Ruth, in Ruth's office in a white-collar organisation. (Hedges and hesitations in bold.)

 1 RUTH: okay when do you need to make a decision
 2 KER: **well um** /Re- + Re-\
 3 RUTH: /you need to confirm\ today do you
 4 KER: **well** Rene's **sort of um** + doing **some** negotiations
 5   with **some** people this afternoon about our funding **and that stuff**
 6   and **um** she's going to cos the money's there
 7   and /it's **just** that I'd\
 8 RUTH: /yeah oh that's good\
 9 KER: I said to them not to worry about it
10   cos it + **you know** I was changing over
11   and it was gonna be **quite** difficult
12   time off and **da da da da things like this**
13   but she said oh no you should go if you can get it
14   so she /said **just**\ ask and
15 RUTH: /mm\
16 KER: see what they say and I said because if the-
17   if I'm not gonna get paid while I'm doing it then I'm not gonna go
18   and she said okay that's fine but **just** ask **anyway** [laughs]
19   so /that's what I'm doing\ yeah
20 RUTH: /yeah true\

In this excerpt, Kerry recounts a dialogue with a colleague from the organisation to which she is moving (lines 9, 11–14, 16–18) in order to make it clear that the suggestion to ask for funding originated with someone else. Again there is a certain amount of apparently irrelevant detail (lines 4–7), a feature typical of Kerry's contributions throughout the interaction, although in this case it is clear from Ruth's positive response (line 8) that, although irrelevant to the point at issue, it creates a useful (for Kerry) positive effect. In lines 17–19, Kerry is suddenly, and somewhat startlingly, in the context of the preceding discourse, extremely clear and direct, and she again succeeds in eliciting from Ruth a positive acknowledgement *yeah true* (line 20).

Kerry effectively combines in this extract the deferential language appropriate to a less powerful supplicant (the relevant strategies are signalled in bold), with the construction of herself as a young, sensible, professional seeking advice from a more experienced mentor. As a result, she successfully resists for a considerable time Ruth's repeated attempts to keep her on track, and Ruth's efforts to cut through her vagueness, imprecision and mass of referentially irrelevant detail.

Hints

We have discussed how the extent to which people pay explicit attention to the feelings of others, or demonstrate considerations of politeness at work, tends to vary with a range of factors, including, in particular, the power relationships between the person issuing the directive and its addressee. While, as we have illustrated, many contextual factors modify the generalisation, it is nevertheless useful to note that routine directives from a person in authority are more likely to be relatively explicit, while directives 'upwards' tend to include signals of deference and to be less direct. With similar reservations about the modifying effect of social and contextual factors, it is also noteworthy that the greater the benefit to the recipient, the more likely a directive will be encoded indirectly, or even carefully negotiated, as demonstrated in the examples above. In this final section, we examine the least direct category of directives, namely 'hints', illustrating some of the forms they may take at work.

Hints are utterances where the directive intent is not directly or conventionally derivable from the words uttered.[13] Rather, addressees must 'infer what is required from their knowledge of the rules of appropriate behaviour in the context' (Holmes 1983: 106). However, in some contexts these rules allow a rather wider range of potentially appropriate responses than in others.

In our data, it was possible to identify a continuum from situations where the addressee could safely ignore the directive intent of the hint without incurring any penalty, to situations where the required action was so predictable that ignoring it would be regarded as at least rude and, in the context of workplace relationships, potentially insubordinate. Example 3.21, where the participants are both of relatively high status and where the action requested could be considered something of an imposition, illustrates a case where it would have been possible for Fay to ignore the directive intent of the hint.

Example 3.21
Context: Fay and Paula are planning for a meeting of relatively senior personnel in a white-collar institution.

1 PAU: well I guess we'll need a record of the meeting
2 FAY: yeah that would be really useful
3 PAU: it's really important everything's in writing around this issue
4 FAY: mm
5 PAU: since I'll be chairing ++
6 FAY: would you like me to do it this time
7 PAU: well if it isn't too much I mean if you could
8 FAY: okay
9 PAU: that would be great

Paula wants Fay to take the minutes of the meeting they are planning. However, since they are of equal status and taking minutes is often regarded as a clerical task, this has to be carefully managed. The directive is realised as an extended hint (lines 1, 3, 5) which is negotiated between Paula and Fay over several turns, and the significance of the pause (marked ++) at line 5 should not be underestimated. Nevertheless, Fay could have chosen to remain silent, or to suggest an alternative solution to the problem Paula has raised.

Example 3.22 occurred in a hospital meeting where experts from a range of disciplinary backgrounds were assigning patients to different doctors.

Example 3.22
Context: Kath is a senior nurse. Judy is a registrar.

1 KATH: we got another referral from doctor X
2   he's one of your neighbours Judy
3 JUDY: no I can't [general laughter] (Mooney 1980: 15).

Kath's directive in line 2 takes the form of a hint which requires some inferencing. Since Judy is a neighbour of the client, the implication is that it will be less costly for her than for others to take him. Given her higher professional status, Judy could have ignored the directive intent and treated the utterance as information. However, her non-compliant response indicates she has opted for an alternative method of responding.

Hints clearly fit Brown and Levinson's (1987) category of face-threatening acts which are done 'off record', the most indirect strategy they identify. Factors which lead to the adoption of this strategy include a power disparity where the speaker is the subordinate, a degree of social distance between the participants (e.g. relatively new colleagues or colleagues who do not work together regularly), or a situation where the request is very costly to the addressee (in Brown and Levinson's terms the ranking of the imposition is very high). Asking the boss for the use of her laptop, asking the office administrative assistant to go out and buy your lunch, or directing a colleague from another department to deliver a file to you are examples which could satisfy these conditions. We did not record many examples of this kind of hint, since most of our participants worked together routinely, and hence social distance was typically low.

Routine relationships are much more likely to produce examples of hints at the other end of the continuum, i.e. where the required action is so predictable that it can easily be inferred by the addressee. These were much more frequent in our data set. Ervin-Tripp (1976: 44) notes that such hints are typically associated with 'high solidarity closed networks' and may involve irony or humour. *You make a better door than a window* is an example used in the workplace by one colleague to get another to move out of the light.[14] Another colleague's wry comment *I must get that hearing aid!* was interpreted (correctly) as a routine request for his softly spoken colleague to speak louder. (Chapter 6 provides further examples of the use of humour to soften directives.) A similar example involved a manager saying to a senior member of her team *now I need to get that up to them today*, meaning 'read it and get it back to me quickly'. Hints which required such routine inferencing occurred in our data set between people who worked together regularly, as illustrated in Examples 3.23 and 3.24.

Example 3.23
Context: Manager Ruth to policy analyst Kelly with whom she has worked over a long period.

1 RUTH: um now I'm not gonna be back until about bit after three
2 KEL: okay well I'll revise the publication proposal
3 RUTH: so I can look at it then
4 KEL: yeah

Ruth provides a time of return in line 1, rather than any explicit directive. Kelly correctly reads this information, in the light of the preceding discussion, as an indication that Ruth would like a revision of the document they have been working on to be ready by the time she is indicating. The message of the directive is totally predictable and thus easily inferred by Kelly from the context. We found many such cases where directive intent was inferred without any problem by the addressee, despite, in some cases, the apparent obscurity of the directive message to an outsider. Example 3.24 illustrates this point even more clearly.

Example 3.24
Context: Manager Helen to executive assistant Fay with whom she has worked over a long period. They are discussing what needs to be done to follow up the gaps left by a temporary replacement while Fay was on leave.

1 HEL: correct it once and then somehow copy it /down into the other\
2 FAY: /okay yep\
3 HEL: bits
4 FAY: that's possible
5 HEL: um and also putting it as an appendix is easiest probably the easiest
6   way
7 FAY: okay

The directives in line 1 are quite explicitly expressed using imperative forms. By contrast the directive to include the material in an appendix is expressed as a declarative, but in the context of the discussion Fay picks it up immediately and responds to it as a directive. There are many examples of such indirect directives in the data. The directive intent is easily inferred from the social context (role relations, rights and obligations of participants) and the discourse context (preceding and following supporting moves).

Conclusion

People at work simultaneously achieve many different workplace objectives which include getting things done efficiently while constructing and maintaining collegial relationships. These two demands, sometimes labelled transactional vs interpersonal, social or affective goals, are frequently perfectly compatible, since good workplace relationships facilitate many aspects of work. However, as politeness theory predicts, there is sometimes a degree of tension involved in negotiating a pathway through situations where concern for the face needs of participants conflicts with the need to get things done quickly, or where the demands being made go beyond what is appropriate in the light of the addressee's work role or position.

Power and politeness are important considerations in accounting for the way people get things done at work. But they are clearly not the only considerations. In this chapter we have illustrated ways in which different kinds of directive reflect participants' relative weighting of a range of different factors. Direct and explicit directives tend to be most frequent in routine instructions from superiors to subordinates, unless the superior is asking for something out of the ordinary or 'beyond the call of duty'. Asking your PA to do your shopping, or even to stay on at work beyond normal working hours, generally requires more sensitive and subtle negotiation. Mitigated and indirect directives instantiate politeness in action in the workplace and are typically found in interactions between status equals or new colleagues, or in transactions where a subordinate is trying to persuade a superior to do something. However, not surprisingly, the examples in this chapter have only hinted at the wide range of contextual factors that may influence the complex ways in which a directive is realised or negotiated.

In addition to factors such as the relationship between the people involved, the length of time they have been working together, the setting of their discussion, the speaker's assessment of the likelihood of compliance, many other factors may also be relevant. Different workplaces develop different cultures, for instance, a point illustrated more fully in Chapter 6. Hence directives couched in bald unmitigated form are much less frequent in some workplaces, while extensively negotiated directives are unusual in others (cf Bernsten 1998). Addressing a group rather than an individual may be a relevant factor in how a directive is framed, as illustrated in Examples 3.6 and 3.7. Particular aspects of participants' social or professional identity may also be relevant at different points in an interaction and thus affect the way a directive is expressed.

Directives, including indirect directives or requests, are of course just some of the many ways people get things done at work. Vine (2001), for instance, draws attention to the category of 'advice', which she defines as a control act which typically benefits the addressee rather than the speaker. There are many other strategies which can be used to manage a situation and achieve workplace objectives. Those who set the agenda for a meeting or discussion, for instance, influence the direction and structure of workplace talk for that period. Similarly, by summing up at strategic points throughout a discussion, and especially at the end, a person can very effectively impose their perspective or 'take' on what has been decided. These are strategies for getting things done at work which are the focus of the next chapter.

Notes

1. Bullet points indicate the examples are taken from a range of interactions. Line numbering indicates the utterances come from the same interaction.
2. There is an extensive literature on directives dating back at least to the 1970s (e.g. Sinclair and Coulthard (1975); Ervin-Tripp (1976); Bellinger (1979); Craig, Tracy and Spisak (1986); Brown and Levinson (1987)). Vine (2001) provides an excellent summary and critical review. 'Control act' is a more recent, broader and more comprehensive term which includes requests, favours, advice, prohibitions, invitations, and so on (Ervin-Tripp, Guo and Lampert 1990: 308). Following Clyne (1994: 63), we use the narrower term 'directive' since our focus is workplace instructions and requests.

3. See, for example, Pufahl Bax (1986); Weigel and Weigel (1985); West (1990); Clyne (1994); Bernsten (1998).
4. Brown and Levinson (1987: 60) describe such directives as 'bald on record'.
5. See, for example, Ervin-Tripp (1976); Mooney (1980); Pschaid (1992); Clyne (1994).
6. See Holmes (1984) for discussion of strategies of hedging/attenuation and boosting/intensification and Holmes (1995, Chapter 4) for a discussion of their relationship to politeness.
7. This point is extensively illustrated in Vine (2001). See also Blum-Kulka, House and Kasper (1989); Blum-Kulka (1997).
8. See Vine (2001) for a thorough discussion of definitions in this area.
9. These examples are analysed in more detail in Brown and Robertson (2000).
10. Chapter 7 on problematic discourse provides further examples of this pattern.
11. See Stubbe et al. (2000) for a detailed analysis of a larger excerpt from this interaction from a number of different theoretical perspectives.
12. Tom's contribution to this interaction is analysed from a CDA perspective in Chapter 7.
13. See, for example, Clark and Lucy (1975); Ervin-Tripp (1976); Holmes (1983); Blum Kulka et al. (1989).
14. Cf Ervin-Tripp's example 'You make a fine door Sal' (1976: 43).

4

Workplace Meetings

Introduction

For many white-collar organisations, meetings are the very stuff of 'work'. Meetings also make a crucial contribution to the achievement of workplace goals in blue-collar workplaces, such as factories and industrial sites. In both contexts, meetings provide many opportunities for the expression of institutional power and authority relationships. Indeed according to Mumby (1988: 68), meetings 'function as one of the most important and visible sites of organisational power, and of the reification of organisational hierarchy'. As this chapter illustrates, meetings also provide sites for the manifestation of politeness, respect and disrespect, collegiality and solidarity, i.e. various aspects of 'rapport management' (Spencer-Oatey 2000).

Researchers have examined the discourse of meetings from a variety of different perspectives. A number of studies have described the discursive strategies used in the management of meetings (e.g. Barbato 1994; Bargiela-Chiappini and Harris 1997), while others have explored how status is discursively realised in meetings (e.g. Craig and Pitts 1990; Sollitt-Morris 1996), or the complexities of how things get accomplished interactionally through meeting talk (e.g. Drew and Heritage 1992; Willing 1992; Boden 1994; Firth 1995; Sarangi and Roberts 1999). The function of interruptions as manifestations of power in meetings has attracted particular attention (e.g. Edelsky 1981; Woods 1989; Craig and Pitts 1990), and the amount of talk contributed by different participants has also been analysed as an indication of dominance (e.g. Swacker 1979; Edelsky 1981; Holmes 1992; Sollitt-Morris 1996). There is also some research on the extent to which politeness considerations appear to influence participants' contributions to meetings (e.g. Pearson 1988; Scheerhorn 1989; Morand 1996a, 1996b). Overall, however, there is not a great deal of research which examines in detail the ways in which power and politeness are manifested in workplace meetings, or the relevance of power and politeness behaviour in crucial decision-making contexts.

The data we draw on in this chapter comprises 80 meetings from 9 different workplaces, involving a minimum of 2 and a maximum of 18 participants, and ranging in length from 7 minutes to several hours. As described in Chapter 2, the meeting data comprises both audio and video recordings, almost all of which were recorded by the participants themselves. A large proportion of earlier research on meetings has been based on self-report data, interview or questionnaire responses and relatively unsystematic observation (see Williams 1988) or, at best, on data collected in rather artificial settings, such as interactions between student participants in laboratories responding to simulated situations (see Mott and Petrie 1995). Where more naturalistic or 'genuine' meetings have been recorded, they have often involved academics and teachers in department meetings, conferences or seminars (e.g. Swacker 1979; Edelsky 1981; Holmes 1992; Sollitt-Morris 1996). The LWP database of authentic meetings provides an unusually large and varied, and thus a particularly rich and valuable, research resource.

Example 4.1 concisely illustrates many of the features of workplace meetings which will be explored in this chapter.

Example 4.1[1]
Context: Meeting in a large commercial organisation chaired by section manager, Clara, since the usual chairperson is absent. Seth has gone to collect the minutes from the previous meeting which he didn't realise he was supposed to circulate.

```
 1 CLA:  okay well we might just start without Seth
 2       he can come in and can review the minutes from last week
 3 REN:  are you taking the minutes this week
 4 CLA:  no I'm just trying to chair the meeting
 5       who would like to take minutes this week
 6 REN:  who hasn't taken the minutes yet
 7 BEN:  I haven't yet I will
 8 CLA:  thank you /Benny\
 9 REN:  /oh Benny\ takes beautiful minutes too
10 BEN:  don't tell them they'll want me doing it every week
         [general laughter]
11 CLA:  it's a bit of a secret
12       okay shall we kick off and just go round the room um doing an
13       update and then when Seth comes in with the the minutes
14       we need to check on any action items from our planning
15       over to you Marlene
```

There is no doubt who is in charge. Clara declares the meeting open, *we might just start* (line 1), even though one of the members is not present. She deftly ducks Renee's attempt to get her to take minutes by asserting her role as Chair (lines 2–3), and then asks for a volunteer for this task (line 5). She approves Benny as minute taker, *thank you Benny* (line 8), and sets the agenda for the meeting (lines 12–14). Finally, she allocates the first turn, *over to you Marlene* (line 15). Meetings are clearly prime sites for doing power.

On the other hand, in this very brief interaction in which she 'does power' in all the ways described, Clara also pays attention to politeness considerations and affective factors. Her expression of thanks to Benny not only ratifies his role as minute taker, it is also a politeness strategy indicating approval and paying attention to his face needs. And she implies approval of the relational work expressed in the side sequence consisting of Renee's comment *Benny takes beautiful minutes* (line 9), and Benny's humorous response *don't tell them they'll want me doing it every week* (line 10), by adding her own collusive contribution *it's a bit of a secret* (line 11). In other words, she participates in, and thus implicitly endorses, the relational humour which typically marks the opening of a meeting.

Renee, on the other hand, takes a couple of opportunities in this short exchange to inject an element of subversion into the proceedings. Her enquiry (line 3) about whether Clara is taking the minutes is not guileless. While minute taking is shared among team members, it is apparent from a range of non-verbal signals that Clara intends to chair this meeting. Moreover, she then takes over from Clara the responsibility for allocating the role of minute taker by asking for someone who has not already undertaken this duty (line 6). Finally, her compliment to Benny is suspiciously double-edged, since minute taking is not self-evidently a valued skill in such a high-powered team, and this interpretation is further supported by her use of the adjective *beautiful* which is sufficiently 'feminine' to cast doubt on her sincerity. So, although overtly Renee effectively conveys an impression of positive politeness, the arch tone of her 'compliment', together with its ambiguous content, seem likely to raise suspicions about her motives. This brief excerpt thus illustrates some of the complex ways in which power and politeness considerations are inextricably intertwined in a speech event which is often regarded as *the* core of workplace interaction – the meeting.

In this chapter, we first describe some of the different types of meetings identified in our workplace corpus and the dimensions along which they differ. We then examine the discourse structure and strategies of these meetings in relation to both their transactional and interpersonal functions. In the final section, we use two case studies to illustrate in more detail how power and politeness are manifested through the various features of meetings. The meetings selected for these case studies contrast on a number of dimensions and further exemplify some of the specific discourse strategies which are used to effectively 'manage' meeting processes and to develop rapport, while highlighting the complex ways in which managers instantiate power and politeness in interaction.

Types of meetings

Defining a meeting

Some researchers avoid defining what qualifies as a 'meeting', arguing that we can all 'commonsensically recognize a meeting when [we] see it' (Cuff and Sharrock 1985: 158; see also Atkinson, Cuff and Lee 1978: 134). In an informal non-technical sense, any interaction between two people can be described as a 'meeting', but such a definition is too broad to be useful for our purposes. Bargiela-Chiappini and Harris define meetings as 'task-oriented and decision-making encounters' involving 'the cooperative effort of two parties, the Chair and the Group' (1997: 208). This suggests a relatively formal encounter involving at least three people and with reportable outcomes, but none of these factors is crucial. In our data, informal meetings were often an important way in which workplace business got done and not all meetings reflected cooperative effort.

We have opted to focus instead on the *function* of the interaction as our fundamental criterion in distinguishing meetings from other kinds of workplace encounters, and use the term 'meeting' to refer to *interactions which focus, whether indirectly or directly, on workplace business*. This 'business' may or may not be consistent with official workplace goals – after all, for various reasons, employees sometimes have meetings aimed at subverting their organisation's objectives, perhaps because they consider them to be badly formulated, misguided, or whatever. Moreover, while most of the meetings in our database were prearranged, this too is not an essential criterion. Some meetings occurred spontaneously when people encountered each other fortuitously and took the opportunity to discuss an issue of common interest and concern. The meetings in our data set therefore vary greatly in terms of their relative formality and the goals and purposes of the participants. In the next section, we consider the variable characteristics of the meetings in our database more closely, before discussing the relationship between these features and aspects of power and politeness.

Variable features of meetings

Formality

A number of features influence the relative formality of a meeting. The size, length, location and composition of meetings are highly variable and interact with other characteristics such as the style of interaction, the structure of the meeting and the relationships between the participants. These features are most usefully analysed in terms of dimensions or scales, as the framework provided in Fig 4.1 suggests. While not intended as a comprehensive

Large in size	Small in size (2–4)
Formal setting	Unplanned location
Starting time specified	Occurs by chance
Finishing time specified	Finishes 'naturally'
Participants specified	Open to anyone
Formal procedures	Informal style
Explicit structured agenda	'Rolling' agenda
Tightly integrated group	Loosely connected
Mixed gender group	Same-gender group

Fig 4.1 Useful dimensions for comparing meetings

model, the dimensions identified provide a useful comparative framework for our purposes in describing the diverse ways in which power and politeness are instantiated in the discourse practices of participants in workplace meetings.

While very large meetings obviously occur at times in organisations, in practice, 18 was the largest number of participants present in the meetings in our corpus, while the smallest meetings comprised just two people. The smaller meetings tended to concentrate at the less formal end of the scale in terms of interaction style, as well as on a number of other dimensions related to how tightly or otherwise the meeting was structured. Unsurprisingly, larger meetings tended to be more formal according to a number of different criteria, although this was not always the case and we often observed variation in the degree of formality between different parts of the same meeting.

At one extreme there were meetings which were prearranged, usually by or at the direction of a senior person in the organisation, for a specified time and sometimes length, in a specified and often dedicated formal committee or boardroom, with a ratified group of participants. Such meetings typically followed formal meeting procedures and an explicit formal, structured and predetermined agenda (cf Bargiela-Chiappini and Harris 1997: 207). At the other extreme were meetings which occurred by chance in a range of possible 'accidental' locations, such as the corridor, the tearoom, or the office of one of the participants, meetings set up on the spot by mutual (often implicit) agreement or negotiation between the participants. Some meetings had no specified finishing time, but simply continued until one or more of the participants declared or negotiated an end.

By contrast with meetings where those with the right or obligation to attend were clearly specified, other meetings had a more open potential membership. For example, anyone interested could attend a meeting arranged to discuss the organisation's annual Christmas picnic (December is summer in New Zealand), or anyone from the workplace might attend a meeting organised by management to inform workers of new policy initiatives. Again contrasting with meetings that followed formal accepted meeting procedures and where the agenda was structured and explicit, some meetings had a much more flexible and fluid agenda, with topics emerging gradually and 'naturally' and with no explicit, formal control over topics or procedures. Some of these features are discussed in greater detail below. It is important to emphasise that they are in principle independent of each other and are best conceptualised as a range of potential points on a scale or continuum, as Fig 4.1 suggests.

There are, of course, many other features which differ from one meeting to another and which bear a less direct relationship to the formality of the meeting – the relationship between the participants, the roles and relative experience of different participants, the range of topics to be covered, and so on. Here we mention just two additional features which proved relevant in our analyses, namely, participant relationships and gender.

At one extreme, there were meetings in our data which involved people who knew each other very well, who worked together and met daily, and who interacted socially outside work. At the other extreme were meetings which involved participants brought together for a single project who met weekly for no more than two hours for only six weeks, and who then had little or no further contact. Characterising these end points as 'tightly integrated' and 'loosely connected' adequately captures this contrast. This factor affected the amount of small talk, social talk and humour in different meetings. Tightly integrated groups, for example, were more likely to catch up on personal news at the beginning of meetings and tended to generate more humorous sequences (see Chapters 5 and 6).

Some meetings comprised all men or all women, while others had various proportions of each gender. For descriptive purposes we usually simply noted whether meeting participants were the same gender or not, but again in principle, one could assign a meeting to a point on a scale depending on the proportions of women and men in the group. Gender is clearly a relevant variable in the analysis of some aspects of workplace interaction, such as humour and small talk and turn-taking patterns, though this is not an issue explored in any detail in this book. In general, as we illustrate below, overt manifestations of power and authority tend to be most easily observed in more formal, structured meetings; but the ongoing process of constructing, developing and maintaining workplace power and rapport is an aspect of all meetings. It is simply less explicit and overt in small, informal meetings and typically requires more detailed analysis.

Goals and purposes

Although they may not always be explicitly articulated or even acknowledged, every meeting has goals or objectives. Indeed, a common understanding of the purpose of a meeting, and agreement about the roles of different individuals attending, are important factors in accounting for how effectively a meeting runs. Typically, the people attending the meetings in our data set knew in advance why the meeting had been set up – either because they had received a formal agenda, or because its purpose had been articulated when the meeting was arranged. This norm was highlighted when, unusually, someone arrived at a formal meeting unclear about its goals, as illustrated in Example 4.2.

Example 4.2
Context: Four people preparing a board paper.

```
 1 SEL:   Brett knows the purpose of this meeting um I've talked to Dereck a
 2        bit I presume Brett's talked to Vera a bit
 3 BRE:   I really asked her what the [laughs] purpose of it was
 4        /actually as a matter of fact\ [laughs]
 5 VERA:  /[laughs] ( )\
 6 BRE:   and we discussed it briefly at lunchtime [laughs] but I no I had a
 7 VERA:  and we discussed it briefly at lunchtime [laughs]
 8 BRE:   I had a [voc] we wr- we do basically know um
 9 SEL:   right
10 BRE:   but I'm I have some concerns about the project about +
11        the thing that I not sure exactly the purpose of the meeting but
12 SEL:   okay
13 BRE:   we should deal with the purpose of the meeting
        [Selene, the manager and Chair, here provides an extended account of
        the background to the meeting, ending as follows]
14 SEL:   + um and + after much shillyshallying I volunteered to write it
15        as long as it was written in a collaborative way
16        such that I wasn't [drawls] the + author of it +
17        and that's what this meeting is about and that's why it needed to be
18        done before I went away
```

In addition, of course, meetings have various implicit goals which also relate to the organisation's business, such as making the required decisions, achieving the meeting's goals within the allotted time, ensuring the relevant decisions are implemented, and so on (processes which are illustrated below). Our database also includes many smaller and/or less formal meetings where the task-related or 'business' goals are often not made explicit, but are nonetheless what the participants would regard as the *reason* for the meeting. Thus there were meetings to discuss the draft of a report, for example, or to review the structure and wording of an important letter; there were meetings to bring someone up to date on what had happened at a meeting they had missed; there were meetings to plan the back-up procedures required while someone was away; and there were many meetings reporting back on other meetings or activities, or planning for subsequent larger, more important and formal meetings.

Even in very small meetings, participants sometimes quite explicitly articulated what they saw as the purpose of the meeting. In Example 4.3, for instance, Claire indicates that she has sought this meeting to discuss a problem relating to her career development. She is seeking an explanation for the appointment of someone other than her as acting manager.

Example 4.3
Context: Claire with a section manager in his office in a government organisation.

1 CLA: yeah um yeah I want to talk to you about . . .
2   well i- the decision to make um Jared acting manager while Joseph is
3   away

In Example 4.4, Bruce seeks advice with a problem.

Example 4.4
Context: Bruce enters Joan's office in a government organisation.

1 BRU: Yvette gave me these and said . . .
2   um + our er portfolio's supposed or should be doing something with
3   these . . . and er she said you might know something about them
4   so to come and have a chat to you

These are examples of 'on-record', task-related statements, where the participants make at least one of their goals for the meeting explicit.

While some analysts have distinguished many diverse functions of meetings, in broad terms, we found it adequate to classify meetings into three distinct types according to their overt primary or 'business' goals and expected outcomes:

- planning or prospective/forward-oriented meeting
- reporting or retrospective/backward-/backward-oriented meeting
- task-oriented or problem-solving/present-oriented meeting.

Many meetings in fact had elements of all three functions (see Fig 4.2). The category *Planning or forward-oriented* generally includes functions such as *assigning tasks*, *requesting action* and *requesting permission* (Dwyer 1993: 606), while the category *Reporting or backward-oriented* obviously covers the function of reporting back, as well as most instances of more detailed functions such as *giving feedback*, *requesting information* and *updating* (Dwyer

---

- **Planning** or prospective/forward-oriented meeting
  (e.g. assigning tasks, requesting permission or action, strategising, making decisions)
- **Reporting** or retrospective/backward-oriented meeting
  (e.g. reporting, clarifying, giving feedback, requesting information, updating)
- **Task-oriented** or problem-solving/present-oriented meeting
  (e.g. problem-solving, collaborative task completion, information exchange)

Fig 4.2 Main purposes of meetings in LWP database (adapted from Dwyer 1993: 606)

1993: 606). Both of these meeting types tend to be planned in advance. However, meetings in the third category, *Task-oriented or present-oriented* are more likely to arise spontaneously or at relatively short notice.

In one organisation, for example, the overall purpose of the majority of the meetings we recorded could be classified as 'planning'. Although, inevitably, their meetings involved some review components too, the team had been brought together for a period of two days precisely to undertake strategic planning for the next three years. By contrast, the main purpose of the regular weekly meetings of another team we recorded was to review progress. Their meetings consisted predominantly of reports from each member concerning their progress with their area of the team's joint project. Another pattern was illustrated by the daily meetings recorded in one of the factories, which typically had aspects of all three purposes: the team leader generally reviewed the previous day's achievements, set out the objectives for the current day, and addressed any problems that had arisen since the last meeting (see Chapters 3 and 7). We also recorded many short meetings between two or three people which focused on a specific task or problem, such as organising a large meeting or preparing for an overseas business trip, or which concentrated largely on conveying information from a subordinate to a superior who needed to be brought up to date on an issue.

As indicated in Chapters 5 and 6, in addition to these transactional or 'business' goals, meetings also typically have less obvious, frequently unacknowledged and perhaps relatively unconscious politeness functions and social objectives. These include improving rapport and relationships between staff, strengthening solidarity, 'creating team' (Fletcher 1999), and generally paying attention to various aspects of participants' face needs; or, alternatively in some cases, emphasising power and authority and the hierarchical relationships between coworkers, by more clearly demarcating status divisions and employment responsibilities and increasing or maintaining social distance between participants.

In some meetings, for instance, the chair used strategies which emphasised his or her authority, such as very formally marking the opening and closing of the meeting, signalling explicitly each of the steps in the progression of the discussion through the agenda and stating and ratifying each decision overtly and 'on record'. In other meetings the chair downplayed their authority and emphasised the collegial nature of the decision-making process. Different degrees of attention to face needs and rapport maintenance were also apparent. In some meetings, people's contributions were explicitly acknowledged and even praised or provided with positive feedback; in others, there were simply no explicit positive comments in response to contributions. In some meetings, conflict was minimised and disagreement was typically attenuated using hedges and mitigating strategies, while in others conflicting views were expressed more directly, with little verbal evidence of concern for face needs. The case studies below illustrate some of these patterns.

It should be noted that although all participants were sensitive to some degree to these more social or affective goals of meetings, and even to their importance in facilitating the achievement of more referential or task-oriented goals, when asked many of the participants in our research considered that the only 'real' objectives of meetings in work settings fitted into categories such as those identified in Fig 4.2.

How are meetings structured?

Three-phase structure

We turn now to a more explicit analysis of how meetings are structured in terms of their topical organisation (the management of the formal or informal 'agenda'). Our examination of the structure of meetings identified the three phases of meetings which have been validated in many previous analyses (e.g. Fisher 1982; Sollitt-Morris 1996; Bargiela-Chiappini and Harris 1997):

- opening or introductory section
- central development section
- closing section.

Each of these components could typically be identified both in the structure of the meeting as a whole and within subsections embedded within the overall structure. In the opening section participants typically agreed on their agenda or identified the problem to be solved:

- well I just thought we needed to talk this through a bit further
- right we need to make some decisions about where we go next

The central section often comprised an exploratory phase where the issue, or a series of issues, were more fully developed in an open-ended way. In the closing section, the problem was usually resolved, or sometimes 'parked' as too hard, or a course of action was agreed on, or a decision was reached:

- right so that's agreed then . . .
- okay so we're clear on what's needed

Typically, both agenda setting and the decision about when a discussion was complete were strongly influenced by those in positions of power or authority, while other participants contributed more, and on a more equal footing, to the development component.

The following specific example of an interaction between just two people, Ruth, a manager and Barbara, a senior member of her staff, illustrates all three phases clearly (Examples 4.5a, 4.5b, 4.5c). In Phase 1, Barbara opens the discussion by stating the purpose of the informal meeting she is requesting. The women then spend a few minutes clarifying the exact nature of the problem Barbara needs help with.

Example 4.5a
Context: Barbara seeks guidance from her manager, Ruth, in a government organisation.
(Phase 1: Opening phase)

```
1 BARB:  hey Ruth
2 RUTH:  yeah
3 BARB:  I've got a little problem
4        I've finally just had a look at these questions and . . .
5        I've discovered a few difficulties . . .
6        a number of the questions are very leading
7 RUTH:  mm.
```

After several minutes of discussion they begin to explore possible solutions, thus entering Phase 2.

Example 4.5b
(Phase 2: Exploratory phase)

```
1 RUTH:  I hadn't realised the questions were quite so loaded
2        do we have to present the information orally or do we have the
3        opportunity to just provide responses in writing
4 BARB:  we can but it would be an awful lot of work
5 RUTH:  mm
```

6 BARB: and we still don't have any control over how it's used
7 RUTH: or the way in which it's interpreted?
8 BARB: no
9 RUTH: I mean that's a real worry
10 BARB: see cos I mean this question I could do a thesis on that
11 RUTH: mm.

It is noteworthy that the participants actively collaborate in attempting to resolve the problem. Both cooperate in evaluating Ruth's suggestion to provide only written responses (lines 4–7). This exploratory phase proceeds in this style for quite a while longer. The participants' engagement with the issue is signalled by the fact that they speak more quickly in this section, with shorter turns, overlapping speech and a great deal of encouraging and positive feedback. Finally, they reach Phase 3.

Example 4.5c
(Phase 3: Closing phase)

1 RUTH: so where are we at? I mean you're inclined to want to pull back a little
2   bit
3 BARB: yeah
4 RUTH: but to find out a bit more from Ray about expressing our concerns
5   about the way in which the questions are framed
6 BARB: mm
7 RUTH: and secondly about what control we'll have over the way
8   in which the information might be used
9 BARB: mm
10 RUTH: those are the two main things we need to get back to Bob on
11 BARB: rightio I'll ring him then
12 RUTH: okay

In this phase the problem is finally resolved. Ruth sums up their position, they agree on the action to be taken and the meeting draws to a close. Though Barbara, the subordinate, initiated the meeting and set the agenda (*I've got a little problem*), it is Ruth who determines its subsequent structure. Her questions shape the direction of the exploratory thinking and it is she who sums up (*so where are we at*) and closes the meeting. The exchange is pleasant in tone and cooperative in function. The two women treat each other with respect, but there is little explicit linguistic 'facework'. It is a very focused, task-oriented and efficient interaction. While Ruth's input clearly assists Barbara to take the matter forward, she avoids giving the impression that she is taking over.

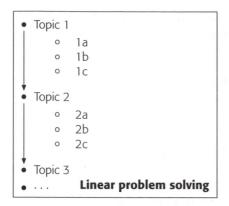
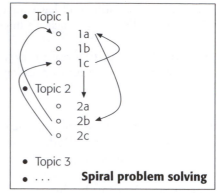

Fig 4.3 Linear and spiral or cyclical patterns

Linear and cyclical patterns

Topic management and turn taking within formal meetings are typically controlled by the chair who has the authority to control the meeting structure, while in less formal meetings they are more likely to be jointly negotiated. However, in the course of analysing both formal and informal meetings in our data, we identified two broad types of topical structure which we describe as 'linear' versus 'spiral' or cyclical (see Fig 4.3). Many meetings had elements of both structures within them, and moved between the two.

Typically, linear sections of meetings tended to follow an explicit or implicit agenda relatively closely, while spiral sections were more exploratory. Not surprisingly, reporting back or information gathering meetings (or sections of meetings) tended towards a more linear structure, which often went hand in hand with a greater degree of formality in terms of turn taking and interaction style. The linear structure reflects most closely the 'traditional' approach to such meetings, where topics are ordered according to a written agenda. Progression between topics occurs in a 'logical' and uniform manner. This pattern is clearly illustrated in Case Study 1 below (p. 78).

In some cases such meetings merely provide a forum where issues are agreed quickly or 'rubberstamped', as in the following excerpt where the chair reads out a series of recommendations and simply confirms the group's agreement (Example 4.6).

Example 4.6
Context: Large meeting in a government department.

1 CHAIR: okay can we go over the recommendations
2   er recommended that we note that capital expenditure is still trailing

3   the capital programme okay
4   er b note the business groups have returned two hundred and seven
5   thousand dollars to the capital pool
6   er c happy to agree to the new capital projects in table five be approved
7   for ninety nine two thousand okay

The influential role of the chair is very apparent in such instances.

However, meetings may also take other forms. One common pattern was a digressional pattern: a basic linear sequence could still be identified, but the participants and/or chair tolerated or actively initiated lengthy side sequences (Jefferson 1972) or 'off-topic' talk. This was particularly common in situations where people met frequently and were accustomed to working together collaboratively on a range of interrelated tasks. As already noted, another pattern was a spiral or cyclical topic organisation. In this style of discussion, the same point often recurred several times, each time receiving a little more discussion and taking the argument a little further. Planning meetings often adopted or developed this kind of spiral or cyclical structure, as did meetings which involved 'brainstorming' or creative problem solving.

In one such example, the group explored a range of possible directions for their activities over the next few months. Several possible directions were initially outlined by the manager. The discussion then ranged freely picking up different possibilities and returning to some options more and more often, until finally a set of agreed preferred objectives emerged. Although this may seem messy and unnecessarily time consuming to those who are accustomed to or prefer a more linear approach, it was apparent that in some cases this pattern of topical organisation facilitated the achievement of other goals, such as greater involvement from the group in the decision-making process, or a more thorough and creative exploration of the available options, both of which resulted in a higher level of 'buy-in' from a team.

Nevertheless, most meetings in our database included elements of both linear and spiral structure, with the precise pattern often depending on the specific topic being discussed. So, for example, a discussion in the staff tearoom about in which restaurant to hold the staff dinner at might be initially predominantly cyclical in structure, with lots of suggestions elaborated in varying degrees of detail and regular return to particular people's preferred choices. But a discussion of when the dinner should be held might be more linear, logically exploring a series of consecutive potential dates. The same group in the boardroom discussing the management of a publicity campaign for the organisation might also follow a predominantly linear style, allowing the logical steps in the campaign to determine the structure of the discussion. On the other hand, the group might use a more exploratory, cyclical approach to the issue of which advertising company to hire.

While many meetings have elements of both linear and cyclical patterning within them, there is nevertheless an interesting correspondence at a very general level between the functions or purposes of a meeting, the nature of the relationship between the participants and the predominant structural pattern which characterises it. As discussed in Chapter 3, the ways in which different types of control acts tended to characterise dyadic interactions was closely related to factors such as the authority relations or status gap between the participants. Thus forward-planning discussions with more senior team members typically involved more advice seeking, for instance, and the managers in the interactions analysed by Vine (2001) regularly diverged from their linear agendas. The discourse structure became more cyclical and the interaction entailed more technical 'digressions' as both parties explored particular points more fully.

A corresponding pattern was observed in meetings between participants who were equal in status and tended to engage in more extended exploratory talk. By contrast, interactions between managers and administrative assistants or more junior staff tended to be characterised by more explicit instruction and requests for action. In these cases, a planning session was more likely to proceed in a relatively linear manner, driven by the manager's agenda, and only in exceptional cases (e.g. where the two had developed a close personal relationship) would this be disrupted by extended explorations of peripheral points.

The overall structure of task-focused or problem-solving meetings also depended very much on the type of problem and the approach adopted by the chair. So, for example, where the problem required logical analysis and a systematic consideration of the steps to be taken in a process, the structure tended to the linear, as in Example 4.6. When the problem required creative thinking and innovative solutions, then brainstorming was a more usual strategy, with the consequence that the meeting structure was more likely to be spiral or cyclical for large sections.

Interestingly, participants themselves were often unaware of the underlying structure revealed by our schematic representations of topic sequencing. They were typically very surprised when we provided evidence of structure in a meeting which they had felt was 'all over the place'. Some found even more surprising our evidence that many so-called 'digressions' served important functions in relation to overall workplace objectives, while other digressions reflected participants' awareness of the importance of politeness considerations, such as the maintenance and strengthening of collegiality and rapport at work.

It will be clear from this discussion that the chair of a meeting or the person of superior status or authority in a small meeting or two-person interaction typically has a great deal of influence on the way the structure of the meeting develops. Some chairs tended to return regularly and explicitly to a basically linear structure after brief cyclical episodes, while others encouraged cyclicity and reimposed linear structure much less often. Other participants influenced the structure too, of course, by introducing digressions or encouraging the detailed exploration of a particular suggestion, or by opposing a particular suggestion and insisting on the exploration of alternative options (see Case Study 2 below for an illustration of this point). People who are 'experts' or who have particular responsibilities or seniority in particular areas are especially likely to be able to influence the direction of the discussion when it relates to their areas of expertise or responsibility. Influence over the structure of a meeting is thus one way in which power manifests itself in meetings.

Attention to relationships and face or rapport management is also evident in some aspects of the structure of meetings. As we will see in Chapters 5 and 6, small talk and humour typically mark the opening and closing phases of meetings. In meetings of groups receptive to humour, eruptions of humour also tend to occur sporadically during the discussion phases of their meetings. Collaborative humorous episodes typically developed, for instance, around the solution to a tricky problem – sometimes as the solution was just beginning to emerge, sometimes just after it had been articulated (see Marra fc). Humour was also a marker of tension release after difficult discussion sections in meetings, especially in workplaces where participants' face needs and work relationships were given attention.

Managing interaction in meetings

Meeting management is a dynamic process in which all participants play a part, whether cooperative or resistant. In this section we briefly survey a range of strategies used by participants to manage the complexity of verbal interaction in meetings and how these strategies contribute to the construction of power and politeness in workplace meetings.

Generally speaking, seniority is an important factor in meeting management. Whether overtly or covertly, those with more status and authority generally have greatest influence on the content and style of meetings, their general structure and the direction taken in the discussion. This applies to meetings of all sizes. When the most senior participant is also the chair, evidence of this influence is relatively easy to identify. In many of the larger meetings we recorded, the chair was also the section manager and thus the person with most organisational authority in this setting. In some contexts, however, the chair rotated around participants week by week, or the meeting was chaired by a project manager who was not also the section manager. This provided an opportunity to observe strategies for meeting management across a range of different roles. We illustrate here just a selection from the range of meeting management strategies we observed, focusing mainly on how they instantiate ways of 'doing power' in meetings.

Setting the agenda

As illustrated above, one of the most obvious ways in which someone can influence the content addressed at a meeting is by determining what goes on the agenda. Managers set work agendas not only in terms of their section's work programme over a period of time, but also at a more specific level for particular meetings. They often made explicit at the beginning of a meeting what they expected to cover and in what order, as in Example 4.7.

Example 4.7
Context: Regular weekly meeting of six men in a commercial organisation.

1 BAR: okay
2 CAL: okay
3 BAR: we're going to do a focus session and
4 CAL: yeah we're um it's a focus session this week...

This strategy of agenda setting can be observed in meetings of all sizes. In Example 4.8 Hera, the manager of a section in a government department, sets the agenda for discussion with her PA, Ana, right at the beginning of the interaction.

Example 4.8
Context: Hera, section manager, in her office talking to her PA, Ana.

1 HERA: okay um now we're about to start with the um + development
2   session this afternoon we've got an outside speaker
3 ANA: okay
4 HERA: which means that you'll be + out here by yourself
5   and I wondered if you wouldn't mind spending some of that time
6   in contacting + while no one else is around contacting the people
7   for their interviews and setting up the appointment times for their
        interviews

Other typical utterances in the data which signalled agenda setting included statements such as:

- what I'd like to do is...
- I've got a couple of things...
- I just wanted to finish off where we got to yesterday
- ...and that's what this meeting is about

These utterances indicate that the speaker is organising the discourse to suit their objectives. Explicitly stating the agenda for a meeting is an effective way of controlling the discourse, and though it was typically used by the chair and/or manager in our data, it is important to note that it is also available as a strategy to others, who may or may not be successful in imposing their agenda. Attempting to set an alternative agenda is one means of resisting sanctioned authority or subverting established power structures. Case Study 2 below provides an example where one participant successfully diverts the discussion for a considerable time to the exploration of her preferred options to resolving a problem.

Summarising progress

Another relatively explicit strategy typically used by more senior participants to manage a meeting was to summarise progress at regular intervals. The devices used for this purpose included making decisions explicit at regular points throughout the meeting with utterances such as the following:

- okay we're going to confirm the policies
- okay so we've dealt with that
- right so we can confirm those recommendations

Again this strategy was used in meetings of all sizes. For instance, in Example 4.5c, after talking informally for some time about the issues involved, Ruth begins to wrap up the discussion by checking her interpretation is shared by Barbara: *so where are we at? I mean you're inclined to want to pull back a little bit*. In this one-to-one interaction, Ruth pays explicit attention to Barbara's face needs. So, even though Barbara provides minimal responses (lines 2, 5, 8) to signal her agreement with each point, Ruth explicitly checks that Barbara agrees with her summary (line 9) *those are the two main things eh*, before moving on to the next topic. By contrast, in Case Study 1 below (see Example 4.15), in a larger and much more formal meeting, the chair summarises an objection from a senior manager in a way that minimally takes account of her seniority, and does not encourage her to persist with her complaint.

These examples illustrate how meeting participants, typically the chairs and/or the managers 'do power' explicitly by controlling the development of the interaction. They state the agenda and monitor the progress of the discussion by summarising, reformulating and confirming understanding. During the process, different managers pay greater or lesser attention to the face needs of other participants.

Keeping the discussion on track

One aspect of the chair's role is to take responsibility for ensuring the agenda is fully covered in the time available. This often involves moving a group back to the agenda topic during or after a digression. This topic control strategy is typically signalled by a discourse marker such as *right*, *so*, *anyway*, *okay*, or even more explicitly, *to get back to the point*, or *getting back on track*. A related strategy is the use of crisp, businesslike statements and responses to contributions from others, a strategy which signals very clearly the speaker's wish to move the discussion along or to deal with a particular issue briskly. In Example 4.9, Selene, the section manager, indicates her perception that the matter under discussion requires quick decisions and urgent action by her brief and concise responses to her staff's comments and suggestions.

Example 4.9
Context: Discussion of the need to brief the Minister.

1 ALEX: well he's er Warren just called me and suggested that we go over
2   and brief him personally
3 SEL: yes if he's here I agree
4 ALEX: and suggested that that you come as well but the trouble is
5   we don't actually know what the implications of this thing are
6   because we don't know enough about what's actually happening
7 SEL: okay but we're gonna have to go in and say it to him clearly

Selene's contributions (lines 3, 7) are pithy and focused and serve to minimise discussion and keep exploration of the problems they face to a minimum. The group knows each other well and overt attention to politeness factors is minimal.

   Another related strategy involves keeping the discussion on track by ensuring people thoroughly cover a topic before moving on or making sure they do not digress. In one meeting, for instance, the manager took a relatively low-key role in the discussion, facilitating contributions from others, but not himself contributing very much. However, at one point he clearly considered that the discussion was moving to a new topic too soon (Example 4.10).

Example 4.10
Context: Large evaluation meeting in a government organisation.

1 CEL: one that I'm am surprised at is [institution] engineering
2 LEN: hang on can we can we stay in the- do this block first
3 CEL: oh okay you want to /do service\ first
4 LEN: /all right\ um + do service first otherwise we'll we'll we'll dart a bit
5   I just want to try and deal with the a- do the scores make sense
6   with people's perceptions . . .

In line 2 the manager, Len, who has been silent for some time listening to the discussion, intrudes to prevent the discussion moving on to the new topic before he is satisfied they have covered all relevant points in relation to the current topic.

Reaching a decision

In many meetings it was important for those involved to reach decisions on issues, and indeed in some cases this was the primary function of the meeting. Decision making is a vital component of meeting management and directing the decision-making process is an important and complex aspect of workplace interaction.[2] Below we provide some brief illustrations of how decisions are arrived at and ratified.

The most overt and simple strategy for managing the decision-making process was to simply state the desired decision. Example 4.11 illustrates how managers and chairs often used this strategy when working with their regular teams and sections and dealing with routine and uncontentious issues.[3]

Example 4.11

Context: Regular weekly meeting of project team in white-collar commercial organisation.

```
1 SAN:  [drawls] um ++ and there's a new issue here
2       which is ongoing training needs
3       is this being examined in the career development project ++
4       so we'll put that against + ms banks shall we
5       who is running the ++ train- er the career development project
6       and is not here to defend herself (4)
7       jolly good
```

In this example, Sandy, the manager, raises the issue requiring a decision, namely, 'who will be responsible for training?' (lines 1–3), proposes a solution, namely, 'Clara Banks will be responsible' (*we'll put that against Ms Banks*, lines 4–6), pauses to allow for a response, and then ratifies the decision *jolly good* (line 7), all in one turn.

The next example provides a nice contrast to Sandy's use of legitimate power above. Example 4.12 illustrates a collaborative decision reached at the end of some discussion about buying a new laptop.

Example 4.12

Context: Discussing the purchase of a laptop.

```
1 JOE:   well i'd just buy it /i mean\ to me it it's
2 WEN:   /yeah\
3 JOE:   /an essential item\
4 WEN:   /( ) essen\tial and
5 MART:  Brett said that if it's over three thousand his approval is needed
```

6   but he said he'd give it ( )
7 JOE: is that our group decision then +
8 DER: do it
9 JOE: fine okay

The different participants all contribute to reaching the decision made explicit by Derek's *do it* (line 8) and ratified by Joe in line 9. Again the participants have worked together for some time and this is reflected in the speed and succinctness of the talk.

More problematic were decisions which had to be made in the context of group dissension and a range of incompatible viewpoints. In such cases, we observed two main alternative strategies: (i) one person made a unilateral declaration or (ii) the decision was negotiated, often at great length.[4] In some meetings, the manager simply stated what was going to happen, despite expressed opposition. Examples of this process occurred especially when it was clear that the manager would be responsible for the downstream consequences of a decision. Clara's direct and non-negotiable declaration *no screendumps*, discussed at the beginning of Chapter 1, exemplifies this point well. However, it is also important to note (as discussed in Chapter 1), that following her veto, some subtle affective 'repair work' was subsequently undertaken, both by the deputy manager and by Clara herself.

Even more dramatic examples of this kind occurred where an expert or a non-chairing manager behaved as a relatively unobtrusive participant until the group appeared to be about to make a crucial decision with which they disagreed (Example 4.13).

Example 4.13
Context: Regular meeting of project team of six men in commercial organisation discussing some new back-up software.

1 CAL: what we'v- what we've actually decided to do is
2   er test it by asking by losing some data or pretending to lose some
3   something significant like everything that's in p v c s
4   like all our documents and all our code
5 BAR: [laughs]
6 ERIC: yeah but d-
7 CAL: and then asking them to restore it
8 ERIC: no don't do that

Eric is the expert in this area and in line 8 he explicitly, directly and unambiguously opposes the decision that Callum announces in lines 1–4.[5]

When a person other than the manager made a unilateral declaration of the desired decision, the ratification of the manager was usually required (explicitly or implicitly) before the decision was firmly recorded, making it clear where the ultimate power and authority lay. Explicit ratifications were sometimes marked with a discourse particle such as *right* or *okay* followed by a positive confirmatory statement:

- okay that sounds really good
- okay so we think two weeks seems realistic then
- okay we're going to confirm the policies
- okay so we've dealt with that
- okay um well I support the paper, the recommendations

However in many cases, the ratification of a decision simply took the form of its explicit restatement by the chair (see Marra fc). Similarly, in cases where a decision was negotiated, sometimes at considerable length, between those who proposed it and those who contested it, the chair's ratification was generally again required before it was regarded as a final decision (see Case Study 2 below).

Analysis of our data also clearly indicates that attending to the face needs of others and nurturing good workplace relationships also play a part in processes like decision making. Participants in a workplace where authority relationships and relative statuses are emphasised and regarded as paramount will more readily accept a unilateral decision on a contentious issue, while workplaces with a more egalitarian work ethic and an emphasis on participation will be more likely to engage in negotiation in such circumstances. As illustrated in Chapter 6, humour is a frequently used strategy to attenuate the face threat of a veto, a contestive or disagreeing statement, or a contentious decision.

Before leaving this topic of the varied strategies used to manage interaction in meetings, it is important to recognise that management strategies may be very subtle and sophisticated as well as overt and explicit. Summarising the discussion, for instance, gives the summariser a good deal of influence over what is overtly recognised as having been agreed, or what is noted as important, as opposed to what is quietly dropped. While the manager and the chair are the most obviously influential roles in relation to meeting management, others also make contributions which may be important in some contexts. Someone explicitly or implicitly recognised as the 'expert', for instance, on a particular topic, may wield considerable influence in a discussion related to their area of expertise. They may veto or dissociate themselves from a decision with which they do not agree and which would reflect badly upon them. So when the team took no notice of Eric's opposition, illustrated in Example 4.13, he (semi-humorously) asked for his dissent to be put on record: *please put it in the minutes that Eric does not think this is a good idea.*

Contributions from less powerful meeting players may 'seed' ideas that are later developed and endorsed by more statusful and authoritative participants. This facilitative role could be seen as a manifestation of deference or politeness, or perhaps as a collegial gesture to assist the team to resolve a problem or decide on a course of action. Conversely, less overtly powerful players can influence the progress of a meeting by initiating digressions, contesting ideas that appear to have general agreement, or to which there is some underlying opposition. The extent to which such behaviours are successful in subverting the goals of the meeting and delaying progress on agenda issues varies in different workplace cultures and depends to no small extent on the management strategies of the chair as well as the tolerance of others for such resistant behaviours.

Doing power and politeness in meetings: two case studies

The discussion so far has indicated that meetings typically serve myriad functions, some conscious and some unconscious, some relating directly or indirectly to high-level objectives and outcomes, and some to more specific short-term goals, some to maintaining or developing strategic collegial relationships, and some to expressing solidarity and support for workmates. The precise balance between these different purposes varies in different workplaces, in different workplace teams and in different meetings of any group. Indeed, the time of year or the day of the week can sometimes influence this balance – typically around budget time meetings tend to be much more goal-focused than just before Christmas, for instance. In this section we take two specific examples to illustrate briefly how power and politeness interact in two particular meetings in contrasting workplaces or communities of practice.

Case Study 1

The first illustrative meeting took place in a government department and was chaired by the chief executive officer. Most of the meeting participants did not engage in regular interaction with each other outside such meetings. They were brought together as 'experts' and senior managers specifically to consider the high-level issues requiring a decision from the executive senior management team. They in no sense formed a tight-knit community of practice. On the other hand, from the perspective of the wider society, these people shared many social characteristics. They were similar in age, ethnicity and level of education and they shared similar views about the functions of the meeting, the way it should be run and the way decisions should be reached.

Meeting structure and the chair's role

An explicit agenda had been circulated in advance. The agenda indicated a start time and a finish time for the four-hour meeting and included not only the ten items to be reported on and discussed, but also the time to be allocated to each item, the time (15 minutes) allocated for afternoon tea and the person responsible for providing the report or leading the discussion of each item was identified.

The chair ensured that the meeting followed this agenda very closely, with a predominantly linear structure and few digressions. Each topic was addressed in turn and any issues relating to it resolved and relevant decisions made, before moving on to the next topic. Progression between topics occurred in a 'logical' and uniform manner, with the transitions clearly marked with topic-management discourse particles:

- **okay** anything else
- **okay** final item email policy
- **okay well** let let's um er if during the course of that discussion you you continue to be uncomfortable let's um discuss it at the time

Moreover, within each topic, the discussion also followed a linear pattern. Similarly, there was a predominance of one kind of decision-making process within the meeting. Generally, an 'expert' in the relevant area presented a recommendation or set of recommendations to the group and the group then approved them, or sometimes briefly discussed and amended them and then approved them. The chair presented the recommendations for the group's approval and then ratified the decision.

Throughout the long meeting, then, the chair focused very consistently on the agenda items, the official topics of the meeting. His style was very businesslike and goal directed. For example, seeking agreement with the recommendations made by the group, he was both very explicit about what was being approved and also very succinct (Example 4.14).

Example 4.14

```
1 CHAIR:  are you happy to agree that the reprioritised projects in table 6
2         be approved for ninety nine two thousand
3         er I'll take it that that was yes
4         and so can we have a a new recommendation e
5         which is er direct the er chief finance officer to advise [department]
6         on what further measures may be appropriate in terms of our capital
7         planning in management to minimise the recurrence in the future of
8         under-expenditure problems
```

Another strategy used by the chair to maintain control of the discussion was to summarise regularly. For example, early in the first meeting a participant expressed her frustration at not having had a report to read in advance. In response, the chair summarised and clarified the implications of her complaint for the benefit of the rest of the group (Example 4.15).

Example 4.15

1 CHAIR: what I understand you're registering your concern about that
2   but not asking for us not to consider the paper is that right?
3 SEL: you've summed it up correctly that I'm uncomfortable

This example nicely illustrates that the focus in this meeting is predominantly on moving the 'business' along. The chair's summary clears the way for the discussion to proceed, thus skilfully containing a potentially time-wasting digression. Nevertheless, at the same time, there is indirect, though minimal, attention to Selene's face needs. The chair indicates that he has noted her concern and he gives her at least the opportunity (though no encouragement) to challenge his obvious desire to proceed with the discussion of the report. This attention to her face needs could be interpreted as strategic, given Selene's seniority, but it is nevertheless an example of a relational as well as a transactional discourse move.

Interpersonal dimension

As suggested by this example, relatively little explicit attention was paid in this meeting to the interpersonal aspects of interaction, to the overt maintenance of warm collegial relationships and to the positive face needs of individuals. The discourse was predominantly 'transactional' in function, with no social or off-topic talk, and very little humour during this meeting.

A very rare exception to the general pattern of proceeding from item to item with little non-referential discourse is provided in Example 4.16 where the chair provides some affective comment.

Example 4.16

1 CHAIR: okay um well I support the paper the recommendations
2   I think you've done an excellent job well done
3   ah I I think we should be explicit about our goals
4   and certainly that's the regime that the government's establishing
5   what the employee relations book was all about
6   laying it all on the table and being explicit
7   I think that Gerald's on to a good point though
8   also about um the need to be clear about
9   what are the higher order goals are here

10	and make sure that we're we're connected into that
11	so perhaps we can craft some recommendation
12	that actually does that linkage Paul

Here the chair explicitly compliments the writer and presenter of the report: *I think you've done an excellent job well done* (line 2), before going on tactfully to express a reservation about the wording of the recommendation (lines 3–6). This is followed by another appreciative comment *I think that Gerald's on to a good point though* (line 7) introducing further suggestions for improvement, and ending with an indirect request that Paul recraft the recommendation (lines 11–12). By avoiding a direct criticism, the chair addresses the face needs of the presenter and saves his face. At the same time, this phrasing could also be interpreted as a strategic move, since it is much more likely that the person responsible will feel positive about what has been decided and will respond to the suggestion if his face needs have been considerately addressed.

Thus even in this case study where the authority of the chair is manifested in such a way as to provide a paradigmatic example of a meeting which is determinedly transactional in its focus, remarkably linear in its structure and businesslike in its style, there is some attention to considerations of politeness and the interpersonal dimension of workplace interaction. The very minimal nature of this attention, however, is brought into focus by our very different second case study.

Case Study 2

The second example is taken from a small organisation whose meetings at the time of our recording were run very democratically, and embedded in a very egalitarian workplace culture with a consensus-seeking, negotiative approach to decision making. Participants interacted daily and frequently in many different work contexts and some also socialised with each other outside work. By contrast with those involved in Case Study 1, the communication patterns in this superficially similar, white-collar, professional workplace could be characterised as 'high involvement' and heavily context embedded, with a strong emphasis on face-to-face interpersonal talk. The boundary between personal and professional life was much 'fuzzier' than for those in Case Study 1 and personal and social talk was frequent, even in 'work' meetings.

The meeting which we consider here contrasts with Case Study 1 most obviously in that it did not follow such a strictly linear pattern of topical organisation and decision making. The purpose of the meeting was to plan the work of the section over the next few months and allocate responsibilities for tasks in the light of anticipated staffing changes, illnesses and some specific problems which had arisen, such as a backlog of filing. In contrast to the other two meetings, the chair in this meeting encouraged wide-ranging discussion and exercised relatively light control over the meeting's progress through the issues on the agenda. As a result the meeting structure is best described as spiral; digressions and shifts back and forth between different topics were common throughout the meeting.

This very different structure from Case Study 1 can be illustrated in relation to the specific topic of the filing backlog which first arose near the beginning of the meeting and then resurfaced regularly throughout. In the course of the meeting, a number of possible solutions to the problem were discussed, some involving a complicated reassignment of duties. As mentioned in Chapter 1, one possible solution, first proposed at a relatively early point in the meeting by the chair, Leila, who was also the section manager, was to bring in external filers, the 'flying filing squad'. A relatively senior team member, Zoe, was clearly not happy with this suggestion and throughout the discussion she raised a variety of objections whenever it re-emerged, as it regularly did.

Rather than imposing the solution she had suggested, Leila, the manager, encouraged extensive discussion of the issue and its impact on related tasks. Examples 4.17, 4.18 and 4.19 illustrate with excerpts from throughout the meeting how she explicitly sought the views of the participants at various points in the discussion.

Example 4.17

```
 1  LEI:  I mean we may not be able to find a solution but that
 2        I mean you're the people who are in the best situation for knowing
 3        that what's your feeling? . . .
 4        I want people to be honest about whether they
 5        if they don't you know even if things come up again
 6        now if you don't feel comfortable say so . . .
 7        you need to work that through it's gonna be +
 8        you know what will work +++ cos I mean
 9        I think you've got a wee bit of a difference here
10        in that you're obviously a little bit uncomfortable about a new set of
11        people and I can understand that because you're thinking consistency . . .
12        does this feel okay I mean I don't want anyone to feel that (6)
13        records are ( )
          [general laughter] . . .
```

Leila clearly states and restates contentious issues (lines 9–11), requests people to make explicit their reservations (lines 4, 6, 7) and overtly seeks agreement before proceeding (lines 3, 12). Similarly, her first response to Zoe's alternative to the 'flying filers' is positive and encouraging (Example 4.18).

Example 4.18

1 ZOE: mm but okay but hang on what are our other options here
2   um we've also got Hannah
3 LEI: mm yeah that's a good suggestion

Leila then allows Zoe to express at some length the reasons for her reservations. Leila's management style, and especially her consultative strategies for assisting the meeting to reach a satisfactory decision, contrast markedly in this respect with those of the chair in Case Study 1.

However, there is extensive evidence that Leila is also a capable and authoritative manager, who controls the discussion and ensures decisions are reached. After the issue has been extensively canvassed, for instance, she firmly but constructively draws the discussion to a close (Example 4.19).

Example 4.19

1 LEI: I think we have the solution here
2   I think the good news is that I'll-
3   I probably don't have to think about recruiting someone else
4 ZOE: oh right

Leila affirms a positive solution, while also explicitly invoking her authority as a manager by referring to her responsibilities for staffing. Her repetitive *I*-statements, illustrated in Example 4.19 but extending well beyond this brief snippet, make it clear that, while she is happy to consult, this type of planning nevertheless falls within her prerogative as manager. She also uses discourse strategies, such as those discussed above, which explicitly control the way in which the interaction develops. She summarises, ratifies decisions, brings the topic back on track from digressions, and so on. In other words, she very effectively 'does power' in meetings, but she does it in a style that is responsive to the features of the particular community of practice in which she is operating.

Leila's sensitivity to the distinctive workplace culture in which she operates is also evident in the attention she pays to interpersonal and relational factors, group dynamics and the face needs of other participants. In addition to more overt strategies, such as complimenting participants on their work and their professional attitudes, Leila also uses humour, and especially self-deprecating humour, to ease tension in meetings.[6] At one point, for example, she tells a humorous anecdote about how she first identified the flying filers by following their van. She presents herself in a slightly ludicrous light, as stretching her head round desperately trying to see their telephone number (Example 4.20).

Example 4.20

1 LEI: and I was trying to sort of /edge round
2   and I was [laughs]\ stretching this way in the car [laughs]
        /[all laugh]\
3 LEI: I was a wee bit like ( ) [laughs]
        [all laugh]

This apparent digression serves a number of useful purposes, by fostering good collegial relationships and reframing her proposed solution in a non-threatening way. Leila closes her short narrative with *I'd found these funny people and Zoe tracked them down* thus subtly pointing out that she and Zoe are a team, and also implying that Zoe must have been open to the flying filers idea at that time.

Towards the end of this meeting, Leila again uses humour, including self-deprecating humour, to reduce the tensions that have arisen in the course of the discussion. She first threatens two people who are about to move from the library section to another section with the fact that they will have to work harder, and then pretends that her own skills are limited to making coffee (Example 4.21).

Example 4.21

1 LEI: /you have to work hard you two\
         /[all laugh]\
2 LEI: no I mean round there [laughs]
         /[all laugh]\
3 EVA: /as opposed to the library\
4 LEI: [laughs] absolutely
         /[all laugh]\
5 xx: /there's a benefit\ I- the coffee's constant round there
6 EVA: [laughs] this is a constant
7 LEI: the coffee is con- yeah I can make coffee
8   /it's one thing I know I can do [laughs]\
9 EVA: /lot of very strong black coffee good\
10 LEI: cos it's one thing I feel confident about
11   /in my cool competency\ making [laughs] coffee [laughs]
         /[all laugh]\
12 LEI: it's one thing I really got a good performance on [laughs]

This humorous sequence provides light relief and tension release at the end of the long meeting in which feathers have been ruffled and people have had to negotiate and sometimes agree to a compromise. The overlapping talk and laughter indicate that the participants are relating well to each other. In particular, it is noteworthy that Leila puts herself in a one-down position, after a meeting in which she has needed at times to be assertive and overtly managerial (cf Kotthoff 1997).

This meeting thus provides a contrast to Case Study 1 along a number of dimensions. First, the discussion is much more democratic, in that all participants' views are explicitly sought, and their reservations and concerns are brought out explicitly and addressed systematically. Second, the strategies used by the chair to exert control over progress through the agenda, the direction of topic development and the decision-making process, are much less overt and more indirect and subtle than in Case Study 1. Finally, in this meeting, a range of politeness strategies is used to pay attention to collegial relations and to the face needs of others, including compliments, expressions of appreciation and self-deprecating humour. So while the chairs in these two case studies both operate effectively in their contrasting communities of practice, they use rather different discourse strategies to run their meetings and to instantiate power and politeness in their different workplaces.

Conclusion

People love to hate meetings and regularly bemoan the fact that there are too many of them, that they go on too long and that they get in the way of their 'real' work. Nevertheless, in many workplaces, especially white-collar workplaces, meetings are the basic forum for communicating information, for planning and organising work schedules, for making decisions and for engaging in collaborative tasks. They are therefore, inevitably, also an important context for 'relational work' (Fletcher 1999) of various kinds. This chapter has explored how meeting participants, whether managers or ordinary workers, balance the sometimes competing demands of doing power and politeness in a variety of different workplace contexts.

We looked first at the big picture – the variable dimensions of meetings and how these interrelate with features such as the degree of formality, the instrumental and affective goals of participants and the discursive patterns and structures of meetings. Some of the ways in which power and politeness interact in the context of meetings were then considered. We illustrated how managing interaction in meetings involves strategies such as agenda setting, summarising progress, keeping the discussion on track and reaching and ratifying decisions, with managers from different workplaces taking more or less account of the face needs of participants in the process. Finally, two case studies were used to illustrate the very different ways in which managers from contrasting communities of practice managed the turn-by-turn interaction in more formal meetings, making use of a combination of linguistic and discourse strategies to assert power and reduce or maintain social distance vis-à-vis their colleagues.

The analysis has highlighted the fact that while there are definite and clear patterns in how meetings are structured and the ways in which people manage the relational aspects of meeting discourse, it is also true that each group is a unique mix of individuals and their experiences, and each group evolves its own particular practices. These practices encompass not only agreed ways of running meetings and reaching decisions, but also include ways of doing relational work and paying attention to politeness considerations at work. In the next two chapters we focus more specifically on affective aspects of workplace interaction, namely, the important contributions of small talk and humour to talk at work.

Notes

1. This example is analysed from a different perspective in Marra (fc).
2. See Marra (fc) for a comprehensive review of the relevant literature on decision making.
3. This example is analysed from a different perspective in Marra (fc).
4. A detailed discussion of one such negotiation is provided in Holmes (2000c). See also Case Study 2.
5. This example is discussed in more detail in Chapter 7, where we focus on problematic talk.
6. Further examples of the humour in this meeting are discussed in Chapter 6.

5

Small Talk and Social Chat at Work

Example 5.1

Context: Participants are gathering for a meeting of a project team in a large commercial organisation. Vita, Tess and Sandy have arrived and are chatting. Sandy is chairing the subproject and meeting. Clara is the section manager.

```
 1  VITA:   when did you last go home
 2  TESS:   I just /got back\
 3  VITA:   /Christmas\ oh have you just come back
 4  TESS:   yes
 5  VITA:   what was it like is it really hot
 6  TESS:   twenty six twenty seven degrees thirty over thirty degrees
 7          on Friday about thirty two
 8  VITA:   it goes up and down eh
 9  TESS:   yeah
10  VITA:   cos I'll be there in about two weeks
11  TESS:   really?
12  VITA:   yeah
13  SAN:    are you going on holiday
14  VITA:   and up yeah well it's to a wedding and um bad time of year to have it
15          I mean February the fourteenth and things . . .
            [weather talk continues for another minute]
            [Ange arrives]
16  VITA:   look at you Ange where are your summer clothes
17  ANGE:   I know I don't really have anything much
18  VITA:   don't you I need to go and buy some more . . .
            [Seth and Clara arrive]
19  VITA:   cas casual day tomorrow
20  CLA:    yes
21  VITA:   is bike shorts too cas bearing in mind it's going to be too hot for
22          jeans
```

23 CLA: I don't care I don't care what people wear they can wear whatever
24   they like
25 VITA: as long as their eggs er oh eggs legs are not too ugly [laughs]
           [laughter]
26 CLA: if they want to wear bike sh- pants that's just fine . . .
27 SAN: is today going to be a fun meeting Seth?
28 SETH: it must be Sandy is looking smart
           [Peg arrives]
29 PEG: Sandy disgraced himself on the weekend
30 TESS: yes what's this story about your um stag party
           [laughter]
31 PEG: now you've upset him /Tessa\
32 CLA: /how are you feeling now Sandy\
33 SAN: well I'm feeling a bit sore still but I'm fine . . .
           [others arrive]
34 SAN: today seeing as Clara has had um three lovely weeks of holiday . . .
           [several seconds of banter about how long Clara has actually been
           away]
35   um it's a really good chance for everyone to give her a um briefing
36   or a more detailed briefing perhaps of what's happened in the last
37   three weeks um so if we could go round the table um looking to review
38   the subprojects

Example 5.1 provides a paradigmatic illustration of small talk in the workplace. These instances of small talk occur as team members wait for everyone to arrive at the beginning of the first meeting of this project team for the year. As the excerpts illustrate, this team's small talk covers a wide range of topics, including the weather, people's holiday activities, clothes and recent and future social events. There is a good deal of humour and lighthearted banter (e.g. lines 25, 29, 30, 34), as the participants re-establish contact after a period away from work. Finally all the participants have arrived and Sandy, the chair, gets the meeting underway.

Despite the efforts of anthropologists and sociolinguists over many decades, small talk is popularly disparaged; indeed its very label suggests it is trivial and not worth taking seriously.[1] This negative perception of small talk, and more generally of social chat and gossip, as marginal and purposeless reflects the fact that such talk is often defined, explicitly or implicitly, as talk which is *not* concerned with serious information and which is not task oriented. Social talk is, at least officially, banished to the peripheries of work time and formally confined to breaks. Yet, things are often more complicated. It is not generally possible to parcel out meaning into neat packages of referential or transactional meaning on the one hand and social or affective meaning on the other. Talk is inherently multifunctional. Every interaction simultaneously expresses both propositional or referential content and social or affective meaning (Holmes 1990a: 254).

As suggested in earlier chapters, a social constructionist framework highlights the dynamic implications of this observation in ongoing interaction and specific workplace practices. In every social encounter participants are unavoidably involved in constructing, maintaining or modifying the interpersonal relationship between themselves and their addressee(s). Adopting this perspective, social talk, including small talk, cannot be dismissed as a peripheral, marginal or minor discourse mode. Though often treated as invisible and 'disappeared' or erased from the official record (Fletcher 1999), social talk is an important means by which we negotiate the dimensions of politeness and power in interpersonal relationships at work; a crucial function of talk with significant implications for ongoing and future interactions.

The analysis which follows is in two sections. First we discuss features of the distribution, structural positioning and extent of small talk and social talk in a variety of workplace contexts,[2] and the relevance of these features in the analysis of power and politeness at work. Then we explore the complex functions of social talk at work, describing its obvious contribution as a politeness device and suggesting a less obvious role in the construction and maintenance of power relationships.

The distribution of social talk in the workplace

Where and when does social talk occur at work? One answer to this question is that it occurs at times and in spaces which are officially designated for non-work or social activities, activities when workers are free to develop and strengthen collegial relationships. But, as indicated by Example 5.1, this is clearly not the whole story. While it is true that social talk occurs at work breaks ('smoko', coffee breaks, lunch, etc.), it is not the case that it *only* occurs in such intervals; nor is it the case that only social talk occurs in such times and places. Our data suggested that non-work-related social topics (family, sport, TV, weekend activities, health) were more likely to predominate at social breaks such as morning tea and breaks between meetings. But even in these contexts, work-related topics such as leave eligibility, preferred shifts or overtime often infiltrated the interaction. In organisations where talk (as opposed to practical activity) was core business, this was even more common. We have one recording, for example, where the topic of a sticky interview with the boss occupied most of a lunch break between two close work colleagues, and many more examples where talk about colleagues and work-related events dominated the tea break. We focus here, however, not on the invasion of social time by work talk, but rather on the distribution of social talk within official work time, where it clearly functions as a positive politeness or solidarity oriented strategy.

Small talk as a boundary marker

Small talk is typically, but not exclusively, found at the boundaries of interaction, as well as at the boundaries of the working day. In this position it serves to soften the transition to work by attending to the addressee's positive face needs. Greeting and parting exchanges which occur in the opening and closing phases of interactions are obvious manifestations of small talk. Our data indicates that the first encounter of the day between work colleagues can be considered an obligatory site for small talk. Its absence at this point is marked, justified only by an emergency requiring urgent attention to a specific task. (The boss who entered the office issuing orders first thing in the morning was rare – and unpopular.) Initial encounters were typified by references to the weather (*lovely day*), recent shared activities (*great concert last night*), and ritual enquiries after well being (*how's things?*). Such exchanges between work colleagues occurred in passing, as well as at the beginning of planned activities. Though formulaic they served a ritual face attending function, a point elaborated in the next section.

When people gathered for meetings, small talk was common, as illustrated in Example 5.1. In addition to its social functions (discussed below), such talk filled in time while participants waited for the meeting to begin. The management of small talk in this context provided many opportunities to observe the manifestation of power relations in the workplace. Calling a meeting to order or halting a digression from the agenda were ways in which managers and meeting chairs exercised their authority and met their workplace responsibilities. As illustrated in Example 5.1, as soon as a sufficient number of people had arrived, the social talk was usually interrupted by the person chairing the meeting. Example 5.2 illustrates this same pattern in a different organisation.

Example 5.2
Context: People are gathering for a meeting in a government department. Monica is the chair. Helen is to do a presentation.

1 LES: I met your um friend Marie Cross last night
2 MON: oh good + how is she
3 LES: she's fine really lovely
4 MON: what was that at

5 LES: that was at that thing um the international institute thing ++
6 MON: [inhales] okay + this is everybody isn't it except Gavin when he comes
7 HEL: just tell me Monica when you think you're ready for my bit
8 MON: yeah really I just wanted to sort of + um sort of just use this opportunity
9   to get a bit of a review on where we're at with . . .

Monica, the chair, has the right to declare the meeting open, but she is dependent on a certain critical mass to make it worthwhile to begin. Thus one of the main functions of Monica's exchange with Leslie is to fill in time until enough people have gathered to justify starting the meeting. This is evident from Monica's inhalation followed by a framing discourse marker *okay* (line 6) which signals a shift from pre-meeting talk to the opening of the meeting (cf Stenstrom 1994). Similarly, in the soap factory where we recorded, workers chatted while waiting for the team leader to formally start the morning briefing meeting. In Example 5.3, an accident on the previous day (where powder was sent down into clean machines in error) provides the topic.

Example 5.3

Context: 6am team briefing meeting. Helena and Sam discuss previous day's disaster until team leader Ginette opens the meeting.

1 HEL: that was a shit of an afternoon wasn't it +
2 SAM: could've been worse
3 HEL: do you think + . . .
4 GIN: Weka half an hour late ++ okay (4)
5   good morning everybody it's just lovely to see you all this morning

In line 5, after enough people have arrived, Ginette asserts her authority, ends the small talk and declares that the meeting has begun.

Small talk is also common at the end of interactions. After a short inter-action, it typically takes the form of a brief *see you later* or *give us a bell* ('phone me'). Longer discussions sometimes lead to more protracted disengagements, serving a range of functions, especially attention to ad-dressees' face needs (see below for discussion of some extended examples). Here small talk provides a transition assisting people to 'come back to earth' as one contributor put it, after a session of hard work, or serve a positive politeness function of re-establishing cordial relations following intense and occasionally heated debate. (Humour can serve the same purpose, as illus-trated in Chapter 6.) Even after a mundane, regular session of delegating tasks, small talk can reorient participants to their personal rather than their role relationship, as Example 5.4 demonstrates.

Example 5.4

Context: Helen, the section manager has been delegating jobs to Rebecca, her PA.

1 REB: I finally got + the the names transferred from the CVs onto the +
2   ont- onto the labels to send out the thank you letters yesterday
3 HEL: oh good let's get that one done . . .
4 REB: okay
5 HEL: okay
6 REB: and how's Sam?
7 HEL: he's just fine

The preclosing sequence (lines 4–5) *okay okay* signals that the work is completed. Rebecca starts to leave and as she gathers up her papers she asks
about Helen's partner (line 6), a typical example of small talk at the end of a
meeting. In this position small talk has the potential for development into
more extended social talk, but equally it can be brief and formulaic, simply
marking the end of the encounter with ritual positive politeness.

Another point at which small talk occurred was when the personnel
involved in an interaction changed – when someone left or someone new
arrived to join an interaction. In some respects, these change points parallel
openings and closings; they are internal boundary points. However, because
they were often technically 'interruptions' to the business of the continuing
participants, small talk was generally minimal and confined to routine phrases
(*how's things?, how are you?*) which in this context elicited routine minimal
replies (*fine, good*), or, in some cases, no overt response. Small talk is thus
typically distributed at the boundaries of workplace interactions. It serves
the discourse function of marking transitions between different phases of an
interaction, while also functioning as a formulaic politeness device.

Boundary marking is a typical function of small talk at work, but it is not
obligatory – at least within the confines of the working day. This optionality
distinguishes transactional discourse from discourse in many other contexts.
While we must beware of making assumptions in this respect because of the
limitations of our data, there is some evidence that work interactions may
begin without preamble, as illustrated in Example 5.5.

Example 5.5

Context: Kate, a relatively senior person in the organisation, addresses Anne, the
computer adviser, as Anne walks through the office.

1 KATE: can I just talk to you?
2 ANNE: yeah
3 KATE: I got your message saying that you'd set up the Turner ID for me
4 ANNE: yep
5 KATE: but I can't log on to it yet cos I don't have a + code number
6   or anything

The preamble, checking availability, satisfies minimal politeness requirements. The discussion then continues with Anne explaining how to resolve the problem. Clearly small talk is not obligatory in some types of work transactions. Most obviously in our data, initial 'greeting' small talk seemed to be treated as dispensable in transactions which were signalled as brief requests for assistance or information, or where an agenda had been set in advance, and/or where participants were working according to agreed explicit time constraints. Initial small talk was also dispensed with when participants had made contact earlier in the day. This feature thus distinguishes small talk in the workplace from its occurrence in other contexts.

Interestingly, however, when initial small talk was dispensed with in this way, attention to face needs sometimes surfaced later. For instance, later in the interaction above, Kate apologised for having accosted Anne so peremptorily at the opening of the encounter, saying, *sorry I'm a bit mean doing this and when you're just walking in*. Kate then went on to introduce another request for advice – the apology, in other words, was used in this case to 'legitimise' an extension of the interaction beyond the brief request for assistance first requested. At a later point, however, Anne diverged from their work talk and introduced personal talk, and Kate was captured; in the circumstances she could not politely avoid listening to an account of Anne's personal problems (see discussion of Example 5.16 below). Again, the importance of taking account of the wider context of workplace talk is apparent in attempting to interpret 'what is going on'.

Social talk inside work talk

The boundaries between work talk and social talk were by no means rigid and social talk regularly infiltrated business or on-task talk in the workplaces in our corpus. Most obvious and easiest to identify were spells of social talk between workers on the job in contexts where talk was not a component of the core business. The distinction was usually clear between talk about hanging out the washing in a day-care centre versus an after-work party, or talk about cleaning the work equipment versus putting a house on the market or holiday plans. Shifts between such different discourses could generally be easily identified, as in Example 5.6, where Ginette and Jim shift back and forth between social chat and task-oriented talk (in bold).

Example 5.6
Context: Two factory workers on a production line are gossiping about a mutual acquaintance.

1 GIN: she's not married eh
2 JIM: she has been . . . she's got a partner ++
3   think his name's Willow ++ it's not what I would try . . .
4 GIN: oh no I wouldn't even think you would do something /like that\

5 JIM: /oh (to hell) with you\
6 GIN: [laughs] **(12)**
7 GIN: **[voc] + two more sets of four** . . .
8 JIM: I've got a sort of like I've got a ( ) weekend
9   you know Saturdays Sundays and stuff
10   so four days get the four days off
11 GIN: four days off ++ all you need /is\ +
12 JIM: /sweet man\
13 GIN: all you need is one day's overtime and you're sweet eh
14   **on four by four**

Ginette and Jim gossip about an acquaintance between lines 1 and 3, followed by a typical (for this team) exchange of jocular abuse (lines 4–6).[3] There is then a 12-second pause while they monitor machinery which is interrupted by the work-focused utterance *two more sets of four* (line 7). The discussion next shifts to the relationship between overtime and time off (lines 8–13) and this time the discussion is cut off by the demands of the production line which dictate on-task work talk (line 14). The distinction between social talk (lines 1–6) and work talk (lines 7 and 14) is crystal clear. However, note that the discussion in lines 8–13 illustrates a fuzzy category, namely work-related talk, rather than on-task talk. This is clear when it is interrupted by strictly on-task talk at line 14. Social talk, as well as work-related but off-task talk, serves as light relief from the repetitiousness and predictability of the job (cf Pilkington 1998).

Within contexts where talk was more central to the organisation's business, people also digressed from the official topic and social discourse sometimes totally displaced task-oriented discourse for a period. Participants introduced personal information ('gossip') about people whose names came up in the course of a business-oriented discussion, for example, or introduced ideas for recreational activities while planning a business trip (see Example 5.10 below). While not necessarily addressee oriented in focus, these instances of social talk typically served the function of building solidarity through the sharing of personal information. These digressions provided temporary relief from the more serious core business topics and were usually light-hearted and often humorous.

People typically moved very skilfully from discourse which was clearly 'core business' to talk which was social in its motivation, and back again. While the transitions are reasonably clear cut in Examples 5.1 and 5.2, with the managers explicitly indicating it is time to start the meeting (Example 5.1, lines 33–34; Example 5.2, lines 6, 8), the transition is often less abrupt, with business talk at the end of an encounter shifting after a mutually negotiated completion to social interpersonal discourse as in Example 5.4, or small talk at the beginning of an encounter gradually shifting to work talk, as in Example 5.7.

Example 5.7

Context: Two young women meeting to discuss a joint project.

1 ILS: so how are things amongst your um +
2   your holiday how was your holiday?
3 MAR: oh it was really funny the holiday was like really really awesome
4 ILS: right
5 MAR: and then my first day back I was just like kicking back +
6   in my desk just just still really relaxed /and I\
7 ILS: /trying to get back into it [laughs]\
8 MAR: yeah and a girl from my- a woman from my section came up and said
9   oh [inhales] do you want to do this horrible speech that I have to give
10   in front of students for work day they had career work day thing
11   and the students have to come in to the building /and I said\
12 ILS: /yeah\
13 MAR: yeah yeah sure I'll do it and she goes [surprised tone] really
14   I thought I'd have to get down on my knees and BEG
15   and I was going oh no no it's cool
16   and I'm sure it was because I was just you know still in holiday mode
17   cos I don't normally like speaking in front of anyone [laughs] but
18 ILS: yeah
19 MAR: yeah I agreed (to) and it was fine
20 ILS: so you might have um taken er a while
21 MAR: so [laughs]
22 ILS: longer t- to come to the decision (would you) [laughs]
23 MAR: yeah oh yeah I would have gone no no go away
24   but yeah it was really good
25 ILS: it was a good trip oh (okay)
26 MAR: yeah but now back into it again
27 ILS: yeah things are pretty full on here
28 MAR: yeah I can imagine
29 ILS: mm sort of working I just did my first submission + for the minister

This extract illustrates very nicely both in form and, as it happens, in content, the gradual shift from polite formulaic small talk in which Ilsa enquires about Mary's holiday and pays attention to her face needs, to discussion of a submission for the Minister, a topic which is firmly in the work domain. It is accomplished in this case via a discussion of the effects of a holiday on Mary's attitude to a work request. The ending of the interaction, in particular, illustrates the conversational skill with which the two negotiate the transition back to work talk. Mary's evaluative comment (line 24) *but yeah it was really good* marks the end of her answer to Ilsa's question (line 2) *how was your holiday?* Ilsa's reformulation (line 25) *it was a good trip*, indicates agreement to the topic closure. Mary acknowledges the closure *yeah* (line 26) and then (literally) moves the topic to work *but now back into it again*. The topics of their talk thus mirror the chronological progression holiday and then back to work. Ilsa then picks up the topic and starts to bring Mary up to date with where things are at. Polite social talk serves as a bridge to the main business of the encounter. There are many examples where the transition from small talk to the business of the meeting is similarly skilfully accomplished. As Coupland, Coupland and Robinson note, small talk is flexible and malleable; social exchanges have 'unique bridging potential – relationally and interactionally' (1992: 226).

This discussion of the distribution of small talk and social talk at work has indicated some important discourse functions served by such talk: (i) as boundary marker, easing transitions between phases of workplace interaction; (ii) as time-filler and source of tension-relief, or informality, during more task-oriented workplace activities.[4] The elasticity, flexibility and adaptability of social talk make it ideal for these purposes: it can expand or contract according to need. The length of social talk exchanges in our data reflected a wide variety of factors. The place and time were obvious influences. Where it occurred in passing, small talk was typically brief, performing its canonical function of creating and maintaining social relations within a broader context in which the primary avowed goals of the organisation predominated (see Examples 5.8 and 5.9 below). Small talk is undemanding in terms of topic and intellectual content and infinitely flexible in terms of length. It can be picked up and dropped with minimal discoursal effort.

Where it occurred at morning tea or lunch breaks, small talk provided a natural bridge to more extended social talk, as well as to the work-related, 'shop talk' which dominated many tea and coffee breaks.[5] Office-based social talk tended to reflect the influence of other factors, such as how well the participants knew each other, the relative status of participants and how busy they were, as well as the norms of the organisational culture. Some of these factors are discussed in the next section which focuses on the more global social functions of non-task-oriented talk at work.

Social functions of non-task-oriented talk at work

While small talk clearly serves the discourse function of marking boundaries and transitions in workplace interaction, it also performs important social functions by constructing, expressing, maintaining and reinforcing inter-personal relationships between those who work together. In the workplace, this not only involves the positive politeness or solidarity oriented functions discussed by Laver (1975, 1981), it also involves attention to the way people 'do power' at work. This section illustrates ways in which apparently peripheral and innocuous phatic exchanges can serve pivotal roles in furthering the interpersonal and sometimes instrumental goals of those involved.

Doing collegiality in the workplace

Paying attention to the face needs of others is a crucial component of 'doing friendship' (Holmes 1995; Coates 1996). In the workplace, the equivalent activity can be described as 'doing collegiality' or 'doing solidarity'. Small talk is an obvious example of discourse which is oriented to positive face needs. In the workplace the exchange of greetings, complaints about how busy life is, promises to get in touch for lunch, coffee, and so on, are examples of small talk tokens that serve this positive politeness function.

Example 5.8
Context: Joan and Elizabeth pass in the corridor.

1 ELI: hi Joan
2 JOAN: hi how are you
3 ELI: oh busy busy busy
4 JOAN: mm terrible isn't it

Example 5.9
Context: Jon and May pass on the stairs.

1 JON: hello hello /haven't seen you for a while\
2 MAY: /hi\
3   well I've been a bit busy
4 JON: must have lunch sometime
5 MAY: yeah good idea give me a ring

In these examples, workmates use small talk to 'do collegiality'. They indicate mutual good intentions as they construct, maintain, repair or extend their collegial relationships. Jon's use of *sometime* (line 4) in his invitation, is an indication of the largely symbolic status of the interchange, and this is ratified by May's equally non-specific suggestion that he ring her (line 5); no precise time or date is mentioned (cf Wolfson 1983 on invitations). Among workers who, at least superficially, accept their organisation's objectives, reference to how busy one is serves as an ideal small talk token. It indicates an orientation to the 'proper' goals of the workplace, while also providing an acceptable account of why social relationships receive less attention than might be expected of good colleagues: in other words 'busyness' is an acceptable excuse for perfunctory attention to interpersonal relationships at work.[6]

Nevertheless, doing collegiality at work often entailed making time within the demands of the workplace routine for talk about non-work topics, and some workers were more inclined to do this than others. Small talk tokens for these workers more typically related to time off than to 'time on' at work. Example 5.7 illustrated workers warming up for the day's work interactions. Talk about holidays and leisure activities typically provides a gentle introduction to work talk. It warms people up socially, oils the interpersonal wheels and gets work started on a positive note (cf Laver 1975: 221; Tannen 1994: 65).

Within an interaction, too, social talk can serve the politeness function of oiling the interpersonal wheels, as Example 5.10 demonstrates. The official topic of talk between Esther and Paddy, two policy analysts in a government ministry, is the necessary preparations for a business trip to Korea. At one point, however, the discourse moves to a discussion of Esther's plans for a weekend in Japan on the way to the business meeting in Korea.

Example 5.10

Context: Esther and Paddy are planning the details of an overseas business trip on which Esther will accompany a senior member of the Ministry.

```
 1 EST:  um and also then he gets there on a Tuesday afternoon or something
 2       I think and we'd have the Monday then we thought we could
 3       perhaps look at some [word deleted for reasons of confidentiality]
 4       protection stuff in Japan /before\ he turns up
 5 PAD:  /mm\ okay
 6 EST:  it also gave us a weekend in between in which we could just sort of
 7       go [exhales] [acts out collapsing] [laughs]
 8 PAD:  yeah
 9 EST:  so for a day and a half or so and then pick up when AJ came back
10 PAD:  mm and Japan is an interesting place
11 EST:  and I got a really good I mean it'd be ideal for me in terms of
12       I've a really good friend who left and is living there at the moment
13       I haven't seen her for months
14 PAD:  which er which er area
15 EST:  um she's in + in Nagata or some it's you know where Tokyo is
16 PAD:  mhm
17 EST:  it's sort of straight up . . .
18       so I mean if I got a chance to go and see her that would be ideal
19 PAD:  yeah yeah
20 EST:  and I'll perhaps do that over a weekend
```

In lines 11–20, by offering Paddy personal information in the midst of the work discussion, Esther is helping build their interpersonal relationship. Another example occurs in the middle of an interaction between a manager and her PA who has been away for a period. The manager is recounting some of the problems that she had experienced in explaining the filing system to the temporary replacement, and she then says with a sigh of relief *oh it's nice to have you back*. This appreciative comment inserted in the middle of task-oriented talk, has the function of providing social oil, reasserting the importance of the sound and effective working relationship which has been developed between the two women.

The end of a workplace interaction is another important position for social talk which attends to the addressee's politeness needs. It mitigates a possible sense of rejection and 'consolidates' the relationship (Laver 1975: 232). It eases the transition from transactional, work-focused, on-task talk about a particular topic to more relational talk. Example 5.4 above illustrates this point and Example 5.11 provides another instance. Although it looks superficially like a greeting, this occurrence of *welcome back* in fact comes at the end of a concentrated interaction focusing on what Hana needs her PA to do, an interaction in which she says several times that it is nice to have Beth back.

Example 5.11
Context: Hana, a manager, is briefing her PA, Beth, on jobs to be done.

1 BET: and the election briefing
2 HAN: yeah oh ++ I think we've cancelled that ++ you might need to check
3 BET: yeah
4 HAN: I'm fairly sure that's been cancelled ++ the panel on Friday afternoon's
5   been cancelled so everyone will just have to + cope on their own
6 BET: pardon
7 HAN: well it's nice to have you back welcome back
8 BET: yes had a very good holiday [tut]
9 HAN: and feel well rested? so where did you go?

Hana finishes the 'work' talk and then shifts to interpersonal social talk via a formulaic small talk greeting (line 7) *it's nice to have you back welcome back*. In the absence of the evidence that such authentic data provides, one would never predict that a greeting such as *welcome back* would occur at the end of an interaction. Its positioning suggests it is a signal of relaxation at the end of the task. Hana switches from a style associated with managing the task to paying more attention to the personal relationship between her and her interlocuter, which until this point has taken a back seat. The small talk serves as a bridge to more extended social discourse. Hana's questions (line 9) *and feel well rested? so where did you go?* provide the addressee with an opportunity to elaborate and extend the social talk well beyond formulaic phatic communion.

Small talk is, then, an obvious means of 'doing collegiality' in the workplace. It enables people to pay appropriate attention to the positive face needs of their colleagues. Where it must be brief, it serves as an acceptable, formulaic nod towards collegiality. Alternatively, where time is not so pressing, more extended social or interpersonal discourse is an important means of constructing and maintaining collegial relationships in the workplace.

Doing power in the workplace

Small talk at work can contribute to the construction not only of collegiality but also of power relationships, as mentioned above in relation to the management of small talk in meetings. A CDA approach is particularly useful in analysing small talk from this perspective. As outlined in Chapter 1, Critical Discourse analysts assume that people habitually enact, reproduce and sometimes resist institutional power relationships in the ways they talk and write. From this perspective, those in power may adopt 'oppressive' and/or 'repressive' discourse strategies to elicit conformity from subordinates. 'Oppression' is the open expression of power, while 'repressive discourse' is a more covert means of exercising 'top-down' or coercive power, in which superiors minimise overt status differences and emphasise solidarity in order to gain their interlocutor's willing compliance and goodwill. Fairclough notes that it is those in positions of power who decide what is correct or appropriate in an interaction. He comments that they also have 'the capacity to determine to what extent ... [their] power will be overtly expressed' (1989: 72), and that in recent years the overt marking of power has been declining. Along with this decline has gone a reduction in formality (Fairclough 1992) and a process of 'conversationalising' public discourses (Fairclough 1995). Similarly Ng and Bradac (1993: 7) discuss strategies for 'depoliticising' the message in order to exercise covert influence over the attitudes and behaviour of others. Power, it is suggested, is increasingly expressed covertly and indirectly – it is hidden.

In Chapters 3 and 4 we outlined a variety of ways, both overt and covert, in which people 'do power' and get things done at work. So, for example, particularly in meetings, the senior participants generally set the agenda, give direct orders, express explicit approval of the actions of others and summarise decisions. But they also employ a variety of less direct, less overt and more subtle means of 'doing power', one example of which is the way they generally 'manage' small talk and social talk at work. The egalitarian work ethic of many New Zealand workplaces seems to have resulted in a situation where, rather than being relinquished, power has gone underground (Sollitt-Morris 1996). The management of small talk and social talk at work can be regarded as one example of subterranean power construction.

Apart from the first contact of the day, small talk is usually optional. But it is generally the superior in an unequal interaction who has the deciding voice in licensing small talk and social talk (cf Hornyak cited in Tannen 1994: 223–4). In unequal encounters the senior person typically sets the agenda and this includes how much small talk and social talk is permitted or considered acceptable during workplace interaction. The extent to which the discourse of work may be de-institutionalised, the extent to which the world of leisure will be permitted to encroach on the world of work is largely in the hands of the superior. In the following extract Carol, Ruth's PA, uses as a small talk token the topic of the tape recording (lines 2, 4) which has become routinised in this workplace. Ruth, however, does not allow the topic to develop, but instead moves quickly to business.

Example 5.12
Context: Ruth walks in to give her PA some typing which needs correcting.

1 RUTH: hello
2 CAR: hello missus- Ms Tape [laughs]
3 RUTH: huh?
4 CAR: I said hello Ms Tape
5 RUTH: who's Ms Tate?
6 CAR: TAPE
7 RUTH: TAPE oh yeah yeah I'll drive everyone up the wall
         [Pointing to the typing Carol has done for her]
8   is that a space or not + it is a space
9 CAR: [quietly] no it's not a space it's not a space

The superior has the right to minimise or cut off small talk and get on to business, and Ruth here resists attempts to use small talk as a bridge to an extended session of social talk. Because of the routine character of small talk it is possible to use it equally as a transition to work talk or to social and personal discourse. By responding formulaically and minimally, Ruth keeps the small talk to a ritual function. In another workplace, the manager's good-humoured warning to meeting participants to *settle down*, during a digression which had become a bit raucous, had the same function of indicating to her team that it was time to switch from off-topic talk to business.

It is also possible for those in more powerful positions deliberately to use small talk to 'manage' or influence the behaviour of others. So, for example, because small talk is associated with the peripheries of interaction, a senior person can use small talk as a strategy for bringing an interaction to an end. In Example 5.13, the manager, Hana, signals to her PA that the business of the interaction is completed by switching to small talk. This leads to more extended interpersonal social talk, but Hana keeps it relatively brief by introducing (via the discourse marker *now listen*) a related issue involving work arrangements.

Example 5.13
Context: Beth is Hana's PA and she has just returned from holiday.

1 BETH: so no it was good I didn't have to worry about meals
2   I didn't have to worry about bills or kids or um work or anything just
3   me
4 HANA: just a holiday for you
5 BETH: yeah + [tut] it was UNREAL [laughs]
6 HANA: now listen are you going to be wanting to take time off
7   during the school holidays

By contrast, in a similar interaction with Jocelyn, an equal in the organisational hierarchy, the off-topic social talk is more extensive and the transition to a closing is carefully negotiated between the two women. Jocelyn's extensive account of her 'time out' is not cut by Hana and, as illustrated in Example 5.14, she responds to Hana's potential pre-closing *that's neat* by indicating she is ready to go.

Example 5.14
Context: Hana and Jocelyn, two managers, are finishing a planning meeting. They have been chatting about Jocelyn's non-work activities.

1 HANA: excellent
2 JOC: it was good + very good
3 HANA: oh excellent oh
4 JOC: yeah
5 HANA: great Jocelyn that's neat
6 JOC: must go
7 HANA: mm okay
8 JOC: all right?
9 HANA: okay thanks

By suggesting that those in positions of power tend to manage and often to limit small talk and social talk during work interactions, this discussion has assumed that subordinates have a greater vested interest in developing such talk with their superiors than vice versa. This interpretation is supported by American research using a questionnaire to study small talk in two business organisations (Levine 1987). The results suggested that while employees appreciate the opportunity to engage in social talk with their bosses, the employers preferred to restrict such talk to non-personal topics. There was extensive evidence in our data that subordinates responded very positively to off-topic digressions and to social talk initiated by superiors. Such topics were generally extended and developed by subordinates in a variety of ways (see Chapter 6 on humour).

On the other hand, the ways in which superiors managed small talk and social talk were much less uniform than Levine's research suggests, perhaps because our data was drawn from a wider range of workplaces and from recorded interaction rather than responses to a questionnaire. While it is true, as illustrated above, that superiors often took the initiative in bringing off-topic talk to a close, it was also the case in a number of work teams that superiors frequently initiated such talk and were willing participants in social talk initiated by others. This was particularly true in teams where there was an emphasis on solidarity and good team relationships, and at points where tensions needed releasing. Leila, for instance, the manager in Case Study 2 in Chapter 4, allowed off-topic social digressions to take their course at points in a meeting where tensions were running high. The CEO of another organisation permitted extensive digressions at certain points during an intense three-day strategic planning meeting. Example 5.15 illustrates Ginette, the manager of a factory team, recounting how she handed out Easter eggs to her team.

Example 5.15
Context: Ginette, team manager, is talking to mates in the control room.

```
 1 GIN:  [laughs] I gave one Easter egg I gave
 2        you know those little coin- chocolate coins
 3        gave Russell a five cent [laughs] chocolate coin + (   )
 4        get this you fucking give it back
 5 ?:    (     )
 6 GIN:  [laughs][mimics Russell] can I have a egg no
 7 PET:  he came here yeah /he\
 8 ROB:  /yeah\ yeah
 9 PET:  did he
10 ROB:  you gave him a Easter egg when he came runnin- running down
11 GIN:  I gave him a whole heap . . . [laughs]
12 TON:  cheeky bastard
13 GIN:  I gave him a whole handful
14 ROB:  oh [laughs] yeah
15 PET:  I says to him go g- go and get some
16        he says Ginette told me to fuck off
```

This is clearly off-topic talk, initiated by Ginette and it continues for some time. The Easter break is approaching and work takes a back seat for a while; social talk is tolerated and even encouraged. The same pattern was identified in a plant nursery at the end of the week's work. Superiors were more likely to license social talk at such times, especially in contexts where work involved physical labour.

The workplace data also provided evidence that subordinates in an interaction do not always accept their superior's construction of a situation. The very permeability of the boundaries between social talk and work talk means that managing social talk may be problematic for those in power. Talk is a potential site of resistance and challenge (Bergvall and Remlinger 1996); some kinds of talk can be characterised as 'resistant political activity' (Kingfisher 1996: 536). So there was sometimes a suggestion of resistance to a superior's repression of social talk, especially if the subordinate had reason to feel exploited or manipulated, a victim of 'repressive discourse'. The interaction between Kate and Anne, introduced in Example 5.5 above, illustrates this point. Kate, the superior, initiates the interaction pretty much head-on without any small talk to ease into her request for assistance (which is also an indirect complaint). Anne is faced with a problem when she has scarcely settled back to work after some time away. As mentioned above, Kate later apologises, but uses the apology as a licence to introduce a second problem. Once she has responded to both problems, Anne asserts her right to some consideration and uses small talk as a channel to social talk which enables her to air her personal problems.

Example 5.16a
Context: Anne, computer adviser, talking to Kate, a more senior policy adviser beside Kate's desk.

1 ANNE: yeah it was a real bummer me not coming in yesterday
2   /but I was absolutely wrecked\
3 KATE: /oh don't worry I worked it out\ for myself and I didn't need to use it

Kate responds to the first part of the comment and overlaps the more personal discourse. Effectively, she focuses on the transactional aspect of the utterance. Anne persists:

Example 5.16b

1 ANNE: I got up and I I just was so exhausted and I thought
2   gee I just wanted to cry
3 KATE: oh you poor thing

At this point Anne has moved from small talk to very personal self-disclosure. Kate is faced with the option of being overtly and explicitly rude, or of listening to Anne – the price, perhaps, of trying to obtain advice more speedily than if she had booked Anne's time. She responds sympathetically to Anne's self-revelation. Anne then continues with her story of stress. She has effectively resisted Kate's attempts at repressive discourse and asserted her own interests. The interaction ends only when Kate's PA interrupts.

Example 5.16c

1 NAN: would you like to speak to Mr D?
2 KATE: oh yes I would
3 ANNE: okay
4 KATE: thanks

The interaction then winds up with references back to Kate's problem and Anne offers to come round and check it later. Other similar examples involve small talk used by a subordinate as a precursor to a request for a day's leave (see Example 5.17), small talk leading into a request for support for a promotion, and small talk as a preliminary to seeking permission to leave work early one day. The subordinate uses the small talk to reduce social distance and emphasise their good relationship with their superior, before requesting a 'good' that only the superior can bestow. Superiors vary in the ways they respond to such talk. Finally, they have the right to cut it short and proceed to business, as illustrated in Example 5.17.

Example 5.17
Context: Tom enters Greg's office to request a day's leave.

1 TOM: can I just have a quick word
2 GREG: yeah sure have a seat
3 TOM: [sitting down] great weather eh
4 GREG: mm
5 TOM: yeah been a good week did you get away skiing at the weekend
6 GREG: yeah we did + now how can I help you
7 TOM: I was just wondering if I could take Friday off and make it a long
8   weekend

Greg effectively resists the small talk with his brief responses, suspecting perhaps that Tom's reference to skiing is not entirely disinterested phatic talk, but may involve a strategic component too. In a meeting in a different organisation, the chair says firmly after an extended social digression *we're going to go on now*, and she returns the discussion immediately to the next topic on the agenda.

Though we have focused in this section on the relationship between differential status and the management of social talk, there are obviously many other relevant factors which account for the precise ways in which interactions progress, and the degree of explicitness with which people 'do power' in interaction. So, for instance, the urgency of the task at hand may override all social niceties, or the closeness of the relationship between two people may reduce the relevance of status differences. Conversely, people may dispense with social talk when they are not concerned to nurture or develop social relationships. Contextual factors must always be considered.

The analysis has suggested that the management of social talk can be regarded as an undoubted but generally indirect and polite manifestation of workplace power relations. Superiors typically determine whether and to what extent there will be social talk within an interaction, and they may explicitly use small talk and social talk as a means of managing a variety of aspects of an interaction.

Conclusion

The distinction between work talk and small talk is often difficult to draw. There is a continuum from one to the other, with many different kinds of 'off-topic' workplace discourse functioning in interesting ways in between.[7] This ambiguity provides a rich resource which may be exploited by participants in workplace interaction. Off-task talk at work ranges from narrowly defined formulaic greeting and parting exchanges to more expansive personally oriented talk. Crucially, it must be identified in context, defined by the way the participants orient to the discourse and the often subtle and ambiguous functions they achieve through its strategic use.

The first section of this chapter explored some of the distributional characteristics of social talk at work, as well as their related discourse and politeness functions. Boundary-marking small talk tends to occur at the openings and closings of social encounters and at transition points within an interaction, easing the entrances and exits of participants and bridging the gaps between different discourse events at work. Social talk also occurs within workplace interaction. In some work contexts it provides relief from boredom; in others it provides light relief from the intensity of the workplace talk, or the tension of a disagreement, or a brief social intermission in a 'full-on' work session. Small talk in the workplace functions like knitting; it can be easily taken up and just as easily dropped. It is a useful undemanding means of filling a gap between work activities. Social talk oils the social wheels. At the beginning of an interaction, it assists the transitions from interpersonal or social talk to work or task-oriented talk. At the end, it provides a means of finishing on a positive note, referring, however briefly, to the personal component of the relationship following a period when work roles and responsibilities have dominated the interaction.

There are many alternative ways of filling silences and providing light relief at work – singing, daydreaming, fantasising, and so on. What broader functions does social talk in particular fulfil? Why do workers choose this particular method of filling gaps and relieving tension? In the second half of the chapter, we discussed some of the complex functions of social talk in the workplace, demonstrating how apparently peripheral and innocuous phatic exchanges can serve pivotal roles in furthering the interpersonal (and sometimes transactional/instrumental) goals of those involved. Small talk is flexible, adaptable, compressible and expandable. It can be as formulaic or as personal as people wish to make it. These characteristics make small talk eminently attractive as a tool in managing workplace relationships. It expresses and reinforces solidarity; it is a way of 'doing collegiality'. But it may also serve as an overt or covert expression of power relationships. People use and respond to small talk as one strategy for 'doing power' in the workplace. Management of small talk is one way in which superiors constitute their organisational control, though of course subordinates may challenge, resist or subvert the discourse.

Small talk has much in common with humour, the topic of Chapter 6. Both are predominantly other oriented and affective in function, and their importance in workplace interaction is frequently underestimated. Newcomers often find that learning how to contribute appropriately to interaction at work breaks, getting the tone right and knowing how much or how little small talk to contribute, and when, are among the biggest challenges in fitting into a new workplace. Because of its complex functions and its (typically overlooked) importance as a component of workplace culture, similar problems often arise in managing humour. The contribution of humour to manifestations of power and politeness in workplace interaction is the focus of the next chapter.

Notes

1. See, for example, Malinowski's (1949) discussion of 'phatic communion'; also Laver (1981), and Coupland (2000).
2. The data collection method is described in Chapter 2. As indicated there, in most cases we gave control over what was to be recorded to the contributors and in all workplaces people were free to delete embarrassing or confidential material (though in fact they rarely did so). One of the consequences of this methodology is that observations about the distribution of small talk and social talk at work must be treated with some caution. Although we emphasised that we were interested in *all* types of workplace talk, including social talk and personal talk, it is clear that some contributers assumed that we were most centrally interested in the talk they classified as 'work talk'. Hence, especially in the early stages of the project, contributers sometimes did not turn on their recorders until what they considered the 'real' beginning of a

meeting, for example, and stopped the tape at what they assessed as the end of a work interaction. Nevertheless, we did collect a good deal of social talk in the workplace, especially in the meetings which we videoed, but the inevitable limitations of the data represented in our sample should be borne in mind, particularly in relation to comments on the distribution of such talk.

3. See Chapter 6 for a discussion of the functions of jocular abuse in this work team.

4. See Laver (1975) for further discussion of these functions in everyday discourse. Linde (1988) also describes how helicopter crews pick up and drop social chat as the demands of work ebb and flow.

5. It can be argued that social talk, and the networking that it facilitates, is just as important to the achievement of the organisation's goals as business talk – though this is not always acknowledged. See Fletcher (1999) on the concept of 'relational practice', the invisible support work that facilitates a good deal of effective business in the workplace.

6. The culturally specific nature of the underlying values reflected in Examples 5.8 and 5.9 is worth noting: e.g. in some cultures such invitations would be considered genuine rather than symbolic and 'busyness' would not be permitted to displace attention to interpersonal relationships and face needs.

7. The continuum from on-task business talk through work-related social talk to off-task social talk and small talk is discussed in some detail in Holmes (2000c).

6

Humour in the Workplace

Example 6.1

Context: Regular meeting of a work team. The team have been discussing a complicated issue arising from a document provided by another section of their organisation. Finally, Yvette, the team leader sums up.

1 YVE: okay clear as mud
[general laughter]

Like small talk, humour is a valuable multifunctional resource in workplace interaction. In discussing the structure of meetings in Chapter 4, we mentioned that many meetings are punctuated by bursts of humour, which tend to occur at strategic points. The opening and closing phases of meetings are obvious sites for humour. Like small talk, humour also occurs within meetings, often at topic transition points, but more distinctively, as illustrated in Example 6.1, following a difficult or complex discussion.[1] Humour releases tension, reaffirms group solidarity when it has been tested or challenged and provides what Max Eastman (1936) calls a 'momentary mental vacation'.[2]

Example 6.1 is a typical tension-releasing one-liner: it involves a simple and even conventional verbal twist to a familiar phrase (*clear as a bell*), and while it is not particularly funny to an outsider, it is greeted with laughter by co-participants. Most workplace humour is inextricably context bound in this way so that utterances which generate hilarity among work colleagues often appear obscure and opaque to outsiders. This is a reflection of one of the most basic social functions of humour – it serves to create and maintain solidarity, a sense of belonging to a group (e.g. Hampes 1992; Hay 1995; Morreall 1991; Ziv 1984).

But humour is also a relevant resource in the construction and management of power relationships in the workplace (e.g. Coser 1960; Brown and Keegan 1999; Pizzini 1991). Humour typically constructs participants as equals, emphasising what they have in common and playing down power differences. It is therefore a useful strategy for softening face-threatening acts such as directives and criticisms. It is equally available as a sweetener for even riskier speech acts such as insults and challenges; humour can license a challenge or provide an acceptable vehicle for contesting authority (cf Kotthoff 1996; Holdaway 1988). The first section of this chapter identifies and illustrates some of these functions of humour in workplace interaction.

The second section of the chapter uses a community of practice framework to focus in more detail on the actual practice of 'doing humour' at work. Three teams from different organisations provide case studies, illustrating the different ways in which humorous exchanges are constructed and the different styles of interaction which develop among different work groups. Humour provides one way of characterising contrasting workplace cultures, as well as insights into different attitudes to power and politeness, or more specifically, different ways of doing power and solidarity at work.

Functions of humour in the workplace

The obvious function of Yvette's remark *clear as mud* (Example 6.1) was to lighten the atmosphere and re-establish group harmony. It also served, however, at a more specific level, as a critical comment on the writing style of those who had produced the document which the team was discussing. At yet another level, it constructed or reinforced a boundary between intra-organisational sections, while simultaneously aligning Yvette, the team manager, with her team members, rather than with the wider organisation. Such multifunctionality is typical of almost every instance of authentic discourse (e.g. Holmes 1982; Tracy and Coupland 1990), but it is perhaps especially characteristic of humorous comments. So although we attempt to disentangle distinct functions for the purposes of analysis, it is important to remember that any particular utterance or discourse sequence is typically multifunctional, simultaneously expressing meaning at a number of different levels. With this caveat in mind, we examine how humour functions to construct harmonious workplace relations, as well as the uses of humour in relation to various aspects of 'doing power' at work.

Nurturing harmonious work relationships

Amusing workmates

The primary function of talk at work is avowedly the furtherance of the organisation's objectives. Humour is thus an interesting discourse strategy in workplace interaction, since its relationship to the achievement of workplace goals is typically indirect. Its most obvious contribution is in the construction of good relationships or solidarity between work colleagues. To the extent that an attempt at humour succeeds in amusing workmates, it contributes to social cohesion at work (e.g. Blau 1955; O'Quin and Arnoff 1981; Holdaway 1988). Example 6.2 is a very clear illustration of humour functioning to construct and strengthen harmonious workplace relationships. It is a short excerpt from a conversation during an afternoon tea break, most of which consisted of light-hearted banter of this kind.

Example 6.2

Context: Three colleagues discussing the problems which arise when someone is unexpectedly summoned to see the Minister.

```
 1  EVE:  I think we need a ministry suit just hanging up in the cupboard
 2        /[laughs]\
 3  LEI:  /you can just\ imagine the problems with the length /[laughs]\
 4  EVE:  /it would have\ it would have to have an elastic waist so
 5        /that we [laughs]\ could just be yeah
 6  LEI:  /[laughs] yes that's right [laughs]\
 7  EVE:  bunched in for some and [laughs] let it out
 8  LEI:  /laughs\
 9  EVE:  /out for others\
10  LES:  and the jacket would have to be /long to cover all the bulges\
11  LEI:  /no I'm quite taken with this\
12  LES:  /so\
13  EVE:  /[laughs]\
14  LEI:  /now that\ that is very nice
```

The three colleagues construct a humorous 'fantasy' sequence (cf Hay 1995), an imaginary scenario describing an all-purpose suit which could be used by anyone unexpectedly summoned to see the Minister. All three particip-ants contribute, though Leila's role is largely supportive, providing com-ments which indicate enjoyment and endorsement of the idea. These women are clearly 'doing collegiality', developing a humorous sequence for mutual amusement.

Shared humour emphasises common ground and shared norms. A humorous comment which elicits a positive response (such as a laugh or a smile), as illustrated in Example 6.1, indicates that the speaker shares with others a common view about what is amusing – thus creating or main-taining solidarity, while also enhancing the speaker's status within the group. A collaborative, interactively constructed sequence of the kind illustrated in Example 6.2, indicates even more clearly that colleagues are on the same wavelength. Example 6.3 is a similar example from a meeting in a differ-ent organisation, but here the humour emerges from the business of the meeting.

Example 6.3

Context: Planning meeting of a group of colleagues. They are discussing the need to coordinate the taking of annual leave to ensure minimum negative impact on the work project.

1 HEL: people might have to take some leave by that stage as well with this
2   sort of panic before the end of November
3 WILL: oh I'm saving up all mine [laughs]
4 SEL: well people could panic early [laughs]
          [general laughter]
5 HEL: never happens
          [general laughter]
6 SEL: well the HR coordinators might crack the whip /so that people
7   panic early yes\
8 TONI: /I planned to panic early by taking\ the school holidays off but that
9   didn't work [laughs]

People's problems with getting prepared ahead of time elicit the suggestion from Selene that they need to *panic early* (line 4) – something of a contradiction in terms since the notion of panic is almost inextricably tied to last-minute pressures. The group clearly share a common reaction to the notion and this is a good example of them 'doing collegiality' through humour. The humorous scenario is interactively achieved or jointly constructed: Helen's comment (line 5) and Toni's contribution (line 8) both build on Selene's humorous suggestion, and she herself elaborates it further (line 6). This is also a nice instance of what Fletcher (1999) labels 'relational practice', i.e. strictly irrelevant talk which nonetheless contributes both to the smooth running of the team and to the achievement of its objectives.

In our data, there are many sequences of witty repartee between colleagues and workmates which serve this function of constructing and strengthening social cohesion. Discussing funding problems, for instance, a group from one government department began with flippant humorous suggestions such as *run a cake stall*; another group discussing the same problems facetiously suggested *levies on cage fighting* as a source of funding. (More typically such sequences require extensive explanation to be fully appreciated by readers.)

Shared criticisms of others can also serve to cement solidarity between work colleagues; a criticism endorsed by others indicates common values and attitudes. Critical comments were often a source of amusement for coworkers, as illustrated by Example 6.4.

Example 6.4

Context: Two young Maori men are discussing plans for a formal presentation which will involve the use of the Maori language by another Maori colleague. Maori is a second language, acquired after childhood by all three men.

1 TOM: Sam's probably the fellow who's had the most experience of them all
2   but god his pronunciation it's [laughs]
3 KIT: [laughs]

Sam's pronunciation of Maori is clearly beyond description; indeed it is so embarrassing that it is a source of shared humour for Tom and Kit. The inexplicitness of this exchange is typical of much workplace humour; it reflects shared background knowledge, experience and understandings. Tom and Kit reinforce their shared in-group status with such exchanges.

Similarly, in Example 6.5, Marlene uses transparent understatement to amuse the group by referring openly to what was a major disagreement between her and Sandy.

Example 6.5
Context: Marlene is reporting to a regular meeting of a project group in a commercial organisation.

1 MAR: [drawls] um Sandy and I had our status update meeting
2   and I'd have to say it was um it got a LITtle bit heated /[laughs]\
3 SAN: /[laughs]\
4 MAR: but we still love each other
       [general laughter]

This is skilful bridge-building as evident from the fact that Sandy laughs first, indicating appreciation of the diplomatic way Marlene has reported their disagreement. Marlene then overstates the warmth of their reconciliation *but we still love each other* (line 4), providing amusement and tension relief, and in the process explicitly strengthening group cohesion.

Self-criticism or self-deprecation is another potential basis for workplace humour which typically enhances social cohesion. In Case Study 2, in Chapter 4 (Example 4.21), Leila, the team manager humorously claimed that her workplace skills were limited to making coffee. In this example, Leila used humour to lighten the tone and, in particular, to put herself down at the end of a long and difficult meeting in which she had at times expressed herself authoritatively. This self-deprecating humour contributed to team collegiality by appealing to shared attitudes and beliefs in a workplace where modesty was highly valued.

Example 6.6 illustrates a rather different situation where self-deprecating humour is used by a subordinate who has made an error. The humour serves to excuse an embarrassing memory lapse (see also Example 6.21 below).

Example 6.6
Context: Fay, the section manager, is talking to her administrative assistant, Pam, who has finally located a file which she has no recollection of creating.

1 PAM: oh well I must have done it
        [both laugh]
2 PAM: oh isn't that gorgeous . . .
3 FAY: when did you send it?
4 PAM: ++ it's a mystery to me [laughs]
        [Fay laughs uproariously]
5 PAM: it really is

Pam first creates a positive context by explicitly admitting her culpability rather than denying it (line 1). She continues by describing her lapse as *gorgeous* (line 2), rather than, say, 'terrible', and by comically exaggerating – rather than diminishing – her ignorance with a dramatic pause followed by *it's a mystery to me* (line 4). Pam thus preserves her positive face by amusing Fay, and the successful humour strengthens the sense of camaraderie between the two, in an interaction which could have turned out very differently.

Because it is intended to amuse, humour almost always has an element of solidarity among its many meanings (though solidarity with whom is a factor considered further below). But constructing collegiality is not typically its pre-eminent function in much work-oriented, as opposed to socially oriented, interaction.[3] Leila's self-deprecation (Example 4.21) created social cohesion, not only by causing amusement, but also by de-emphasising status and power differences between participants in the interaction. Humour thus also serves a strategic purpose within a meeting where tensions have sometimes run high, and where Leila has needed to emphasise her authority at times. Similarly, Pam's honest admission of her incompetence amuses Fay and appeals to her sense of solidarity, but since Fay is Pam's boss, it also serves a strategic function of disarming criticism. Interestingly, in work contexts involving people of different levels of authority, instances such as Example 6.6 were less frequent than instances where the superior initiated the humour (cf Pizzini 1991; Sollitt-Morris 1997). Clearly, the mediation of power relations is an important function of humour in workplace interaction, as illustrated in the next section.

Maintaining good work relations

Humour makes a major contribution to workplace harmony, and hence indirectly to work efficiency, by virtue of its mitigating or hedging effect on 'controlling' speech acts, such as directives and criticisms. As discussed in Chapter 3, directives are canonical instances of face threatening acts (FTAs) (Brown and Levinson 1987): They impinge on the autonomy of others. By softening the force of a directive, a speaker pays attention to the face needs of the addressee(s), recognising and respecting the addressee's basic 'want to preserve self-determination' (Brown and Levinson 1987: 70). There are many means of mitigating a directive, as illustrated in Chapter 3, including linguistic hedges (e.g. *perhaps*, *maybe*), modal verbs (e.g. *might*, *could*), pragmatic particles (e.g. *sort of*, *you know*) and prosodic devices such as a rising intonation contours. Humour is another such device.

In our workplace data, humour was more often used to soften directives between equals than by bosses to subordinates, while directives upwards were relatively rare and typically treated as humorous per se (cf Mooney 1980). The very idea of a subordinate giving the boss a direct order was regarded as intrinsically humorous (see Chapter 3). The boss or the manager has a right to give orders, but directives from one colleague to another, where there is no formal institutional basis giving one person the right to direct the other's behaviour, clearly needed to be carefully phrased to avoid causing offence. Between status equals or near equals, then, humour proved a popular strategy for attenuating the force of a directive. Softening with humour simultaneously expresses concern for the addressee's face and signals goodwill and positive cooperative intent; in other words, humour serves to maintain good relations and negotiate respect between participants, as Example 6.7 illustrates.

Example 6.7
Context: Two policy analysts, Kate and Melanie, are discussing a proposal. Kate suggests Melanie should take away the proposal and work on it further.

1 KATE: well we've just about done it to death I think
2   it's about ready for you to give give it mouth-to-mouth
3   resuscitation do you think
         [both laugh]

Kate attenuates her directive to Melanie with metaphoric humour based on the notion of the document as a living entity. The use of *we* (line 1) emphasises the collegiality at the basis of Kate's relationship with Melanie, while the incongruity of the metaphor provides the humour attenuating the directive, which might otherwise threaten that collegiality. Between close colleagues, humour used in this way sometimes developed into good-natured banter, a jointly constructed humour sequence, where the person on the receiving end of the directive challenged its initiator, as shown in Example 6.8.

Example 6.8
Context: Vince and Aidan are working through a proposal.

1 VIN: you're not on page four yet?
2 AID: yes
3 VIN: [laughs] /[laughs]\ [laughs]
4 AID: /I've been there and come back\ [laughs]

Vince wants Aidan to speed up, but in the interests of maintaining good relations, he does not want to be overtly directive. He conveys his message by an indirect strategy, using a high pitched incredulous and humorous tone for a comment which could be interpreted as a criticism of Aidan's slowness. Aidan retaliates, however, with a humorous challenge to Vincent's implication about his speed. Thus complex messages are conveyed in an acceptable way. Humour enables Vince to convey a directive which recognises Aidan's face needs, while Aidan preserves his dignity as well as responding appropriately to Vince.

When superiors mitigated their directives, most used standard politeness strategies or epistemic devices such as tags, modal particles and indirect structures, rather than humour (see Chapter 3), suggesting that humour may typically function as a particularly 'strong' hedging device. This suggestion finds support from the fact that superiors sometimes used humour to soften an implied criticism, as in Example 6.9.

Example 6.9
Context: Manager, Beth, to administrative assistant, Marion, who is chatting to a secretary.

1 BETH: okay Marion I'm afraid serious affairs of state will have to wait
2   we have some trivial issues needing our attention
           [all laugh]

There are several indications that Beth's utterance is motivated by politeness and oriented to Marion's face needs. The use of the pronouns *we* and *our* function to align the manager and the administrative assistant, expressing solidarity; and the source of the humour itself – the ironic downgrading of their on-task work to *trivial* compared to the social talk or work gossip in which the other two women were engaged – also serves this purpose. However, in addition to the directive, there is also an implicit criticism of Marion. She should be getting ready for the meeting and instead she is chatting. This kind of context greatly favoured the use of humour in our data; i.e. humour functions to attenuate the explicit or bald enactment of power by a superior over a subordinate.

Examples 6.10 and 6.11 provide further brief illustrations of the same pattern – humour used by a superior to a subordinate to mitigate criticism – but in two very different work contexts. In both cases the criticism is overt and there is a large audience. Without the humour such public reprimands would be harsh indeed.

Example 6.10
Context: 9am meeting of white-collar group from commercial organisation is well under way when Rob Blair arrives late.

1 SAN: however it's a service we've provided for our customers
2   good afternoon Mister Blair
3 ROB: I forgot it was on
       [general laughter]

Example 6.11
Context: 6am briefing meeting of factory team is well under way when Sue arrives late.

1 XM: there's run upon run upon run so that's I'd do at least five or six
2 GIN: good afternoon Sue
3 LES: good afternoon Sue
4 SUE: hi everybody I'm here

In both these examples, the manager used humour to maintain good relations, while nevertheless conveying the message 'you're late!'. The requirements of institutional roles at work often make face-threatening acts unavoidable; in such contexts, humour provides an acceptable attenuation strategy. It is coopted as a strategy for mediating between competing discourses – those of politeness and power.

Licensing a professional challenge

The examples discussed so far illustrate ways in which humour is used to construct and preserve good workplace relations, to indicate positive intent and concern for the feelings of addressees and to mitigate overt realisations of power – in other words, to express politeness. We turn now to instances of humour used as a subversive strategy: e.g. to mask risky negative messages to an equal or superior; to challenge another's point of view; or to contest a superior's authority. Humour serves in such cases as a socially acceptable cloak for face attack acts in the workplace.[4]

Jocular abuse

Jocular abuse or a joking insult is the simplest case where humour licenses a face attack act, and, at its most benign, it serves largely as an expression of solidarity (Hay 1995). Jocular abuse is much more common in some workplaces, among some workplace groups and in some work contexts than others (a point to which we return below). Indeed, for some work groups, jocular abuse seems to be a continuous source of entertainment. Example 6.12 is a typical exchange between members of a factory team.

Example 6.12
Context: Two male production workers on the factory line talking during a lull in their work.

```
 1 PET:  oh man I'm starving I am starving . . .
 2        I might go and join the war remind me of the old days the army
 3        and the front row . . .
 4 DAV:  you'd be the first one to get shot
 5 PET:  why /what makes\ you say that
 6 DAV:  /you're so\ you're so big
 7 PET:  [warningly] brother
 8 DAV:  it's very rare that a bullet will miss you
        [general laughter]
 9 PET:  yes /that's not on\
10 DAV:  /look at the\ size of your stomach
11 PET:  that's NOT on (3)
12 DAV:  actually they'll close their eyes and sh- fire a shot
        [general laughter]
13 PET:  [drawls] oh I see
14 DAV:  they got no problem missing that
```

As this example illustrates, jocular abuse in blue-collar workplaces often focused on personal characteristics such as weight or looks and functioned primarily to construct solidarity rather than to license a challenge to an individual's professional workplace skills.

More obviously subversive in their intent are the following examples of jocular abuse between team members.

Example 6.13
Context: Team members interacting in a variety of organisational contexts.

* Barry hasn't read the reports
* Callum did fail his office management word [laughs] processing lessons
* [blokes] can't multi-task . . . it's in the genes
* the heart was there but the mind wasn't
* you don't have enough work to do Barry
* you're trying to wind up Dudley are you
* [laugh] + [yells] some time today'd be nice (i.e. 'hurry up')

In these cases the professional competence of the target is being impugned and, potentially at least, this is a relatively serious matter in the context of workplace interaction. The target is typically just one member of a larger group and the (often minimal) humour which cosmetically 'lightens' the criticism typically takes the form of overstatement, irony or sarcasm (see Hay 1995).

Conversely, a group member's over-zealousness may become the target of jocular abuse. In Example 6.14, Celia is abused for 'breaking ranks'. By finishing her work ahead of others she challenges group norms and 'shows up' her colleagues.

Example 6.14

Context: Three women from a government department discussing proposals they are working on.

1 VAL: and Celia's finished her proposals I'm sure [laughs]
2 CEL: on the last one
3 VAL: ah you sod
       [all laugh]

The humour is generated by the incongruity of the strong term of abuse *sod* in the professional office work context between colleagues. At one level, there may be an element of underlying aggression based on envy, reflected in the fact that an insult is the chosen response. However, insults between those who know each other well are also signals of solidarity and markers of in-group membership: i.e. 'we know each other well enough to insult each other without causing offence' (cf Hay 1994; Kotthoff 1996). Humour encodes the criticism or insult in an acceptable form.

Jocular abuse of this kind occurs in a variety of contexts in the workplace. Colleagues used abusive terms such as *rotter*, *sod*, *bitch* and *bastard* in situations where they wished to contest the addressee's professional actions, but to do so in a collegially acceptable way, for example, when a colleague passed on an unwelcome job, volunteered them for a task, suggested they should be the person to respond to a tricky client, and so on. Humour provided a socially acceptable 'cover' for their protest. In other words, jocular abuse often functions as a covert strategy for face attack, a relatively polite means of registering a veiled protest.

Challenging authority

Because it constitutes such a threat to face, jocular abuse tends to be restricted to those who know each other well. The examples discussed in the previous section focused on jocular abuse between relative equals at work. But people who work together at different levels of the institutional hierarchy over long periods get to know each other well too. And though jocular abuse was far more common between equals, there were cases in our data where subordinates used humour to hedge insults to superiors.[5] As mentioned above, people sometimes protested about tasks assigned to them, or responded to criticisms with humorous abuse (e.g. *oh shut up*, *what a rotten trick to play on a girl*, *bullyboy*, *slave-driver*, *unjust unjust*, and so on). But these jocular insults have different force between status differentiated participants than between equals. Directed upwards they are slightly risky and, however jocular, there is an underlying contestive component to the message.

In such cases humour functions to license the challenge from subordinate to superior. Such challenges may be lighthearted and involve relatively trivial issues, as illustrated in Example 1.5 (*you should have got it in writing*) where

Ivan used humour to lighten the tone of the exchange, while simultaneously conveying an implicit criticism of his superior. But humour can also serve as a shield for more serious criticism of a superior and as a cloak for the expression of 'socially risky' opinions by subordinates (Winick 1976). In Example 6.15, Bob casts doubt on his senior's judgement.

Example 6.15
Context: Chairperson, Henry, planning with Bob, a more junior staff member, a strategy to trounce opposition at a meeting.

1 HEN: they're bound to fall over as soon as you present this stuff
2   it can't be refuted
3 BOB: let's just hope they've been reading the same textbooks as you
        [both laugh]

The humour serves as an instance of contestive discourse, attenuating and thus concealing what could be considered the effrontery of a critical speech act in such a context. Bob is effectively conveying scepticism about Henry's views, and indicating he is less confident than Henry about the predicted outcome. By embedding his different judgement and sceptical evaluation of their chances of success in a humorous utterance, Bob renders it more acceptable. And, of course, humour also renders Bob's implied critical judgement and different opinion less accessible for challenge by Henry because it is not explicitly 'on record'.

In Example 6.16 a sarcastic comment about a report written by a manager from a different section of the organisation (who is not present) can be analysed similarly.

Example 6.16
Context: Regular weekly meeting of IT project team in large white-collar organisation.

1 CAL: I didn't count the pages
2 BAR: didn't you [laughs]
3 CAL: it's just one and a half feet high
4 BAR: is it one and a half feet? that's a better measurement
        [general laughter]

Callum conveys his criticism of the unreasonable length of the report by a sarcastic comment about its height, which is not a typical way of measuring written reports! Barry's utterance (line 4) first expresses supportive astonishment and then quite explicitly endorses Callum's adoption of a non-conventional measure, indicating that he shares Callum's view that the report is unreasonably long. In these cases, then, humour provides an acceptable vehicle for expressing subversive attitudes or aggressive feelings (cf Rodrigues and Collinson 1995; Ackroyd and Thompson 1999).

In a meeting of a group of women in another organisation (the focus of Case Study 2 in Chapter 4, as well as Case Study 1 below) a sarcastic comment serves as an acceptable vehicle for indicating irritation with a particular style which is inconsistent with the group's generally egalitarian approach to management.

Example 6.17

Context: Meeting of a work group in a white-collar professional organisation to plan changes to systems.

```
 1 LEI:  mm ++ Emma the reason I put you up there as part of the solution is
 2       I think that you're going to be quite a large part of finding out
 3       just I mean you have a much better idea than any of us
 4       well you're the only person actually /knows anything about\
 5 KER:  /[laughs]\
 6 EM:   /about what\
 7 LEI:  /the nominations\ /[laughs]\\
 8 EM:   /well as I\
 9 LEI:  and /the practical working\
10 EM:   /subtly tried to say\ earlier Leila
11       I actually [laughs] don't know what's going on with it
12 ZOE:  what a wonderful boss you must be
13       delegate delegate delegate way to go [laughs]
         /[general laughter]\
14 LEI:  /well it's just been\
15       it's a bit more of a mess than what any of us thought
```

Leila is the target of two critical comments in succession, one more overt than the other. Emma first laughingly refutes Leila's assumption that she is the most knowledgeable person and therefore the most suitable person for the task being allocated (line 11). Though this is a contestive utterance, with Leila and Emma competing for the floor (especially lines 6–10), both are also laughing throughout this exchange and the tone is friendly. By contrast, the tone with which Zoe's apparently humorous compliment (lines 12–13) is delivered is distinctly less friendly, and the humour in fact serves as a cover for an implicit criticism of her superior's authority. Zoe effectively has her cake and eats it too; she conveys her professionally risky message, criticising Leila's management techniques, in a socially acceptable form. As with jocular abuse, it is difficult for a superior to challenge criticism framed as a humorous comment without losing face.

To sum up, humour is used at work to construct and maintain good relations with work colleagues. It serves as an interesting politeness device, not only in establishing good relations between colleagues, but also by mitigating or softening less welcome messages such as directives and criticisms. When used to attenuate unwelcome messages to subordinates, humour indicates concern for maintaining good workplace relations by those in positions of power and authority. Humour is an effective way of 'doing power' less explicitly, a subtle device for getting things done in a socially and professionally acceptable manner. Used by subordinates to soften unwelcome messages to superiors, humour serves as a critical discourse device, a contestive strategy, providing one of the few acceptable means available to challenge, if only temporarily, the existing authority structures. In the next section, we consider in more detail the ways in which workplace humour contributes to the construction of power and politeness in different communities of practice.

Humour and workplace culture

Even cursory observation indicates that the quantity of humour (most obviously evident in the amount of laughter heard) varies in different workplaces, in different teams and in different contexts within a workplace. Not surprisingly, then, a more detailed analysis of the humour produced in meetings of specific work groups in different workplaces identified considerable variation in the amount of humour produced. At one end of the spectrum, a well-established, cohesive factory team produced a high average of one instance of humour every two minutes, while at the other end a group of regional managers from a white-collar organisation, who met only sporadically, produced less than half that amount. This distribution was also understandable given that the factory work was intellectually undemanding and relatively routine, leaving team members free to use their wits in other ways to relieve boredom, while the strategic planning in which the professional managers were engaged provided fewer obvious opportunities and incentives for humour. As the discussion above has suggested, however, it is not just the amount of humour which varies in different contexts; the ways in which humour is used at work is at least as important in characterising different types of workplace interaction. In this section we examine the ways in which humour contributes to the construction of a distinctive workplace culture in different communities of practice (CofPs).

Workplace culture comprises the knowledge and experience that enables people to function effectively at work or, expressed less formally, familiarity with 'the way we do things around here'.[6] Humour is clearly one aspect of workplace culture. Knowing how to participate appropriately in workplace interaction is an important passport to social integration and managing humour is one aspect of this participation. Perhaps, most obviously, not 'getting' a joke brands you as an outsider.

As noted in Chapter 1, members of a CofP regularly engage with each other in the service of a joint enterprise. They share a repertoire of resources which enables them to communicate in a kind of verbal shorthand which is often difficult for outsiders to penetrate. Humour is one aspect of this. Ways of realising 'harmonious or conflictual workplace relationships' (Wenger 1998: 125), for instance, clearly include humour, as illustrated in the previous section. 'Shared ways of engaging in doing things together' and 'certain styles recognized as displaying membership' (Wenger 1998: 125–6) point to the relevance of different styles of humour in constructing workgroup membership. The number and kinds of 'insider jokes' provide further obvious criteria for differentiating workplaces from one another. In what follows we focus on three work groups from different organisations as brief case studies, identifying relevant parameters for distinguishing the contribution humour makes to the contrasting workplace cultures, and in particular to the ways in which power and politeness are played out at work.

Case Study 1

The first case study is an office-based work unit in a relatively small, white-collar 'knowledge industry' organisation, with predominantly female staff. One of their meetings was used as Case Study 2 in Chapter 4. Using Wenger's (1998) three criterial features for a CofP (mutual engagement, joint enterprise and shared repertoire), this group can be described as a relatively tightly knit, cohesive community of practice, with a high involvement communication style. They engaged with one another many times a day in a variety of ways: in formal meetings, informal problem-solving sessions and in social chat in their workspaces and at breaks. They shared a clear sense of joint enterprise which went beyond doing the tasks at hand to encompass the pursuit of certain ideals relating specifically to their organisation's objectives. And they often jointly constructed a highly interactive and typically supportive communicative style which was particularly evident in their humour.

Sequences of collaborative humour and amusing anecdotes were commonly interleaved with the business at hand during formal meetings and other discussions in this community of practice, indicating a workplace culture where relationships were valued and nurtured. In the meeting used as a case study in Chapter 4, the group worked very hard to reach consensus on a controversial issue. Leila, the manager and chair, was aware that Zoe, a senior member of the team, was unhappy about the solution being considered. In Example 6.18, Leila presents Zoe and herself as in accord on a related matter, and then skilfully uses humour to compliment Zoe on her ability to 'mother' new staff, which raises a laugh from the group as a whole.

Example 6.18
Context: Meeting of a work group in a white-collar professional organisation to plan changes to systems.

 1 LEI: Zoe Zoe and I'd been talking I mean one we're gonna need Zoe
 2   um anyway to do handing over with the other librarians
 3   when they come /on\ board and I think that
 4 KER: /yeah\
 5 LEI: they're probably going to feel a need for a little bit of mothering
 6   and I think Zoe will be good at that
 7   and the /other thing she's been\
 8 KER: /[laughs]\
 9 LEI: really good with Kerry I've watched her [laughs]
10   I've seen her doing it
11 EM: mother librarian
12 LEI: she'll be sort of the great aunt librarian /[laughs]\
        /[general laughter]\

Leila's humorous compliment indicates appreciation of Zoe's mentoring skills, eliciting agreement from Kerry (line 4) and a collaborative contribution from Emma *mother librarian* (line 11). The use of humour to lighten the tone and head off the threat of overt conflict is consistent with the team's preference for a consensual style of decision making. Moreover, the characterisation of authority relationships in 'familial' terms is another typical strategy for defusing potential conflict and playing down power differences.

Zoe is not mollified, however, and Example 6.17 above illustrates how she manages to convey her dissatisfaction with Leila's approach in a socially acceptable way. Her comment *what a wonderful boss you must be, delegate delegate delegate, way to go* (lines 12–13) is framed as a compliment, but it is a barbed one in the context of this work group where status differences are generally minimised, and cooperation and consensus emphasised. In the real world of conflicting goals, all is not sweetness and light, even in the most harmonious of workplaces, and sarcasm and irony are salient indicators of disaffection or resentment, as illustrated further in the discussion of Case Study 3 below.

Towards the end of the discussion in this meeting, as a solution begins to emerge, there is a good deal more collaborative, jointly constructed humour reflecting relief that a solution is in sight (Example 6.19).

Example 6.19
Context: Meeting of a work group in a white-collar professional organisation to plan changes to systems.

      [laughter throughout this section]
 1 LEI: Emma you are part of the solution in that I think that ( )
 2 EM: I only want to be part of the problem
 3 XX: really
 4 LEI: [laughs] [in fun growly tone] don't you dare be part of the problem

5   I'll keep on giving you vitamin c bananas [laughs] chocolate fish

6   [laughs] I gave I gave um I you know everyone had chocolate fish

7   last week but Emma had more chocolate fish than anybody

8   the only thing was she had holes in her teeth /[laughs]\

9 EM: /I couldn't eat them\

10 LEI: she couldn't eat them [laughs]

       [general laughter]

The way Leila shares information about the holes in Emma's teeth and jokingly threatens to feed her with various goodies simultaneously reinforces the supportive team culture and constructs Leila in a nurturing role. Once again 'family' roles provide a vehicle for the humour, which is collaboratively achieved. Emma plays the role of recalcitrant child (line 2) to Leila's benevolent, authority figure (lines 4–8). The extent to which they are 'in tune' is indicated by Emma's provision of the resolution to Leila's narrative *I couldn't eat them* (line 9), which is echoed and reinforced immediately by Leila *she couldn't eat them* (line 10).

Example 4.21 also occurred towards the end of this meeting and, as mentioned in that chapter, the humour clearly signalled tension relief at the end of a complex discussion. The interaction is characterised by a great deal of cooperative overlapping and laughter. It is a collaborative achievement nicely exemplifying how the group reconstructs its valued cohesive relationships at the end of a meeting where goodwill has been stretched. Consensus is achieved on important decisions and is then literally enacted in the interactional style of the group at this final point. The overall effect is one of a high energy, friendly and good-humoured exchange, with many of the features of 'all-together-now' talk, identified by Coates (1996) as characteristic of the talk of women friends.

In their work breaks too, members of this CofP interact in supportive and cooperative ways, as illustrated in Example 6.2. While Eve and Lesley collaborate to describe features of the hypothetical all-purpose Ministry suit, Leila laughs and makes supportive comments *yes that's right* (line 6), *I'm quite taken with this* (line 11), *that is very nice* (line 14). Throughout the episode there is laughter from all three participants. Lesley seamlessly links her contribution to Eve's description with a coordinating conjunction *and the jacket would have to be long* (line 10), while Leila, the group leader in more task-oriented contexts, here takes the role of appreciative audience, contributing consistently positive evaluative responses, including laughter (lines 3, 6, 8), which overlap throughout with the descriptive contributions of the other two. This example nicely illustrates the detail of the way in which humour functions to construct and maintain particular kinds of work relationships. Maximally collaborative talk of this type is a means of 'doing collegiality', while Leila's background role in this exchange, compared to her role in meetings she chaired, demonstrates again how power and authority are played down where possible in this community of practice, as well as how power and politeness are constructed differently in different social contexts.

In terms of workplace culture, then, there is considerable emphasis on consensus-based decision making in this community of practice. Power and status differences are downplayed, and group membership is highly valued. The team's use of humour reflects these priorities. There is a good deal of laughter in the group's meetings, much of the humour is jointly constructed and collaboratively developed, and most of it is positive in its pragmatic effect. Where conflict arises, humour sometimes serves as a vehicle for the expression of dissatisfaction, or to mask a covert challenge to what is perceived as an overly 'managerial' style. Overall, however, the humour which characterises this workplace culture is an accurate reflection of the friendly, supportive work relationships of the group.

Case Study 2

The second case study is a blue-collar, multicultural, male-dominated but female-led, factory-based team within the manufacturing industry. On the three criterial features, this work group constitutes a very tightly knit and highly cohesive community of practice. Their level of mutual engagement on a day-to-day basis is not uniformly high, as the packers and manufacturers work on different floors of the factory, and there are long intervals where individual team members may not need to communicate with one another. However, the team has daily briefing sessions, individuals have regular contact with one another in the course of their 12-hour shifts, they see one another at 'smoko' (tea/coffee breaks), and there is regular social contact between many team members outside work hours. They are a very cohesive group with a real sense of joint enterprise and high motivation, both in terms of completing immediate tasks during each shift and meeting longer term goals, such as continuing to outperform other production teams. Teamwork is highly and explicitly valued, something which is further reinforced by the Polynesian cultural background of a majority of the team, which tends to privilege the group over individuals.

One of the more noticeable ways in which these characteristics are reflected in the discourse of this group is in the high proportion of humour which pervades their talk. As mentioned above, there was a higher proportion of humour in the team meetings of this group than in any other work group we recorded. Moreover, the style of humour favoured by the group was sparky, contestive and competitive; i.e. rather different from the supportive, collaborative humour more characteristic of meetings between members of the team in Case Study 1. The factory team had a well-deserved reputation for uninhibited swearing and constantly joking around and 'having each other on'. Their particular blend of verbal humour, jocular abuse and practical jokes contributed to a unique team culture and generally helped to create positive relationships within the team. These kinds of playful yet highly competitive and 'in your face' strategies for building solidarity are well documented as common characteristics of all-male groups (e.g. Kuiper 1991; Coates 1997; Kiesling 2001).

Example 6.20 provides a typical illustration of how members embed the team culture and low-key humour into routine task-oriented interactions.

Example 6.20
Context: Ginette the team leader talks to Russell in the manufacturing section via the intercom.

1 GIN: copy Kiwi copy Kiwi
2 RUS: what's up
3 GIN: stand by and I'll give you the figures bro
4 RUS: yep go
5 GIN: for the line 1 acma rainbow flight we need 24 tonnes 24
6 RUS: yo bro

Ginette, the manager, is participating in a longstanding team ritual when using the intercom, by the mock-serious use of ham radio conventions like *copy Kiwi* (line 1) and *stand by* (line 3) to initiate the interaction with Russell. Her use of his nickname *Kiwi* (line 1) and the familiar and friendly term of address *bro* (line 3) when addressing Russell, and his use in return of *bro* (line 6) are also characteristic of the way this team interacts.[7] Example 6.21 of humorous self-deprecation by Sam illustrates the way such low-key humour is endemic, naturally woven into team members' mundane workplace interactions.

Example 6.21
Context: Sam and Helen are working side by side on the factory line.

1 SAM: I dunno where my I dunno where my knife went (4) disappeared
2 HEL: there it's there
3 SAM: oh shit see that's what happens when you're running around
4   like a blue arsed fly [laughs] . . . you forget where you put things

Example 6.21 above is a more obvious example of the sort of no-holds-barred contestive humour that is commonplace between members of this team. This kind of teasing, focusing on personal characteristics, was common currency among team members, and an obvious way in which they constructed and reinforced team solidarity. Ginette, the team manager participated fully, often deliberately initiating humorous escapades to counteract boredom and maintain morale amongst the team. A classic example occurred on April Fools' Day when she tricked several team members into ringing the zoo to ask for 'Mr Lion', much to the mirth of their colleagues.

Ginette's routine use of humour to emphasise team cohesion and solidarity has much in common with Leila's use of humour to release tension and emphasise collegiality at strategic points in the meeting outlined in Case Study 1. What is very different, however, is first the type and style of humour which characterises the interactions within each team. The office-based team's humour is typically anecdotal, gentle and unthreatening, and often attracts support from others who collaborate to develop and extend it. The factory team's humour is largely abusive, robust and contestive, with team members frequently vying competitively for the floor to top each other's humorous sallies. In both cases, however, the effect is to reduce power differences between team members and their managers, and to emphasise social connection ahead of individual status (cf Tannen 1990).

A second difference is the way the factory team leader uses humour in conveying her more explicit face attack acts. The white-collar manager, Leila, is rarely overtly critical, especially in large meetings, preferring indirect strategies for indicating areas for improvement. Ginette, by contrast, is frequently extremely direct and critical, using explicit imperatives, often reinforced by strong expletives when addressing the group as a whole (as illustrated in Chapter 3). However, she is also skilled in using humour to ensure the team pay attention to her message. In Example 3.6 (repeated in part here for convenience), she begins with a no punches pulled style, characterised by explicit directives, and appealing to individuals not to let the rest of the team down, but she ends with humorous bathos.

Example 6.22
Context: Regular 6am team briefing meeting. Ginette is telling the packers that there have been serious delays caused by their mistakes with documenting the packing codes.

1 GIN: check the case . . . make sure you check them properly
2   cos like I said it's just one person's stupid mistake
3   makes the whole lot of us look like eggs +++
4   check them properly . . .
5 GIN: please fill them out properly fuck youse
         [general laughter]

Ginette uses very direct forcefully expressed imperative forms (lines 1, 4), but she includes an amusing simile (lines 2–3), based perhaps on the idea of getting egg on one's face, and she ends her long harangue (the example is edited) with the bathetic *please fill them out properly fuck youse*. The comic mix of imperative form and forceful expletive, alongside the formally polite *please*, and the friendly colloquial pronoun *youse*, an in-group solidarity signal, elicits appreciative laughter from the team.

This mix of critical abuse and humour is what distinguishes Case Study 2 from Case Studies 1 and 3. It is a distinctive interactional style which depends on close and trusting relationships between all group members. Example 6.23 illustrates Ginette in her stride at 6am at a morning meeting where it is quite clear that everyone is not present.

Example 6.23
Context: Regular 6am briefing meeting of factory team.

1 GIN: good morning everybody it's just lovely to see you all this morning +
2   just can't imagine my life coming into work not seeing you every day +
3   nice to see you all well
       [general laughter and a range of indecipherable responses with tone of good-humoured riposte]
4 GIN: one one three +++ nice to see everybody's here on time +++

Sarcasm and jocular insult is thus the normal currency of this team's interaction and Ginette foots it with the best of them. As people gradually drift in, Ginette maintains her ironic tone to comment on their tardiness, as also illustrated in Example 6.11 above. She uses humour very effectively to maintain attention, creating a sparky, engaged interactive style, while simultaneously getting over her message that people are expected to arrive on time for morning meetings. She ends the meeting with a genuine but good-humoured challenge (Example 6.24).

Example 6.24
Context: Regular 6am briefing meeting of factory team.

1 GIN: if you don't finish it by six o clock you're staying here
2   until you do finish it ++ that a good deal
3 MAN: that's good news give me the bad news now . . .
4 LES: the bad news is that Russell is a liability for all of us
       [all laugh]

In terms of workplace culture, then, this community of practice can be described as a highly cohesive and solidarity oriented workplace, with team membership highly valued. Team members express their close relationships with a wide range of teasing, practical jokes and jocular abuse. By contrast to Case Study 1, decision making in this team is often unilateral and, in such cases, decisions are conveyed downwards clearly and explicitly. Directives and criticisms are commonplace. In this context, humour functions importantly to maintain good workplace relations. The team leader participates fully in the team horse-play, but she also uses humour as an attention-grabbing device and a means of rendering her most 'in your face' criticisms palatable.

Case Study 3

The third case study is another very different kind of work group. It involves a team of experts in a white-collar, information technology (IT) organisation, with a predominantly male workforce, brought together to work on a specific project with a fixed time span. The team members met weekly for ten weeks to work on the project. Using Wenger's three criterial features for a CofP (mutual engagement, joint enterprise and shared repertoire), this work group can be described as a rather loosely knit community of practice, with a relatively low involvement communication style. Although they were engaged in a joint enterprise or project and they 'talked the same language', namely IT jargon, members' commitment to each other was temporary and variable. They met only once a week for a couple of hours. This group resembles the kind of CofP described in Wenger's more recent work (Wenger and Snyder 2000), rather than the more traditional CofP illustrated by the previous two cases. They are a group of people 'bound together by shared expertise' (2000: 139). The length of the project defined the life span of this CofP and members' degree of commitment largely depended on the extent of their contracted contribution and their level of responsibility within the project, factors of which they were very aware.

Status in the organisational hierarchy and power, including expert power, were salient variables for the members of this group, as their discourse indicated in a variety of ways, including the type of humour which occurred. Unlike Case Study 1, where power differences were played down using the discourse of negotiation and consultation, in this group responsibilities were frequently made explicit and members were very clear about relative rights and obligations. Example 6.25 illustrates this nicely.[8]

Example 6.25
Context: Regular meeting of a project team in a commercial organisation discussing some new back-up software.

```
1 CAL:  what we'v- what we've actually decided to do is
2       er test it by asking by losing some data or pretending to lose some
3       something significant like everything that's in p v c s
4       like all our documents and all our code
5 BAR:  [laughs]
6 ERIC: yeah but d-
7 CAL:  and then asking them to restore it
8 ERIC: no don't do that
```

```
 9 CAL:   we won't really lose it
10 ERIC:  yeah right and what you're going to do is have a file that's three weeks
11        old overwritten over the top of all your um stuff that's um current
12 BAR:   mm
13 ERIC:  don't do that at all
14 CAL:   no we're going to protect some
15 ERIC:  [laughs]
16 JAC:   that we're not that we haven't updated
17 ERIC:  don't do it
18 JAC:   no?
19 ERIC:  no
20 JAKE:  you don't tr- /you you don't\ trust them
21 ERIC:  /please please put it\
22        please put it in the minutes that Eric does not think
23        this is [laughs] a good idea
          [general laughter]
```

Clearly this is a group of experts using their own linguistic repertoire (e.g. lines 1–4 in particular). However, on this specific issue Eric is the one with the relevant expertise and he makes it very clear (lines 6, 8, 10–11, 13, 17, 19) that he disagrees with what Callum is proposing (see Chapter 7 for more detailed discussion of Eric's discourse of disagreement). When it appears that, despite his explicit on-record disagreement, his advice will be ignored, Eric resorts to a formal request that his opposition be recorded in the minutes of the meeting (lines 21–23). The formality of Eric's request (emphasised by his reference to himself as *Eric* rather than as *I*) elicits laughter because it sounds incongruous in the context of the meeting, which is in most other respects relatively informal in style.

This example is a good representation of the kind of humour which characterises the interactions of this group. It arises very directly from the business at hand, it is concerned with issues of power and it takes the form of ironic overstatement. Eric uses humour to get his message across in an acceptable form, but the underlying message is deadly serious.

In keeping with their rather competitive attitudes and tendency to define and defend their own expert patches, the discourse style of this group is considerably less collaborative than the style of the other two work groups considered above. There are few instances of supportive, positively oriented, jointly constructed humorous exchanges (such as illustrated by Example 6.2 concerning the fantasy Ministry suit). Rather, this team specialises in sarcasm and their preferred style of delivery is a short, pithy one-liner to the jugular. Most of the instances in Example 6.13 were taken from meetings of this group. Examples 6.26 and 6.27 are in the same style – sarcastic one-liners. In Example 6.26, Eric comments on Callum's tendency to want things explicit, suggesting he is unnecessarily pedantic.

Example 6.26

Context: Regular meeting of project team in commercial organisation.

1 ERIC: [smiling voice] Callum has to ask

In Example 6.27, Callum is the instigator of the ironic humour. He is responding to criticism that he has left the wrong date on a memo.

Example 6.27

Context: Regular meeting of project team in commercial organisation.

1 CAL: I find it hard being perfect at everything
     [general laughter]

This sarcastic contestive style of humour is the most characteristic pattern throughout the meetings of this group. Sometimes, however, like the members of Case Study 2, this professional team join in jocularly abusing each other, as illustrated in Example 6.28.

Example 6.28

Context: Regular meeting of project team in commercial organisation discussing a long report.

1 DUD: have you read it?
2 BAR: I have
3 DUD: have you already?
4 BAR: [laughs]
5 JAC: and and Callum's read it already
6 BAR: [laughs]
7 DUD: you don't have enough work to do Barry
8 BAR: I read it I was up till about ( ) no /[laughs]\
9 JAC: /[laughs]\
10 ERIC: well I was up till about midnight last night too
11 CAL: surfing right?
12 ERIC: no
13 BAR: [laughs] surfing the net

The humour takes the form of challenges to professional expertise and competence, a recurring theme for this team. Dudley's jocular insult (line 7) is based on the assumption that a high workload is the norm for this group. Seriously boasting about how hard you work (lines 8, 10) is clearly acceptable and serious. In the same vein Callum challenges Eric's claim that he worked late with the accusation that he was *surfing right* (line 11), and Barry supports Callum *surfing the net* (line 13) when Eric denies the charge.

In another interesting example, the group collaborate more constructively to indicate to Jacob, an American expert who has been seconded to the organisation precisely for this project, that he does not in some senses fully 'belong' to the group.

Example 6.29

Context: Regular meeting of project team in commercial organisation. The team are discussing an 'outside' meeting they plan to attend.

1 JAC: do you want me to come as well?
2 CAL: um hmm /[laughs]\
3 DUD: /don't wear a\ don't wear a [company name] tie
4 BAR: [laughs] yeah you can go incognito
         [general laughter]
5 JAC: hide in the back row
         [general laughter]
6 BAR: just don't say anything . . .

Here the meeting participants make humorous suggestions about the conditions under which Jacob may accompany them to the function. In this jointly constructed humorous sequence, the participants are oriented to a common topic with a shared goal of mutual amusement. Each contribution expands and elaborates the underlying proposition 'you can come only if you don't identify with us', an insulting suggestion, and an example of jocular abuse which is the primary source of the humour. Each participant competes to outdo the previous speaker with a witty contribution (lines 3, 4, 5, 6). The basic message conveyed is that Jacob is an outgroup member. He belongs to an outside organisation and the team members here repudiate – in a jocular way – the validity of his membership of *their* team. Jacob, however, knows this group's membership criteria and he is able to join in the humorous sequence with his own contribution, using a similar grammatically minimal clause, *hide in the back row* (line 5). This is a rare example of the team working together to construct a humorous sequence. It illustrates that no group fits into a category perfectly; reality is always messy and analytically challenging.

In terms of workplace culture, then, this community of practice is relatively loosely knit. On the whole, membership of this particular team is not regarded as a primary commitment for team members. Power and status of various kinds (including expert status) are highly salient and a frequent focus of attention, including sarcastic and ironic attention. Decision making is thus an uneasy mix of authority based and consensual in style, which proves a constant source of contestation and challenge, often delivered in a superficially humorous tone to render it more palatable. While the group becomes gradually more integrated over the weeks of the project, the predominant discourse style, evident in their humour in particular, is a contestive, one-at-a-time (Coates 1997), non-collaborative, individual style, with contributions typically competing for the floor.[9]

Conclusion

Humour is a valuable resource in workplace interaction, a highly flexible discourse strategy which typically builds and maintains good relationships at work. Workmates use humour to amuse each other during work breaks, to release tension at strategic points in workplace interaction and to relieve boredom on the job. Humour also mitigates the impact of directives and criticisms and takes some of the sting out of insults. As a discourse strategy, then, humour is a useful means of constructing solidarity, paying attention to the addressee's face needs and 'doing power' in a socially acceptable way. Generally, the higher the threat to the addressee's face, the more likely the message will be presented in at least superficially humorous packaging.

Humour can also be considered a distinctive feature of workplace culture, with considerable variation in the amount and type of humour which characterises workplace interaction in different communities of practice. Looking more closely at the humour of three specific work teams revealed interesting differences in the detailed interactional practices of each team. In the team in Case Study 1, where power and status were downplayed and smoothly attained consensus was an important goal, humour was predominantly supportive and positive in pragmatic effect and typically collaborative in style; jointly developed, supportive humour sequences were common. The team manager used humour to facilitate progress in areas where difficulties were apparent, and subversive or contestive humour was relatively rare.

A much more robust style of humour characterised the interaction of the team which was the focus of Case Study 2. Jocular abuse was the common currency and team members, including the team leader, were adept at 'roasting' each other in a variety of ways, including practical jokes. While jointly constructed sequences occurred, they typically involved trading jocular abuse. Often the boundaries between power and solidarity were fluid and humour was an interesting indication of this, with all team members, including the team leader, considered fair game. However, when necessary the team leader asserted her authority, skilfully using humour to convey unvarnished criticism and directives in attention-grabbing and acceptable ways.

The team who constituted Case Study 3 paid much more explicit attention to status and power distinctions than the team which was the focus of Case Study 1, who downplayed them, or the team in Case Study 2, who accepted and took them for granted, i.e. power was not an issue. For the team in Case Study 3, power was a salient and contestable dimension and this was reflected in the way humour was used by group members. This group specialised in subversive, contestive humour, typically conveyed in pithy, sarcastic or ironic one-liners which often challenged the competence or expertise of other group members. When they collaborated to produce more extended sequences, these frequently functioned in similar ways, attacking other group members for real or concocted inadequacies.

The discussion in this chapter has illustrated the fact that humour is often used to reduce tension, to manage potential conflict and to contribute to the management of problematic situations. In the next chapter, we focus more specifically on problematic talk at work, including the kinds of problems that arise in workplace interaction when goals of the managers and the managed are not in perfect alignment.

Notes

1. Holmes (2000d) provides the following definition of humour, as well as a discussion of the literature in this area: 'Humorous utterances are those identified by the analyst, on the basis of paralinguistic, prosodic and discoursal clues, as intended by the speaker(s) to be amusing and perceived to be amusing by at least some participants.'

2. There is an extensive literature on the functions of humour: e.g. Martineau (1972); Ziv (1984); Ervin-Tripp and Lampert (1992); Graham, Papa and Brookes (1992). Hay (1995) provides an useful summary. For discussion of the tension release function of humour in the workplace, see, for example, Consalvo (1989); Hatch and Ehrlich (1993); Ädelsward and Öberg (1998).

3. By contrast in Hay's (1995) analysis of humour in friendship groups, the construction of solidarity or social cohesion was the overriding and ubiquitous function of humour.

4. Austin (1990) provides an interesting discussion of face attack acts. Kuiper (1991) illustrates jocular abuse in a rugby changing room and Holmes (2000d) provides further discussion of jocular abuse in workplace interaction.

5. It is interesting to note that jocular abuse was rare downwards from superior to subordinates, especially in white-collar workplaces. It is possible that insults, even if attenuated by humour, too obviously constitute abuses of power in the workplace, and that they are thus avoided due to legislative restraints. However, a parallel pattern was noted by Hay (1995) in her analysis of jocular abuse in friendship groups. Newer and less well-established group members received less abuse than longer standing and well-integrated members.

6. Quote from a managing director (Clouse and Spurgeon 1995: 3).

7. Although *bro* is an abbreviation of *brother*, and therefore more commonly used as a solidarity marker between males, it is nevertheless not unusual for it to be used in addressing women who are members of the in-group, particularly in Polynesian contexts.

8. Part of this rich example was used in Chapter 4 to illustrate the role of the expert in decision making. It is analysed from a different perspective in Chapter 7.

9. The contrasts in the discourse style and humour used in different meetings illustrate the relevance of gender as well as workplace culture, since the participants in Case Study 1 were all female, while those in Case Study 3 were all male. We mentioned in Chapter 4 that gender sometimes surfaces as a relevant social variable in workplace interaction and this is a case in point. It is not, however, an issue which we pursue in this book (see Holmes and Marra fc; Holmes, Marra and Burns 2001; Stubbe 1998b; Stubbe et al. 2000).

7

Miscommunication and Problematic Talk at Work

Example 7.1

Context: Jan, a branch manager, and Heke, a policy manager are engaged in a meeting in Heke's office in a government organisation.

```
 1 JAN:    what- what happened to Marama? + was-
 2         I presumed that Marama was going was that MY misunderstanding +
 3 HEKE:   [drawls] OH
 4 JAN:    to the + /[ministry]\
 5 HEKE:   /[ministry]\ + I presumed she was going as well (1.5)
 6         /okay [laughs] okay so she just didn't\ show at all
 7 JAN:    /[drawls] well [laughs] so\ no + and + well that's not like Marama
 8 HEKE:   no ++ no oh well ++ I have no idea
 9 JAN:    okay so can you /check\ that out? I've just got back unfortunately
10 HEKE:   /all right\
11 JAN:    because I WAS in a bit of a situa/tion where I don't know\the detail
12 HEKE:   /yes\
13 JAN:    of the research very well
14 HEKE:   no
15 JAN:    um so I couldn't go into much
16 HEKE:   [softly] for god's sake
17 JAN:    explanation ++ BUT we did get from them um
18         they've got no problem in developing the proto/col\?
19 HEKE:   /[tut]\ [high pitch] GOOD GOD okay all right sorry I'm just + a little
20         bit-
21 JAN:    so + can can someone get onto them and organise a meeting
22         immediately if not sooner +
23 HEKE:   okay (4)
```

Miscommunication and problematic talk could be described as occupational hazards of organisational life. Example 7.1 provides a typical illustration of the sorts of things that can go wrong and shows how, even in cases where a potential problem is avoided, or where a tricky discussion results in a constructive resolution to a particular issue, misunderstandings and differences of opinion inevitably take time, energy and relational skill to work through.

The actual misunderstanding Jan refers to in this example was in itself relatively minor. Marama had not turned up as expected to a meeting with another organisation and so Jan, the section manager, had been left to contribute to a discussion where she did not have all the information she needed. There are a number of possible explanations – Marama may not have received the information about the meeting, she may not have understood that she was required to attend, or she may simply have failed to ensure Jan was informed that she could not come. However, whatever the reason, Marama's non-appearance at an important meeting with an external stakeholder resulted in embarrassment for Jan, a senior manager, and had the potential to derail some sensitive negotiations. Although she gives Marama the benefit of the doubt, *was that MY misunderstanding* (line 2), Jan nevertheless feels obliged to follow the incident up with Marama's line manager, Heke, in part to prevent a recurrence, but also to get him to organise some 'damage control' in the form of another meeting. In doing so, she enters into problematic discourse of a different kind, a discourse where the interplay between the enactment of power and politeness is especially foregrounded, an area which is the explicit topic of later sections of this chapter.

However simple or complex the underlying cause, ineffective or problematic communication in a workplace can have highly visible and costly negative outcomes, both for the individuals concerned and for the organisation as a whole. The potential consequences range from relatively minor and easily repairable interruptions to the smooth flow of work or communication between colleagues, as in Example 7.1, through to more serious disruptions to productivity or workplace relations. In one workplace we studied, for example, a simple failure to clarify a message led to a costly production line outage when a new product was pumped through a hopper before it had been cleaned after the previous production run. Many employment tribunal cases on public record in New Zealand identify interpersonal miscommunication as a key contributing factor in the escalation of workplace disputes.[1] Published communication, management and legal case studies also frequently report on and analyse problematic dealings with 'difficult' colleagues or clients, as well as structural problems relating to organisational communication processes.[2]

Workers clearly put a good deal of effort into communication at work and into the construction of workplace relationships through talk. When things go wrong the practical consequences are often very visible. Participants in our project reported that communication problems of various kinds were of ongoing concern, affecting relations between colleagues in the same teams, in different sections of an organisation, or between management and staff. The notion that we can and should become 'better' communicators also has wide currency (cf Cameron 2000). However, our analyses, supported by informants' self-assessments of individual interactions, indicate that on the whole, people did a remarkably good job of communicating effectively with their colleagues on a day-to-day basis, as measured by the achievement of their stated and implicit transactional goals and the (apparent) maintenance of smooth working relationships during particular interactions. (See Example 7.10 below for an illustration of how appearances can be misleading.) Obvious instances of miscommunication, such as the one referred to in Example 7.1, are far less common in our data than our informants' reported perceptions might lead us to expect.

Throughout the preceding chapters, we have explored the complex ways in which power and politeness are played out in everyday workplace interactions, in contexts where the explicit focus is (or is expected to be) on the task at hand. We have looked at how people use a range of direct and indirect strategies to balance their relational identities and instrumental goals in particular contexts such as meetings, or when trying to get others to do things, and how they make strategic use of 'off-task' talk such as humour and small talk to achieve both instrumental and interpersonal goals. We have seen how interactants constantly perform a delicate discursive balancing act in their attempts to get tasks done, while at the same time managing their relationships with their coworkers. This interplay between the imperatives of power and politeness is especially foregrounded in cases of miscommunication and problematic discourse – indeed it is the tension between sometimes conflicting relational goals and the imperatives of the task at hand which often renders such talk particularly problematic in the first place. In this chapter, we turn the spotlight on the glitches, the hitches and the hiccups of workplace interaction, and we focus quite explicitly on the management of problematic talk at work. We first discuss examples where the referential or information content of the message is the source of the problem, and we then turn to examples of a much more frequent type of problematic talk, where power and politeness are the fundamental issues.

Miscommunication

Example 7.1 provided an instance where a manager was left in an embarrassing situation as a result of what she, diplomatically perhaps, interpreted as a genuine misunderstanding. In interpreting what had happened, Jan inferred that crucial information had not been transmitted from one person to another.

This interaction occurred in a white-collar professional environment and the consequences involved inadequate communication between organisations. In small businesses and factories, by contrast, misunderstandings may result in more concrete evidence of failure to meet workplace objectives, in the form of a drop in the level of material outputs, as in the case of the unclean hopper mentioned above. Example 7.2 provides a more extended analysis of a similar misunderstanding which developed on the factory floor, a misunderstanding which has been referred to in earlier chapters and one which, like the uncleaned hopper, entailed potential economic consequences for the organisation, as well as loss of face for the team responsible for the errors. In Example 7.2, the team manager is outlining the problem and identifying its basis.

Example 7.2
Context: Regular early morning briefing meeting. Ginette is telling the packers that there have been serious delays caused by mistakes with documenting packing codes.

```
 1  GIN:  the um the [product] that was packed on the other two shifts
 2        line two was put on hold because the pack code was wrong
 3        and that should have been picked up a lot earlier on the packing line
 4        but it wasn't
 5        and that's because the checks aren't done properly
 6        they're done like this bullshit it's not checked properly
 7        now the day before yesterday was it the day before yesterday Lesia
 8        we did the same thing we did exactly the same as the other two shifts
 9        did not checking what we're packing people just take it for granted
10        what's on the outside on of those cases and packets are right
11        when I went over to check the line three check list
12        it didn't have the pack code right . . .
13        when you do the checks check the case off the lay card
14        if they don't match there's something wrong stop the line
15        if the lay card says you've got five numbers on
16        you should have five numbers on the pack code
17        that's what you put in there not four
18        just cos it's got a zero on there doesn't mean it doesn't count
19        it does count so make sure you check them properly . . .
20        cos like I said it's just one person's stupid mistake
21        makes the whole lot of us look like eggs (5)
22        check them properly [laughs]
23        we shouldn't blame Lesia cos he's got a good memory . . .
24        please fill them out properly fuck youse
```

As illustrated in earlier chapters, the patterns of power and politeness on the factory floor are very different from those of the white-collar office context. Ginette pulls no punches in communicating her message here; she is both direct and directive. In terms of directness, she identifies the problem very explicitly: i.e. there is a recurrent issue with the packing codes in that *the checks aren't done properly* (line 5), behaviour which causes production delays: *line two was put on hold because the pack code was wrong* (line 2). Next she gives very clear and detailed instructions about what ought to take place (lines 13–16). Then she analyses the problem further and identifies what she surmises is the source of the problem – a misunderstanding of the significance of a zero in the packing code *just cos it's got a zero on there doesn't mean it doesn't count* (line 18). Ginette here moves from an unforgiving analysis of the team's past errors to a very clear and explicit account of what needs to be done to rectify them, and why. Unlike Jan in Example 7.1, in identifying the problem, Ginette is not primarily concerned with face saving, although by laying the blame squarely at the door of her team and insisting that they accept collective responsibility for the mistake, she avoids embarrassing the individuals who were actually at fault.

Finally, however, she shifts to a different and more affective level of communication, in her appeal for an improvement in future behaviour (lines 19–24). While she uses the inclusive *we* in her earlier analysis (lines 8, 9), she also clearly indicates her supervisory role and responsibilities with the use of *I* (line 11). In the final section, she has recourse to consistent solidarity-oriented techniques, pointing out that one person's error *makes the whole lot of us look like eggs* (line 21). Again she identifies as a team member (she uses *us* not *you*). Just as she has avoided in the earlier section pointing the finger at any individual, here she quite specifically, though jokingly, lets her second in command off the hook, *we shouldn't blame Lesia cos he's got a good memory* (line 23). She concludes with the kind of team-building jocular abuse (line 24) which, as illustrated in Chapter 6, forms the basic currency of positive politeness in the interactions of this team.

This example illustrates how the dimensions of power and politeness are interwoven in Ginette's handling of a serious misunderstanding in the factory. Here she plays the tough boss, adopting direct and explicit strategies which communicate the problem clearly, and which also instantiate her authority as team leader. At the same time, however, she pays attention to the face needs of team members by avoiding laying blame on any individual, appealing rather to their team loyalty and solidarity. She also indicates that she is a boss who can have a laugh with her team by engaging in the kind of swearing and abuse which is the team's common currency. These are all strategies which reflect her strong orientation to maintaining team morale, and her ability to balance her management responsibilities with her continued acceptance as one of the team.

Two further examples from the factory data, also based around this specific problem, provide further illumination of the way workplace miscommunication may be handled, and the importance of power and politeness in analysing what is going on.

Example 7.3
Context: Lesia and Sam are on the packing line discussing how to follow Ginette's instructions regarding the packing codes.

1 LES: but now they try to take out the zero no more zeros
2 SAM: no cos the zero doesn't mean anything the zero is a nothing
3   that there is the main one four five six seven
4   but the zero zero is only just something in front of it . . .
5 LES: but why do you think you would say that
6   when Ginette was explaining that this morning
7 SAM: oh I wasn't over here
8   I only just just realised this morning when you come over you see . . .

Lesia begins by identifying the problem as Ginette has outlined it, namely, people have mistakenly been deleting the zeros in the packing codes (line 1). Sam challenges this and provides an explicit example of the error that Ginette has earlier identified, by arguing that the zeros have no meaning (lines 2–4). At this point Lesia appeals to Ginette's authority and cites her early morning lecture on the topic, at which point Sam admits not paying attention during the meeting, and backs down (lines 6–7).

This is an interesting example, suggesting how easily miscommunication can be compounded if a single person did not hear the explanation. If Sam had been more pig-headed or assertive, or if he had been in a position of greater power than Lesia, it is possible that his mistaken version would have won the day. The excerpt illustrates, in fact, how a misunderstanding can be rectified, but it takes more than a simple assertion to convince Sam. An appeal to authority is what finally convinces him. In another interaction involving Sam and a different team member on the packing line, the same effect is achieved by an appeal to the team ethic, and especially the notion introduced at the end of Ginette's briefing, that if individuals do not make an effort to sort this problem out, then not only will they lose face themselves, but they are letting the whole team down.

In Example 7.4, used to illustrate mitigated directives in Chapter 3, we see Ginette in action again, this time talking one to one with Sam, who is very obviously still a little confused. Again, what is noteworthy is Ginette's skill in combining clarity of explanation with attention to the affective dimensions of the interaction.

Example 7.4

Context: Ginette, the team manager, is talking to team member Sam on the packing line about the packing codes.

```
 1  GIN:  what do we have on here
 2  SAM:  four five six seven
 3  GIN:  why have you put four five six seven
 4  SAM:  cos I was taking it off that one but gonna take it off that one
 5  GIN:  you don't take it off that one
 6  SAM:  no er well yeah I did I know I was my- that was my mistake
 7  GIN:  yeah
 8  SAM:  yeah
 9  GIN:  no the way you did it this morning is good that's what we're supposed
10        to do (9) see how important important the checks a- are you know
11        if you do them properly
12  SAM:  well I yeah I'm usually pretty good on on that sort of thing now so-
13  GIN:  yeah
14  SAM:  if you go by the book you can't go wrong
15  GIN:  that's right . . . just remember that when you're doing the check list
16        you put down what YOU find not what it should be
17        so you're checking against what it should be
18        if it don't match then there's something wrong
```

In this one-to-one interaction Ginette uses quite different strategies to those she used when talking to the whole team. She adopts a range of facilitative, coaching strategies to help Sam see for himself what he has been doing wrong (line 6) and what is right, and she gets him to the point where he acknowledges how important it is to pay attention to detail and do the checks (line 14). She asks questions (lines 1, 3), provides supportive feedback (lines 9, 13, 15), expands on Sam's contributions, and finally sums up what they have agreed (lines 13–18). It has taken all morning, but at least for this worker the misunderstanding has finally been resolved.

We were very fortunate to be able to track in some detail the progress of Ginette's attempts to rectify a misunderstanding on the factory floor. Few misunderstandings are so clearly identified and explicated, and the chances of recording not only the original statement of the problem, but also a range of follow-up interactions, are vanishingly small. Our data allowed us to trace the negotiation of the problem through a series of interactions on the factory floor between different team members throughout the day following the morning briefing session. As a result we were able to see the many and varied strategies that participants used to resolve the problem, ranging from very explicit and direct denunciations of incorrect behaviour, to appeals to authority and team solidarity to ensure the problem did not recur. It is also worth noting that the final resolution of the misunderstanding was not achieved in a single interaction. It took a series of related interactions in different settings with different interlocutors, using a range of direct and indirect strategies, and invoking affective as well as referential meaning, for the message to finally 'get across', as Ginette put it. Throughout these various interactions, appeals to authority or power as well as to mateship or positive politeness emerged as important dimensions in the analysis.

In what follows, we turn to the consideration of somewhat different and typically more common kinds of problematic talk, drawing out and analysing in more depth some of the underlying tensions and conflicts which have been referred to in earlier chapters. Problematic talk frequently revolves around issues of power and there are many ways of managing the tensions that such issues generate in the workplace. In what follows we focus in particular on strategies associated with politeness and authority in managing problematic talk: for example, the use of linguistic politeness strategies, and especially attenuating devices, the use of directness and indirectness, and appeals to institutional power and authority of varying degrees of explicitness. To illustrate the complex ways in which these strategies are invoked in workplace interaction, we focus on a number of problematic interactions in which a power differential of some kind is involved.

Negotiating with the boss

In earlier chapters we have discussed a number of situations where an individual was faced with a communicative challenge which involved negotiating with a superior. In Chapters 1 and 3, for instance, we provided excerpts from an interview in which Kerry sought permission from her acting manager, Ruth, to take leave to attend a conference. The analysis of the negotiation identified a range of vague language, hedging and information avoidance strategies used by Kerry to obfuscate the nub of the issue, namely that she was seeking leave with full pay, despite the fact that she intended shortly to leave the organisation. Chapter 3 also illustrated the indirect strategies people use to get those who are not subordinates to assist them. Example 3.21, for instance, showed Paula and Fay negotiating over who was going to take the minutes of a meeting. And in a problematic encounter, in a different organisation, Claire used the strategy of ostensibly seeking advice from her manager, Tom, in order to indirectly register a complaint about being passed over for the job of acting manager (we examine Tom's contribution to this interaction from a CDA perspective below). All these encounters illustrated the discursive skills involved in handling a problematic workplace issue.

Example 7.5, an encounter between two individuals at different levels in a government department, provides some interesting similarities and contrasts in terms of how a problematic issue is managed by the less senior participant. Kelly is a policy analyst and Katie a senior policy analyst. Kelly is seeking Katie's advice about possible titles for a publication. She begins by reporting her own negative opinion of the title that has been proposed at a meeting which she missed. The problem Kelly faces is that she does not know Katie's views of the proposed title and she must therefore tread warily in disclosing her own views. Although they are on good collegial terms, Katie and Kelly are not especially close friends; hence this is a tricky encounter for Kelly. She negotiates her way through the problem by adopting linguistic strategies which present her views very tentatively, while attempting to establish Katie's views as she proceeds. To highlight her strategies we have put the hedging devices Kelly uses in bold.

Example 7.5
Context: Two policy analysts at different levels in the hierarchy of a government department discuss the proposed title of a department publication.

```
 1 KEL:  okay it's about the title for the [name] publication
 2 KAT:  oh yeah
 3 KEL:  and there was a meeting to discuss the titles when I was away
 4 KAT:  yeah
 5 KEL:  I mean you know I was supposed to be there but it's just that I've
 6        got a little bit of a concern about this is the sort of thing that um
 7        [tut] is being opted for like the [title] but I sort of think that um
 8 KAT:  that's been used
 9 KEL:  well also you see I suppose my concept of what we want to convey
10        is not something that sound we- we sort of don't want to sound like
11        it's an agenda we're trying to push because we're political
12        right I think what we what it needs to convey is um
13        something that's more about um how you how +
14        you actually build in the differences be- you know that work
15        bring about to get good quality advice
16        do- do you sort of know what I mean
17        like it's cos o- I'm trying to think who we're targeting
18        I just think that word goes- puts them right off
19 KAT:  yeah
20 KEL:  and I was trying to think of a
21 KAT:  it's a very political word
22 KEL:  well that's right I mean and it I just wonder if if our market
23 KAT:  yeah
```

24 KEL: is **actually** policy managers and policy analysts
25   we should **actually** go for something different
26   do you think is that your sort of gut feeling about that
27 KAT: yes I do actually I think these are all awful
28 KEL: yeah [whispers] so do I
29   so I'm **just** trying to think of some alternatives
30   **I don't just say look I think these are awful** but th- that's your
31   **is that your sort of feeling about it too**
32 KAT: yes I do I think none of them are usable at all I think
33 KEL: oh good okay no **I don't think** they are either
34 KAT: they're either wimpy or silly or politically misdirected
35 KEL: yeah

Kelly's propositions are heavily hedged and attenuated. They leave her room to escape if she finds that Katie does not agree. In other words, her strategies for handling this problematic situation superficially resemble those used by Kerry in Example 1.4, in seeking permission to obtain conference leave with pay. Though their motivations are very different, their discursive strategies have much in common, since in both cases their aim is to avoid placing the full facts on record too explicitly. In addition to attenuation devices, however, Kerry uses vagueness, introducing a good deal of apparently minimally relevant additional information which served to obfuscate the central issue. By contrast, Kelly is always on topic, but because they are heavily hedged, her central propositions are not always easy to identify. Her strategy is to play for time so that Katie can indicate where she stands on the relevant issue.

In stark contrast to Kelly's discourse, Katie's statements are expressed very succinctly and directly, and they are largely unattenuated: *that's been used* (line 8), *it's a very political word* (line 21), *actually I think these are all awful* (line 27), *none of them are usable at all* (line 32), *they are either wimpy or silly or politically misdirected* (line 34). These direct statements are reminiscent of Ruth's challenges in her encounter with the evasive Kerry in Chapter 1, though Katie's intent (as we know from our ethnographic interviews) is very different from Ruth's, as is the effect her utterances have on her addressee. As the interaction develops, it becomes clear that they are functioning as explicitly supportive feedback, intended to reassure Kelly that Katie shared her reservations about the proposed title.

These examples suggest that the linguistic politeness devices of hedging and attenuation are important resources in managing problematic talk, and that is undoubtedly true. But another important resource for participants in handling confrontational interactions which threaten their face needs, is to emphasise their own status and competence. In the encounter between Tom and Claire, for instance, which we analyse further below, it is noteworthy that Claire attends not only to Tom's face needs but also to her own. As illustrated in Chapter 3, she assiduously avoids any kind of direct confrontation, but rather uses indirect strategies and generously hedged propositions which allow Tom a range of avenues with which to defend his position. At the same time, however, she asserts her own strengths, and extracts agreement about them from Tom, as illustrated in the excerpt in Example 7.6.

Example 7.6

Context: Claire has sought a meeting with Tom, the overall manager of the area in which Claire's section is located in a government organisation.

```
 1 CLA:   well I did when I was in + the old [section]
 2        I used to pick up work oh for Peter all the time . . .
 3 CLA:   I've been here for two and a half years now
 4 TOM:   mm mm
 5 CLA:   so I'm fully au fait with the internal workings of [name of organisation]
 6 TOM:   mm
 7 CLA:   which I think policy management's largely about um is is knowing that
 8        and who to go to when to go to how to go about it . . .
 9 TOM:   I would've had no difficulties in in um er acting you into the position
10 CLA:   mm . . .
11 TOM:   you know um had I + probably thought about it
12        or or um had this conversation you with you bef-
13        I would've been quite happy /um\
14 CLA:   [tut] right well /( ) let you know [laughs] yeah\
```

In these snippets from the interview we see how Claire draws explicit attention to the fact that she has been at the organisation for a considerable time (line 3), that she knows how it works (line 5), that she has had experience of replacing those senior to her (line 2), and that she knows what policy management involves (lines 7–8). She is direct and clear in these assertions: there are no hedges, no modal verbs, and no attenuating devices. The pragmatic particle *I think* (line 7) is used in a 'deliberative' sense (Holmes 1990b), to add weight to the proposition and suggest that she has relevant and thought through views about the job. These strategies are clearly effective since Tom's response concedes that perhaps he had not given these points sufficient thought (lines 11–12).

With considerable skill, then, Claire manages to elicit an acknowledgement from Tom that she has the necessary abilities to perform the role of acting manager, and a commitment that next time the opportunity arises she will be seriously considered for the position. Clearly, managing problematic talk 'upwards' involves a range of discursive skills, including the sophistic-ated use of a range of linguistic politeness strategies. But how do those who are managers handle the communicative challenges presented by those who work under their direction? How does problematic talk look from the perspective of the boss?

Negotiating 'downwards'

As we have illustrated throughout this book, there are many ways in which individuals can present their supervisors and managers with communicative challenges, and these often require considerable relational skill to negotiate. In Chapter 1, for instance, Ruth, the manager, effectively challenged Kerry's attempt to obfuscate the issue of leave with pay by adopting a very direct approach, and by appealing to the department's established institutional procedures. These two basic strategies frequently recur as means of man-aging problematic talk, i.e. the use of discursive directness and strategic indirectness on the one hand, and the invoking of institutional authority on the other.

Consider, for instance, the interaction between Tom and Claire, men-tioned above, which was analysed from Claire's perspective in Chapter 3. Claire presented Tom with a number of difficult issues in an interview ostensibly sought to seek his advice. In the course of the interview Claire indicated that she was dissatisfied with the way that she had been treated and implied that she felt discriminated against. This was undoubtedly problem-atic talk from the perspective of Tom, her section manager. He was faced with a situation where he was being subtly accused of passing over someone capable of being appointed to a position, for a range of reasons which, though never explicitly specified, inevitably reflect badly on his managerial integrity.[3] Tom's main strategy for managing this problematic situation involved adopting a conservative line, one which subtly underlined his authority and his right to make decisions. As illustrated in Example 7.7a, Tom appeals to the institutional status quo, the taken for granted assumptions about the way things operate in the organisation: things have to get done, managers have to make the best decision in the light of their assessment of the situation – that's the way things work here, he suggests.

Example 7.7a
Context: Claire has sought a meeting with Tom, the overall manager of the area in which Claire's section is located in a government organisation.

1 TOM: yeah I don't think it's a it's a question of er favourability
2   I mean it was a question more practicalities more than anything else

3   um I was in urgent need of someone to fill in
4   and Jared had done that in the past already

Tom pursues this line of argument further by stating that appointing Jared as acting manager provided the simplest, safest and most efficient solution, and one which followed precedent. Example 7.7b illustrates Tom's repetition of this assertion at several points throughout the interview.

Example 7.7b
(Tom's name in the margin indicates sequential points in the interview.)

1 TOM: er so from my point of view it was simply logistics
2   and what was practically easy that would create the least amount of
3   hassles at that point in time . . .
4 TOM: and it was as simple as that
5   so it wasn't a judgement call on were you better or he w- he better
6   i- it was simply I saw precedents
7   [drawls] and that was the safest course of action in the short time I
8   had . . .
9 TOM: it was simply going on what was the safest ground
10   in respect of what the m- policy manager had done in the past . . .
11 TOM: in lieu of a decision I'll take probably the last decision that was made . . .
12 TOM: I'm more prone to take the least path of resistance
13   or the path that's more known to me
14   which which which really was Joseph had set a precedent before . . .
15   well as I say I didn't er qualify my decision
16   other than look at the precedent

Tom appeals to logistics (line 1), to what *would create the least amount of hassles* (line 2) and repeatedly to precedent, either explicitly (lines 6, 13, 15), or implicitly *what the m- policy manager had done in the past* (line 10) and *the last decision that was made* (line 11). Appealing to precedent to justify his decision is a very conservative response to Claire's concerns, one that assumes and emphasises the inherent 'rightness' of the status quo. As the argument is elaborated by Tom, the word *precedent*, and its derivatives and synonyms, are often closely collocated with the words *safe* and *safest* (e.g. lines 7, 9). In other words, Tom's strategy for managing the problematic talk is to retreat to the safety of institutionalised processes and established procedures which embody taken for granted assumptions about the way things should be done. His appeal to the *safest* procedures, the simplest, most sensible, tried and true methods of dealing with a situation, namely to *precedent*, is a paradigmatic example of the way power relationships are performed and repeatedly reconstructed in interaction.

Similarly, in providing advice to Claire about how she should strengthen her case for future promotion, Tom quite explicitly asserts the importance of her using the 'proper' channels to make her request for consideration for preferment (Example 7.7c).

Example 7.7c

1 TOM: the issue . . . is [drawls] probably one that um +
2   you could address directly with Joseph . . .
3 TOM: you might like to raise that as a development issue with Joseph . . .
4 TOM: because he's your immediate controlling officer . . .

By explicitly referring to Joseph's status as her *controlling officer* (line 4), Tom emphasises his point that Claire should follow established procedures. Indeed, at several points during the discussion, Tom refers to the way he himself follows proper procedures in dealing with those of different status in the organisation, as illustrated in Example 7.7d.

Example 7.7d

1 TOM: there would be very little chance of me crossing paths
2   with the p m the policy manager . . .
3 TOM: um but I'll never override my policy manager
4   unless I thought it absolutely necessary to do that

Here we see Tom consistently asserting the importance of using the correct channels, namely those which the organisation provides to deal with the situation under discussion. His arguments presume the legitimacy of the existing hierarchical relationships and take for granted that Claire should act in an appropriately deferential manner in her dealings with her superiors; a nice example from a CDA perspective of how 'discourse reproduces inequality' (van Dijk 1999: 460).

Overall then, Tom deals with the threat Claire poses by adopting a stance of reassurance that all is well. Skilfully responding to Claire's framing of the interview as 'seeking advice' rather than 'making a complaint', Tom constructs his role as experienced adviser to an acolyte and conducts the discussion in a way that is convenient and unthreatening to the institutional status quo and which minimises the threat to his own managerial face. He negotiates his way through this problematic encounter by using the basic strategies of appealing to institutional authority, to the status quo and to established processes, drawing on the taken for granted assumptions about the rightness of these. This method of dealing with such problems was very common in our data. It was used in the encounter between Ruth and Kerry referred to above, for instance, though it was rarely made quite so explicit as by Tom in Example 7.7.

Interestingly, in the sections where Tom is asserting his right to make the decision he did (7.7b, 7.7d), he uses predominantly direct and clear statements, with relatively few mitigating or attenuating devices. Rather, the qualifiers are typically strengtheners and boosters, e.g. *it was as simple as that* (7.7b, line 4) *simply* (7.7b, lines 1, 6, 9) *absolutely* (7.7d, line 4), This contrasts with sections where he is more oriented to addressing Claire's concerns (7.7a, 7.7c) when he provides excuses (7.7a), and uses indirect directives in the form of suggestions (7.7c), attenuated with hedges and mitigating pragmatic particles such as *I don't think* (7.7a, line 1), *I mean* (7.7a, line 2), *probably* (7.7c, line 1), *could* (7.7c, line 2), *might* (7.7c, line 3).

In this interaction, then, an interaction in which Claire could be regarded as indirectly questioning his integrity and his managerial competence, Tom has recourse to a range of strategies to manage the problematic talk. The means he adopts include strategies which index his authority by referring to established institutionalised procedures, on the one hand, alongside the strategic use of direct statements and pragmatic strengtheners (which under-line his authority), and indirect directives attenuated with pragmatic hedges (which mitigate the threat to his face).

Throughout our data, as mentioned above, it is common to find manag-ers appealing to institutional processes for dealing with problems, or to standard accepted practices and 'the way we do things around here'.[4] In Leila's team, for instance, as illustrated in Chapter 4, the way things are done, and particularly the preferred way for problems to be resolved, is to talk them through until consensus is reached. In the interaction between Jan and Heke referred to in Chapter 3, Jan first suggests indirectly that Heke needs to crack the whip a little with staff who have been underper-forming. When he responds by suggesting they may need to work evenings and weekends, Jan suggests that he should not go overboard and refers to the fact that they belong to an officially 'family friendly workplace' to support her point (Example 3.14). Appeals to institutional norms and standard workplace practices are thus one component in the armoury of discursive resources which managers draw on in negotiating through prob-lematic talk.

Example 7.8 provides an interesting and somewhat more subtle illustra-tion of the ways in which managers may negotiate their way through a potential problem. The problem in this case is that Hera does not want Tracey to proceed with work on a particular project, which Tracey has assumed is part of her area of responsibility.

Example 7.8

Context: Manager to policy analyst in a government department.

```
 1 TRA:   I got thinking after that and I thought + [exhales] I- +
 2        you could kill two birds with one stone
 3        because those projects really hinge on this
 4        having a framework of like /Maori women eh\
 5 HERA:   /well actually\ I've listed that as a /separate\ project
 6 TRA:    /yeah\ yeah
 7 HERA:   that is a project that I've already listed /it's a\ fact it's in fact some-
 8        thing=
 9 TRA:    /so have I\
10 HERA:   =that we're w- again that we are to do according to our outputs
11        but + looking at the current workloads of everyone
12        that's what I've got more or less reserved
13 TRA:    yeah
14 HERA:   for that for that for the new bodies that are coming in (yeah)
15        I mean we got two more new people coming in let's hope
           [knocking sound]
16        cross fingers + and I'm looking for somebody for for the sen-
17        a senior person who's going to be able to manage that as a project
18 TRA:    oh I see . . .
19 HERA:   and you're right in that the work to do with the Maori women's claim
20        and to some extent the um Maori women in decision making
21 TRA:    /yeah\
22 HERA:   /and\ maybe even some of the other little projects to some extent +
23        the issue of the framework is quite a critical one
24 TRA:    okay fine
```

In lines 1–4 Tracey suggests that she should take over a project which is closely related to one she is already working on. Hera lays the groundwork for what will basically constitute an argument against Tracey's suggestion, with two standard signals of a dispreferred response, namely the hedges *well* and *actually* (line 5). She then proceeds to address the issue using a very sophisticated combination of directness and indirectness. On the one hand Hera asserts her authority as the person who has the right to decide how things will be managed in the section. This is most apparent linguistically in the consistent use of 'I- statements': *I've listed that as a separate project* (line 5), *that is a project that I've already listed* (line 7), *that's what I've got more or less reserved for that for that for the new bodies* (lines 12, 13), *I'm looking for somebody for for the sen- a senior person* (lines 16, 17). There is no doubt who is in charge and who makes the decisions here. This explicit assertion of Hera's power is discursively emphasised through the use of repetition (lines 5, 7, 12), and interruption (line 5).

On the other hand, Hera never explicitly says to Tracey 'no you can't take over this project'. Rather she conveys this message implicitly by referring to *the current workloads of everyone* (line 11), and the responsibilities of the two *new bodies that are coming in* (line 14). In other words, she uses this means to tell Tracey that she intends to allocate this work to the new people. When she says she is looking for *a senior person who's going to be able to manage that as a project* (line 17), it is clearly implied that this person is not Tracey but rather will be one of the new staff members. So, while she does not explicitly disagree with Tracey, by sketching out her plans for the project, which do not involve Tracey, Hera skilfully conveys the message that she does not concur with Tracey's suggestion that this is an area she should absorb into her workload.

Hera ends her outline of what is to happen by paying explicit attention to Tracey's face needs. She has implicitly suggested concern for Tracey's workload in line 10, but in concluding her response, she quite explicitly confirms Tracey's analysis of the situation as accurate *and you're right ... the issue of the framework is quite a critical one* (lines 19–23). Tracey's acceptance of the scenario that Hera outlines (line 24) suggests that Hera's attention to the politeness dimension, her concern for the affective aspects of the interaction, makes an important contribution to the satisfactory and smooth resolution of this potentially problematic issue.

Though they concern very different kinds of problems, and occur in very different kinds of workplace contexts, there are obvious similarities between Hera's strategies for addressing the problem raised by Tracey's offer to take responsibility for an additional project and Ginette's managerial strategy for dealing with her team's mistake on the factory line (Example 7.2): i.e. first focus on sorting out the problem, while taking care to avoid undue upset; then pay explicit attention to face needs and affective aspects of the interaction. It is a pattern which we observed repeatedly throughout our data, though of course the transactional and affective components, the dimensions of power and politeness, are not always so clearly distinguishable.

In this section, as in the previous one, we have seen how people draw on a variety of discourse strategies to manage problematic workplace encounters. Those in positions of authority often use direct and succinct statements, sometimes to ensure there is no misunderstanding, sometimes to challenge another's definition of the situation or to identify a point of disagreement. Superiors frequently appeal, either directly or indirectly, to institutionally ratified procedures, to the authority conferred by their position in the organisational hierarchy, to 'proper' processes and the assumed correct ways of doing things. It is also clear, however, that considerations of politeness and attention to people's face needs form an intrinsic component in the negotiations that participants engage in to manage problematic talk.

Problems, power and partnership

In this final section, we focus on two contrasting encounters between people in apparently equal relationships in their organisations in order to illustrate two very different strategies for managing problematic talk, and in particular the issue of disagreement. The first entails very direct and unmitigated disagreement in a relatively formal meeting context. The second involves a much less explicit disagreement avoidance strategy which would have almost certainly gone undetected if we had not had available the information collected in a follow-up interview with one of the participants. The second example, which is longer and analysed in more detail, broadens the considerations of institutional power raised in earlier sections of this chapter, where the focus was on intra-organisational institutional power, to the issue of societal institutional power – the intrinsic and unquestioned institutional power of the dominant group in a society. In particular, this example raises for consideration some of the complex reasons why minority group members might opt for avoidance as a strategy for managing problematic talk.

On-record disagreement as a pragmatic strategy

The first example we address in this section involves a problematic issue which arose within a team of experts in an information technology organisation. The relevant excerpt was mentioned in Chapter 4 as an example of expert power, and discussed briefly in Chapter 6 as an illustration of the ways in which humour can be used to mitigate confrontational talk. We repeat the example here for convenience. Eric is a member of a special project team discussing the trialling of some new computer software. The team brings together experts from several different sections in the company to work on one specific project; hence relations of relative power and authority are much more fluid and dynamic than in an established team. In Example 7.9, Eric makes explicit the fact that he disagrees with what the rest of the team is proposing.

Example 7.9
Context: Regular meeting of project team in commercial organisation discussing some new back-up software.

```
1 CAL:  what we'v- what we've actually decided to do is
2       er test it by asking by losing some data or pretending to lose some
3       something significant like everything that's in p v c s
4       like all our documents and all our code
5 BAR:  [laughs]
6 ERIC: yeah but d-
```

```
 7 CAL:   and then asking them to restore it
 8 ERIC:  no don't do that
 9 CAL:   we won't really lose it
10 ERIC:  yeah right and what you're going to do is have a file that's three weeks
11        old overwritten over the top of all your um stuff that's um current
12 BAR:   mm
13 ERIC:  don't do that at all
14 CAL:   no we're going to protect some
15 ERIC:  [laughs]
16 JAC:   that we're not that we haven't updated
17 ERIC:  don't do it
18 JAC:   no?
19 ERIC:  no
20 JAC:   you don't tr- /you you don't\ trust them
21 ERIC:  /please please put it\
22        please put it in the minutes that Eric does not think
23        this is [laughs] a good idea
          [general laughter]
```

Most of the members of this team could be considered as equals in the organisational hierarchy, yet each brings their own particular area of expertise to the discussion. Eric is the expert on the issue under discussion and he faces the problem that he disagrees with the procedure proposed by Callum (lines 1–4). He first indicates his disagreement with a polite *yeah but* (line 6). He is interrupted at this point, but he goes on to assert his opposition quite explicitly: *no don't do that* (line 8), followed by an explanation, indicating that he believes his colleagues do not understand the consequences of the procedures they are proposing (lines 10–11). He ends with a reinforced repetition of his opposition *don't do that at all* (line 13). At this point it is apparent that his very overt and explicit opposition is beginning to cause discomfort and his colleagues begin to attempt to address his concerns (lines 14, 16). In response to these attempts to provide evidence that they do understand the consequences of what they are proposing, Eric laughs cynically (line 15) and reiterates his opposition for the third time *don't do it* (line 17). Finally, when it appears that despite his repeated on-record disagreement, his advice will be ignored, he resorts to an explicit and formal request that his opposition be recorded in the minutes of the meeting (lines 21–23).

Though Eric's statements of opposition are delivered very seriously, by the third reiteration his tone has an element of pseudo-dramatic warning, a strategy he seems to adopt in recognition of the markedness of his explicit opposition. This tone is sustained in the mock-serious request to have his opposition formally recorded, and his use of the distancing strategy of referring to himself in the third person. The point is further underlined by the understatement of the utterance *Eric does not think this is a good idea*. As mentioned in Chapter 6, the formality of his request, which sounds incongruous in the context of this relatively informal meeting, elicits laughter. The discomfort aroused by Eric's formal opposition to what is proposed is thus resolved through his strategic use of humour. He skilfully underlines the fact that his disagreement stands, while simultaneously defusing the tension this opposition has generated.

This example illustrates a relatively unusual co-occurrence – the expression of explicit, on-record, overt disagreement in a relatively informal meeting of colleagues and equals in a white-collar 'professional' workplace. In accounting for this, it is important to note that although this is a team of equals, it is also a team of experts. In Example 7.9, Eric is the authority in the team on this particular topic, and hence it is less surprising that he is prepared to go 'on record' using direct and explicit discourse strategies to indicate his opposition to the proposal. This is a nice illustration of the relevance of expert power in action (Spencer-Oatey 2000). Eric's expertise and authority is also linked to responsibility. Thus one reason why he needs his views to go on record is to protect himself from the repercussions of what he considers a bad decision that he opposes. The opening example in Chapter 1 provides a similar case. Clara was ultimately responsible for the project under discussion, and hence she had a strong incentive to go 'bald on record' with her veto.

It is also important to note that workplace culture is a relevant consideration. Some workplaces tolerate and even encourage direct expressions of opinion, while others tend to favour greater attention to the face needs of participants. As mentioned in Chapter 6, the project team involved in this excerpt is a particularly competitive group of individuals who belong to a very loosely knit community of practice which emphasises individual responsibility at least as much as team responsibility. Even in this workplace, however, where confrontation is well tolerated, the seriousness and intensity of Eric's expression of opposition appears to require mitigation, in this case through the use of humour. This particular instance of problematic talk is realised and resolved, then, not through overt politeness strategies, as illustrated in earlier examples, nor by avoidance or reticence as illustrated in the next example, but by a skilful combination of in-your-face directness and ironic humour.

Off-record resistance as a pragmatic strategy

The final example of problematic discourse which we analyse in this chapter is in a somewhat different category from those considered previously. It has been selected to illustrate why analysing power and politeness at the local level of a single interaction may not always provide an adequate description or explanation of what is going on. The interaction in question constitutes a one-hour meeting between Aidan, who is Maori, and Hugh, a Pakeha colleague. The two men are evaluating vocational training programmes for Maori students. Aidan and Hugh are peers within the organisation and, as illustrated in Example 7.10a, a typical excerpt from this interaction, there is little overt evidence from the discourse itself that there is anything particularly problematic going on here.

Example 7.10a

Context: Advisers in a government organisation evaluating proposals.

```
 1 HUGH: yeah um the trainees finding their own so there could ++
 2        and that's a flaw with trainees finding their own
 3        is that they could end up sweeping the floor for two weeks
 4 AID:   yeah
 5 HUGH:  um + and by having the trainee find it
 6        the polytechnic gets no input into the the training that's covered
 7 AID:   yeah well the other issue about that thing is that the they're they're
 8        not they're not seeking culturally safe industries places to /protect\
 9        students +
10 HUGH:  /yeah\
11 AID:   and so all that sort of stuff
12 HUGH:  yeah yep
13 AID:   yep um
14 HUGH:  well like there are other ways of making it culturally safe
15 AID:   yeah
16 HUGH:  I mean I I I I mean it's nice to have cultural safety
17        but I think part of that is is the realisation that it's not a
18        culturally safe environment
19        /+\ out in industry
20 AID:   /no\ and yet in the cultural component they're not teaching any of
21        that stuff about how to deal with that
22 HUGH:  right okay yep + yep
23 AID:   and um yeah so the other thing is so how are they supporting
24        students + into into industry you know those sorts of things
25 HUGH:  yeah
```

While this is a very task-focused interaction, at a superficial level at least, it is consistently polite and friendly and overall the two men appear to be engaged in a relatively smooth and uncontroversial discussion where they meet their stated goals in terms of completing a joint task. There is little or no direct manifestation of conflict, problematic talk or miscommunication in the discourse. Nevertheless, our ethnographic data, together with comparative data from other interactions involving Aidan in particular, provide evidence of undetected subterranean problems based in general societal inequalities between Maori and Pakeha, which form an undercurrent to this interaction in a government organisation.

An interview with Aidan provided the first real indication that he perceived his interaction with Hugh to have been problematic, and that that this was part of an historical situation. (We do not have any comparable information on how Hugh perceived things, so this is necessarily a partial view.) Interestingly, it was not the practical outcome of the interaction that Aidan saw as the problem – he considered that they had completed the task expeditiously and without major disagreement. Rather, as indicated in Interview excerpt 7.1, the issue was that Aidan felt uncomfortable with Hugh's style of interaction and considered there to be unresolved conflict between them, which essentially boiled down to a kind of power struggle at both an interpersonal and intergroup level.

Interview excerpt 7.1

now with Hugh, there's a history between me and Hugh, and he's a Pakeha male who brings all those power elements of Maori/Pakeha into what I believe is a Maori process . . . and Hugh I believe was forever arguing.
I think what I'm doing here is saying, to hell with all that bullshit, I just want to get the job done, and I'm not going to play your game of arguing . . . he's easy to get on with, this guy, he's not ugly or anything, I'm just really conscious that he power plays

Aidan reported that he resented and resisted these 'power plays', maintaining a degree of distance between himself and Hugh, for instance, by refusing to be drawn into extended discussion of a topic and just focusing on the task at hand (Interview excerpt 7.2).

Interview excerpt 7.2

I got to the point of saying to this man, you've got a lot to say but there's actually very little substance to what you're saying. I don't know if that's a Pakeha trick in terms of communication, but whenever things get tough it seems to be you need a thousand words to explain what you could explain in five and to me it seems to be a disempowering language technique that if you possibly come up against an articulate minority person, then the way to get around that is to bamboozle with words and jargon; and this guy was really good at that, and I got to the point of saying, I'm not dealing with any of that, we've got a job to do.

The covert problem in this talk is thus a problem involving societal power issues, although it is never articulated overtly. Rather it is played out in the way the discourse is distributed and instantiated between the participants. A comparison of this interaction with a parallel interaction between Aidan and Vincent, another Maori male, provides some interesting insights into the discourse strategies Aidan uses to avoid overt conflict and mask his feelings about Hugh's style of interaction, while at the same time indirectly resisting what he sees as Hugh's 'power games'. These interactions both relate to the same evaluation task and there is no overt status difference between any of the interactants, who are all of similar age and educational background and work at the same level in the organisation.[5] Nevertheless, despite the contextual similarities, there are noticeable differences between the conversational styles of the two interactions. As we saw above, while the interaction between Aidan and Hugh is at the informal end of the scale, it is very on-task and focused, and there are few explicit signals of solidarity or high involvement evident. Instead, Aidan makes assertive use of 'one-at-a-time' turn-taking strategies (Coates 1996), and consistently addresses questions and challenges to Hugh in a stereotypically masculine 'one-up' style (Tannen 1990). In these ways, Aidan manages to present himself both as an able and confident professional in his field who knows what he is talking about, especially in terms of Maori issues, and to consciously place himself on an equal footing with Hugh. Aidan avoids as far as possible going on record with any disagreements, although, as we see in Example 7.10b, when he does (lines 3, 7), he does so fairly minimally.

Example 7.10b

```
 1 HUGH:  I guess to make me um perfectly happy with that sort of thing
 2        I'd like to say the following w- we tutors use
 3 AID:   that's words though Hugh
 4 HUGH:  I I know and and perhaps concreting that + I mean so
 5        I mean every nobody could rattle off that list the crucial
 6 AID:   not everybody does though eh
 7 HUGH:  yeah but and anyone could put it in there but do they do it +
 8        and to make me perfectly happy
 9        I'd like to see examples of um group learning
10        or a description of I'm nitpicking
11 AID:   mm
12 HUGH:  but (I mean) in terms of an ideal + yeah
13        I'd like to see how that that integrates into the whole teaching
14        package think this isn't so bad but a lot of the proposals we're
15        looking at they- they kind of skimp over it
16        and they might give it a couple of mentions
17        like that list or something (though) you're not you haven't got a
18        picture of + you know what (it takes)
```

19 AID: is that a gap then
20   is that what something you want you'd want me to write down

This example illustrates Aidan's strategy for dealing with Hugh. He tends not to elaborate or get drawn into an extended discussion. Rather he lets Hugh talk with only the most minimal of feedback and then changes the subject: *is that a gap then* (line 19). This appears to be a polite strategy for avoiding conflict, but it is one which is so subtle that it only becomes apparent by comparing it with Aidan's usual style of interaction, and after being alerted to it via a follow-up interview (see Interview excerpts 7.1 and 7.2 above). Example 7.11a by contrast, shows how Aidan and Vincent, who know each other very well and interact regularly outside the work context, place a high value on creating and maintaining solidarity through their interactional style.

Example 7.11a
Context: Advisers in a government organisation evaluating proposals.

 1 VIN: um all this stuff is in Maori bro
 2 AID: oh yeah I did read it I did read it
 3 VIN: [laughs] I'm gonna take /photo\copies of that
 4 AID: /yeah\
 5 VIN: well do they ask for these back do they ask for these back
 6   or can we keep them
 7 AID: no you can keep them
 8   but that's what good about some of these things
 9   is the forms that come with them
10 VIN: [laughs] yeah /[laughs]\
11 AID: /you can rip them out eh\ like for the capability stuff and + recording
12 VIN: you're a prof bro
13 AID: yeah

Although the two men are obviously involved in a serious task, they adopt a very informal style and make active use of a wide range of positive politeness strategies designed to maximise the level of solidarity between them, and to reinforce the construction of this as an interaction between Maori men who are both friends and colleagues in a predominantly Pakeha organisation. For example, they address one another as *bro* (lines 1, 12), there is a lot of humour and laughter and there are frequent brief digressions into relevant but strictly speaking 'off-topic' talk.

Aidan is also motivated by a wish to help Vincent, who is a friend as well as a Maori colleague, 'get up to speed' with his new job. The discussion of each point therefore often takes longer than if they were focusing purely on the task at hand, as Aidan takes the time to explain things or provide advice. Aidan's wielding of 'expert power' is humorously acknowledged by Vincent in the excerpt above when he quips *you're a prof bro* (line 12), but in fact, Aidan is careful not to dominate the discussion.

As we see in example 7.11b, when Aidan takes issue with something Vincent says, which he does regularly and vigorously throughout this interaction, his disagreements are heavily mitigated.

Example 7.11b

Context: Vincent has just criticised a proposal for over-emphasising academic content.

```
 1  AID:  the only thing that I would probably contest you about
 2        the um about the university approach
 3        and that I think cos it's a bridging course to university
 4        these guys hopefully gonna feed onto there
 5  VIN:  mm
 6  AID:  so I think that they actually do need an introduction
 7        to that type of um approach
 8        but I think that the crux of it is is
 9        that they're encased in [in maori] tikanga maaori
10        because they're outside the university
11  VIN:  yeah well after writing that I reflected on that and thought yeah no
12        I'm just being I'm just reacting [tut] to um academic snobbery /( )\
13  AID:  /shall I\ take that off
14  VIN:  yeah take it off
15  AID:  apart from that I've just got what you've got just in a lot less words
16        /[laughs]\
17  VIN:  /[laughs] you have to draw it up though\
18  AID:  [laughs] that's a different approach you summarise things
19        and put down your summary thoughts
20        whereas I look for evidence and and bang it out bit by bit +
21        I think that's what I'm doing anyway [tut]
22        where you're very good at summarising things and putting it down
```

Aidan's mitigation takes the form of strategies such as hedging: e.g. *I would probably contest you* (line 1), *I think* (lines 3, 6, 8, 21), *actually* (line 6), *just* (line 15), elaboration and providing reasons (lines 1–7), and redressive positive politeness strategies such as giving praise (lines 15–22). This is typical of Aidan's interaction style with Vincent.

In summary, in his interaction with Hugh, Aidan uses a combination of positive and negative politeness strategies to keep the interaction flowing as smoothly as required in order to complete the task, but without investing any great effort into the long-term relationship as he seems to do with Vincent. The effort that is required to maintain a degree of social distance and resist Hugh's enactment of power, while at the same time keeping up a show of friendliness and collaboration, is probably one source of Aidan's perception of this as an instance of problematic talk. In addition, the history of his relationship and previous interactions with Hugh undoubtedly also contribute to this perception. By comparing the strategies Aidan uses in these two comparable but differently constructed interactions, we gain some insight into how people can make use of quite subtle differences in discourse strategies and styles to politely and constructively negotiate problematic issues such as power in otherwise collegial workplace relationships.

Conclusion

This chapter has attempted to draw together the complex threads of power and politeness, by illustrating the skilful ways in which people manage problematic talk at work. We began with several examples of relatively straightforward miscommunication – where it appeared that the content or message had not been adequately conveyed from one person to another. As we noted, such explicit examples are remarkably rare in workplace talk. We then explored instances of problematic talk involving relational and power issues, and the management of different people's (often competing) face needs in workplace interaction, a much more complex and frequently occurring phenomenon, as the discussion throughout this book has indicated.

The analysis has also demonstrated that the strategies adopted to manage conflict and other kinds of problematic discourse can vary a great deal. At the level of the single interaction they include hedges, attenuators, boosters and intensifiers of various kinds which, along with avoidance and supportive feedback, and positive politeness devices such as humour, serve to mitigate potential threats to face. But we have also indicated how speakers make use of the more 'macro-level' resources at their disposal, such as avoidance of face-threatening acts, variable turn design and appeals to institutional procedures and processes.

The strategies used by participants to avoid conflict and maintain good work relationships illustrated in the examples in this chapter are just as evident in individuals' management of many other kinds of problematic talk. It is seldom a straightforward matter to locate in a stretch of discourse the precise point at which problematic talk or miscommunication can be said to have occurred. The analysis, whether from the perspective of participant or analyst, relies heavily on contextual information at a number of different levels and must always be seen in the light of wider societal discourses of power. Nevertheless, careful analysis of everyday workplace interaction frequently shows people taking pre-emptive action to prevent communication breakdown and to manage potentially face-threatening situations before they can pose a threat to longer term working relationships.

Although, as stated in Chapter 1, 'almost every example of authentic discourse has several layers of meaning', power and politeness consistently emerge as important dimensions constraining the ways in which participants negotiate and resolve miscommunication and problematic issues at work, whether the issue at stake is one of the process or the outcome of a given interaction. Relevant cases seem particularly likely to occur where there is a difference in relative status between the interactants. An analysis of the interplay between power and politeness in such interactions has provided some interesting insights into the nature of problematic discourse. In the final chapter, we consider some of the implications of such analyses for workplace practitioners.

Notes

1. See, for instance, four decisions of the Wellington Employment Tribunal during 1994: *Poumako* vs *National Bank*; *Cadman* vs *Wisharts*; *Smith* vs *Hodder & Tolley Limited*; *Adkins* vs *Turk's Poultry Farm*.
2. See, for example, Tannen (1994); Linde (1988); Hernal, Fennell and Miller (1991); Gatenby and Jones (1995); Sligo, Olsson and Wallace (1997).
3. This interaction is analysed in detail from a range of perspectives in Stubbe et al. (2000). The excerpts discussed here are explored in more depth from a CDA perspective in Holmes (fc). We thank Meredith Marra for her contribution to the original analysis.
4. Quote from a managing director (Clouse and Spurgeon 1995: 3).
5. However, this does not mean there are no *power* differences – Aidan has expert power by contrast with Beth and Vince, who are relatively new to the job, and all three interactions take place in a context where unequal power relations between Maori and Pakeha in NZ society are foregrounded.

8

Conclusion: Some Implications
and Applications

Introduction

The analysis in the different chapters of this book has demonstrated some of
the many and varied ways in which power and politeness are inextricably
intertwined in every workplace interaction. Despite their very different
transactional or business objectives, commercial organisations, factories and
government departments all use talk as one means of achieving them. And in
the process of talking people cannot avoid involvement with the dimensions
of power and politeness. Every interaction at work involves an individual in
the performance of their professional status and authority relative to others,
and equally the dynamic nature of any interaction entails constant negotiation
of social distance or solidarity. In other words, we have tried to illustrate in
the preceding chapters some of the complex means that workers use to 'do'
power and politeness in their workplace talk.

Some chapters of this book have focused more on the transactional business
of different workplaces, while the main focus of others has been the affective
and social aspects of workplace talk. The discussion of directives, or how people
get things done at work in Chapter 3, the analysis of meeting talk in Chapter
4, and the exploration of problematic communication in Chapter 7, surveyed
aspects of what most people would consider the core business of any
workplace. Chapter 5 on social talk and Chapter 6 on humour, on the other
hand, examined the contribution of types of talk that many would consider
irrelevant or dispensable in the workplace context. Our thesis has been that
both dimensions are important in accounting for the complexities of workplace
interaction, and especially in accounting for the manifestations of power and
politeness at work. The content and style of apparently peripheral small talk
characteristic of work groups in an organisation typically make as important
a contribution to the construction of a distinctive workplace culture as the
norms of interaction in weekly meetings. The patterns and types of humour
which develop within a project team are as significant in accounting for its

distinctive interactional style as the way the manager gives directives, or the way problems are worked through. Moreover, every workplace interaction, regardless of whether its primary function seems predominantly transactional or social, inevitably involves the negotiation of relational meaning. As we have seen, workplace interactions are seldom neutral in terms of power and always involve some degree of face work. Spoken discourse provides a finely tuned interactive resource which allows workers to strike an appropriate balance between creating the degree of social distance required to reflect and enact relative status on the one hand, and to signal collegiality on the other, while attempting to meet the requirements of the task at hand and the longer term objectives of the organisation.

We have aimed to demonstrate that these aspects of workplace talk are not only amenable to study, but that the results of such analyses can be useful in understanding the dynamics of workplace interaction. In this final chapter, we select just two areas to illustrate this claim in more detail. We first briefly consider the implications of a small selection from the patterns of interaction that we have described in earlier chapters for one specific group, namely those who are joining a new workplace. Then, in the final section of the chapter, we outline one particular practical application of our analyses, an action reflection model, which, as indicated in Chapter 2, we have trialled with workplace practitioners.

Getting integrated at work

As reflected throughout this book, one of the most challenging aspects of workplace interaction is balancing the demands of the organisation's transactional goals alongside the construction of social rapport with fellow workers. Workplace relationships are typically an important aspect of job satisfaction. While good interpersonal relationships generally mean things get done more smoothly, at times the demands may conflict so that, for example, maintaining good rapport with workmates may entail engaging in talk which distracts from workplace objectives. Alternatively, making sure the team meets the week's quota, or completes an important report may involve paying less attention to colleagues' face needs, at least for a period. We have argued that both functions of discourse, the transactional and the social, are simultaneously relevant in interpreting what is going on, the 'meaning' of the discourse; and both are important in ensuring that an individual fits in at work. This is the challenge that faces any new employee in an unfamiliar workplace, namely, to develop appropriate ways of doing power and politeness in the particular community of practice they are trying to join. Small talk and humour are areas where this challenge is particularly evident and we focus on these for exemplification in this section.

Managing small talk at work

Many researchers argue that social integration is a crucial key to workplace success:

> Relatively subtle aspects of pragmatic language use can inhibit the development of meaningful relationships with others . . . the display of conversational competence can be considered as an essential prerequisite for the achievement of a valued quality of life.

> (Hatton 1998: 93)

Chapter 5 on small talk and Chapter 6 on humour in the workplace indicated some of the complexities of managing social talk at work. To take a specific example, the distinction between work talk and small talk is often difficult to draw. Experienced workers move smoothly and gradually between work talk and social talk, as illustrated in Chapter 5. But the distinctions are often fine and very context related, both in terms of what is appropriate in a particular interaction or setting, and in the culture of a particular workplace or a specific community of practice. Discerning the boundaries and avoiding overstepping them are obvious potential pitfalls for a new employee. Small talk, for instance, typically extends into social talk, and as the formulaic routine components of the interaction reduce, the demands on the conversationalists increase. This is not a problem for many workers, but for those whose communication skills are not well developed, or for whom the workplace is a second language environment, it can be problematic.

This was starkly illustrated by data that we collected from workplaces where workers with an intellectual disability had been placed. Some could manage the small talk and social talk exchanges which were so crucial for their integration into the workplace. Others, however, found it difficult to carry their side of the conversation and to respond and extend social talk overtures appropriately, a problem which has also been identified in studies of non-native speaker–native speaker interactions (Holmes and Brown 1976). Example 8.1 illustrates a typical pattern.

Example 8.1
Context: Three women helpers in a child-care centre at the beginning of the day.

1 SUE: good morning Laura how are you
2 LAU: good
3 SUE: very good got anything exciting on for the weekend
4 LAU: no
5 SUE: you're not going anywhere
6 LAU: um no

In this paradigmatic early morning ritual, Laura, the worker with an intellectual disability, responded appropriately with *good* (line 2) to the formulaic opening in line 1, but failed to pick up and develop the social topic initiated by her coworker, Sue, in line 3. As workplace conversation becomes more of a negotiation and less of a ritual, satisfactory participation poses more of a challenge for some workers, particularly for newcomers.

Another aspect of managing social talk at work is recognising the cues that it is time to get 'down to business' or 'back on track'. As illustrated in Chapters 4 and 5, it is typically superiors who direct discussion back to business after digressions, sometimes overtly (e.g. *getting back to the agenda*), but sometimes using less explicit discourse markers such as *OK, right, now, yes well* and *alright*. Recognising the discourse cues which provide the signal that it is time the discussion got back on track is an important workplace communication skill. On occasion, the shift back to business was very abrupt if the demands of work made themselves apparent before the social talk had been nicely rounded off. In Chapter 5, the conversation between Ginette and Jim on the factory line (Example 5.6) illustrated the typical rapid shifting between social chit-chat and on-task communication which characterised exchanges on the factory line. Ability to shift topic abruptly in such circumstances – both backwards and forwards – is an important aspect of sociopragmatic skill in interaction. In Example 8.2, a discussion of the state of the teeth of one of the participants has developed from the manager's comment that she gave out chocolate fish as a reward in the previous week (see Example 6.19). The shift back to the work topic is quite abrupt.

Example 8.2
Context: Planning meeting in a government department.

```
 1 EVE: I've been putting off going to the dentist for /six months now and\
 2 LEI: /oh no\
 3 EVE: I've got a hole in /my tooth\ [laughs] anyway
 4 LEI: /oh yuck\
 5 ZOE: so if we if we did if if it was Hannah then that leaves you and I in the
 6      library
 7 KER: mhm
 8 ZOE: you've said that you feel that really the records thing really isn't /too
 9      bad\
10 KER: /I think that\ the two of us in the library's fine actually
```

Zoe moves the talk back on track here quite abruptly at line 5, but the other participants pick up the thread promptly and smoothly, an important indication that they are 'tuned in' and 'work' oriented. Management of the smooth integration of social talk within transactional talk, as illustrated here, is one area which can be problematic for newcomers to a work team.

The frequency of small talk and humour and the amount which is appropriate in different contexts are further distributional aspects of social talk which are systematically patterned, and which can pose difficulties for people new to a workplace. Identifying occasions when social talk is dispensable as opposed to obligatory, for instance, is an important aspect of contributing appropriately to workplace discourse. Learning to use social talk to fill potentially awkward silences at the beginning of a meeting or humour to spice up boring stretches of work or gaps between work activities is another challenge to those trying to integrate into the workplace culture. In Example 8.3, like Laura in Example 8.1, Heath fails to pull his conversational weight in an interaction where Mary is clearly trying to maintain good relations and to fill in time as they do a boring weeding job together.

Example 8.3
Context: Mary is working alongside Heath in a garden centre. They are between tasks.

1 MARY: how's your mum?
2 HEA: good
3 MARY: is she ++ has her knee fixed up yet? (3)
4 HEA: no
5 MARY: has her knee got better now?
6 HEA: yes
7 MARY: that's good

Mary is doing all the conversational 'work' here, carrying the conversation. There is a long pause at line 3, as Mary waits for a response, and when they do come, the responses which Heath supplies (lines 2, 4, 6) are minimal. He provides one word replies rather than supplying extra information to keep the conversation alive. Being a good companion at work entails skills in maintaining and contributing appropriately to social talk, as well as task-oriented skills.

The extent to which small talk on personal topics is accepted or even expected as a way of constructing collegial relationships also varies from workplace to workplace. Thus one of our informants reported feeling quite uncomfortable initially when she began work in a new organisation where people routinely shared quite intimate details of their personal lives to an extent that would have been deemed 'unprofessional' in her previous workplace. She eventually became accustomed to this practice, and in fact valued it as an important way in which members of the group provided support to one another, but she remained aware that it presented a potential barrier to the integration of new team members.

We also noted that social talk is used by superiors to maintain good workplace relationships. Language plays an important part in creating a particular kind of work environment. The boss who begins the day with a friendly chat establishes a very different work environment from one who arrives with a barrage of instructions for his or her staff. Conversely, responding positively, but not too minimally or effusively, to small talk is a social skill which workers typically develop through experience. Such skills often present problems to newcomers to the workplace and particularly to those from different cultural or linguistic groups.

Managing humour at work

Another challenging area of sociopragmatic competence is interpreting and understanding the context-bound and very distinctive styles of humour which characterise different workplaces. A sense of humour is well attested as a highly valued attribute of employees. Since humour is a crucial component of different workplace cultures, as illustrated in Chapter 6, this is another area where those joining a new workplace face a steep learning curve. Chapter 6 also illustrated the point that humour serves a range of functions in the workplace. People use humour to emphasise a sense of belonging to the group, or to express solidarity in the workplace. They use it to soften necessary instructions or criticisms, thus paying attention to others' face needs. And they also use it, on occasion, to 'have a go' at coworkers or challenge the boss in a socially acceptable way.

The practical implications of these observations are evident from the fact that humour in the workplace has been big business for many years. Many business organisations report that humour is an important indication of a healthy workplace, and claim to rank a sense of humour very highly among the desirable attributes of employees (Nolan 1986: 28, as cited in Morreall 1991: 360). Hence, not surprisingly, there has been a burgeoning business in humour consultancies offering humour seminars and training. One such business claimed that in the nine months following a humour workshop in Colorado, 20 middle managers increased their productivity by 15 per cent and cut their sick days in half (Morreall 1991). Similarly, the well-known actor, John Cleese, has built Video-Arts into the world's largest production company for films on interpersonal skills training, based on the notion that if mistakes are presented humorously, workers can identify them without getting defensive.

Our analyses suggested that humour was variably distributed in different workplaces, in different work groups and in different work contexts. There was a great deal more humour, for instance, in the interactions of the soap factory work team than in the meetings of groups in government departments. Moreover, as Chapter 6 indicated, the type of humour which predominated in different workplaces was also variable. Jocular abuse was frequent between members of some work teams, for example, while others seemed to prefer witty and succinct sarcastic comments; and jointly constructed fantasy scenarios were a feature of some workplaces. This is another area where the implications of our analyses for new workers are very clear. The amount and type of humour characteristic of the particular community of practice you are joining always needs to be identified and adapted to. Learning to recognise, understand, and if possible, to enjoy and contribute to the humour in a workplace is an important aspect of fitting in.

Again we can illustrate this point with data collected from a workplace in which a young worker with a disability had been placed. In Example 8.4, Aaron, the newly placed worker, did not immediately 'get' the joke his co-workers were making.

Example 8.4
Context: Small talk between workers in a small business at their tea break.

```
 1 AAR:   you got Sky Tom?
 2 TOM:   nah
 3 AAR:   oh right
 4 MIKE:  we got it
 5 AAR:   h- h- how do you watch the game?
 6 MIKE:  he doesn't
 7 TOM:   well my neighbour's got Sky so I go outside and look through his
 8         window
 9 AAR:   oh okay oh right [laughs] that's quite handy
10 MIKE:  got a telescope we go straight through
11 AAR:   yeah that's handy yeah [laughs]
12 TOM:   nah it was on it was on um yesterday
13 AAR:   yeah yeah yeah
14 TOM:   replayed on 3
15 AAR:   oh oh okay oh yeah it was too yeah true yeah
```

The three men have been discussing a rugby game. Aaron takes the initiative and asks Tom if he has the TV channel Sky, since the game was first relayed on Sky TV. It is clear from the tape that Aaron takes literally Tom's joke that he watches it through his neighbour's window (a joke which Mike contributes to with his comment about having a telescope to help). It is not clear whether Tom was teasing Aaron, in particular, in the first place, or whether his 'joke' was aimed at everyone (with the expectation that they would recognise the absurdity of his comment). But Aaron falls most obviously for the tease. Tom relents, however (line 12) and rescues Aaron. When he realises his mistake, Aaron recovers well (line 15). Being teased and made the butt of jokes is normal workplace experience for all workers. Indeed, the fact that Aaron is included in the banter is a sign of social integration in the workplace.

Handling such banter and teasing, and learning to recognise when a remark is intended as humorous or sarcastic, are skills which all workers need to develop, but the challenge represented by such indicators of workplace integration are brought into sharp relief by young workers like Aaron. There is extensive research indicating that these workers often find managing social interaction in the workplace a major problem:

> It is an inability to interact effectively with otherm people, rather than an inability to operate machines or perform job tasks that often causes many mentally retarded adults to get fired from competitive jobs.
>
> (Greenspan and Shoultz 1981: 23)

Chadsey-Rusch (1992: 405) makes the same point: 'A major reason for job loss for persons with mental retardation may be their lack of appropriate social skills.' This research suggests that actual ability to perform work tasks is just the tip of the iceberg in terms of success at work. Social and inter-personal skills proved to be much more significant predictors of workplace success (e.g. Black and Langone 1997; Hatton 1998). Our research has made an important contribution in this area, since previous research was largely based on reported data or questionnaires, rather than actual observation of workers in the relevant workplaces. By collecting data in contexts where young people with intellectual disabilities were working, we were able to identify problematic areas and provide materials and suggestions for the communication skills programmes that they were concurrently attending.[1]

However, many of the points which have proved useful to those assisting workers with intellectual disabilities to successfully integrate into the work-place are just as important for all workers. Sociolinguistic and sociopragmatic competence is an underestimated aspect of workplace success (Clyne 1994; Pauwels 1989). According to a Robert Haft International 1985 survey only 15 per cent of workers are fired because of lack of competence (Sultanoff 2002). The remaining 85 per cent are 'let go' because of their inability to get along with fellow employees. Ability to manage social talk is one important component of good interpersonal relations at work. Analysis of workplace interactions such as those illustrated in this book can provide a starting point in developing relevant materials to assist people to develop these important relational skills.

To what extent can the ability to interpret and produce the subtleties and complexities of everyday talk in a workplace context be taught? Is it possible for workers who are new to a workplace, including workers who are non-native speakers, to acquire the sociopragmatic skills outlined in this book, or even to identify and correctly interpret the complex meanings relating to the construction of power and politeness which we have illustrated? The many sophisticated and experienced workers that we recorded had generally learned, through extensive exposure, to accurately interpret the sociopragmatic meanings conveyed by the participants in workplace interaction, although even then, as we saw in Chapter 7, the potential for misunderstanding is an ever-present pitfall. Our experience suggests that some preparatory training, combined with on-the-job practice of what has been learned, can be a fruitful way of assisting new workers to acquire these skills. The complexity and richness of our data suggests that teachers and communication skills trainers need to demonstrate some ingenuity in providing opportunities for learners to observe, practise, and acquire the sociopragmatic skills involved in the management of areas such as small talk and humour in the workplace. In the next section, we describe a process which we developed in collaboration with several workplaces to explore one practical application of our research.

Reflection as a learning strategy for the workplace

Interview excerpt 8.1

Context: A senior manager explains how job candidates were selected for new positions in her section.

... we've chosen people who are really good open confident communicators at a business level and at an interpersonal level ... so hopefully we've moved the culture ahead a step further by the selection of these four people and ... M and C and I did the interviewing and largely + um obviously we met all the technical competencies we needed but largely we made the choice amongst a HUGE pool of really good applicants on on interpersonal skills ... and communication as being a big part of that + their WAY of working

As the comment from the manager quoted in Interview excerpt 8.1 suggests, there seems to be an increasing emphasis on the need for workers to have well-developed communication skills at all levels and in all occupational groups, a trend which has been noted by a number of commentators (e.g. Cameron 2000; Coupland, Sarangi and Candlin 2001; Scheeres 1998), and can be readily observed in a variety of organisational texts such as job descriptions and advertisements, performance reviews and training plans. A worker's interpersonal skills and style of communication may even be given priority over their technical skills, as illustrated in Example 8.1.

The shift to a 'new work order' (Sarangi and Roberts 1999) which downplays organisational hierarchies in favour of more egalitarian team-based structures provides one possible explanation. The 'linguistic turn' in the social sciences and in the field of organisational communication over the last two decades, which emphasises the discursive processes by which organisations and their members come to be constituted, has also been influential in positioning communication as a key concern for practitioners involved in organisational change and development (Jones and Stubbe fc). As one manager who participated in our research commented: 'You have to be more articulate about what you're doing and why and what you want . . . communication is a lot more open in this place than it was.'

But how exactly might we define a 'good communicator' or 'competence' in interpersonal communication in the workplace? To what extent can individuals acquire and apply the competencies involved in isolation? These questions are central to any attempt to evaluate and develop workplace communication. The traditional pattern of training in workplace communication tends to consist of courses which offer training in a set of discrete, rigidly defined 'skills' and tasks. The participants are then sent back to their workplaces to practise and apply what they have learned. The material in this book has illustrated, however, that there are many different ways of communicating at work and that the specific context of any interaction is crucial to the choice of communication strategy. People adapt their communicative approach according to myriad social, personal and contextual factors. Moreover, we have also illustrated that particular work groups tend to develop their own particular communication strategies and patterns, and experience their own specific problems. No pre-packaged course can hope to prepare people for such communicative diversity and the associated challenges. Rather people need assistance in developing their observational and analytical skills, so that they can identify for themselves the appropriate ways of interacting in their specific community of practice on any particular occasion. Our data provides support for the position taken by critics of narrow competency-based approaches (e.g. Antonacopoulou and Fitzgerald 1996) and suggests that to be of real practical use, training and development in communication must go beyond a narrow focus on individual skills, to encompass a context-sensitive, interactive model of communicative competence.

One approach which the LWP team have developed is known as the Communication Evaluation Development (CED) model (Jones and Stubbe fc). It is based on the individual's observation, reflection and evaluation of their own particular communication processes in their specific workplace. The process adopts a reflexive approach. Participants make observations about their communicative environment, identify specific aspects of their communicative behaviour which they would like to alter or develop and then devote time to practising new communicative strategies which they consider will improve the effectiveness of their workplace interactions. The results of trialling this process suggest that it can be very effective in a range of different work environments.

The model is based on the two key elements of an action learning approach, namely, evaluation (developing insights from reflection on past events and observation of current practices) and planning (applying these insights to future actions). It also draws on the principles of appreciative inquiry, an approach to organisational development which involves looking for what is done well with the aim of finding ways to share strengths with others and develop them further, as distinct from looking for 'problems' and setting out to solve them (Hammond 1996). The steps in the CED process thus entail:

1. Identifying a problem/development issue to be addressed.
2. Analysing what happened in a specific instance of communication involving the relevant issue.
3. Reflecting on ways in which things might have been done differently.
4. Experimenting with ways of approaching the interaction differently.[2]

Exemplifying with material illustrated in different chapters of this book, the managers of an effective factory production team could use this approach to identify, for example, those elements of the team's communicative practice that contribute positively to their performance, so that they can develop these practices and build on them elsewhere in the factory. Alternatively, an individual could use the approach to help work out why they were consistently misinterpreting the urgency of the tasks their manager was giving them, and thus running into trouble when the tasks were not completed according to the manager's expectations. A project leader could use the CED approach to evaluate and address difficulties experienced in managing the agenda in meetings which seemed to result in too many irrelevant digressions. In other words, our experience with the CED model suggests that it can provide a strategy for helping individuals or work teams identify what is actually going on in the relevant interactions, checking their perceptions and expectations with those of others, and allowing them to consider what steps they need to take to improve things from their perspective.

Our work with people in a range of workplaces suggests that the insights gained from the reflective process incorporated in the CED approach is beneficial to a wide variety of people in many different roles in an organisation, and at different levels in the hierarchy in different workplaces. This is nicely illustrated by feedback from people who participated in workshops and follow-up interviews relating to a number of areas of the research discussed in this book. For instance, our research indicates that good managers skilfully balance the need for action with the importance of constructing and maintaining rapport. This typically involves assessing the complex interacting demands of many different contextual factors. One manager reported, for instance, that she became more aware of the range of strategies that she used to get things done with different people in different contexts. Another commented that before being involved in our research she was unaware of the important role that humour played in maintaining good staff relations in her workplace.

People in workplaces also found it useful to reflect on findings from LWP research on interaction processes and structures in relation to their own experience. In one such case, two senior women, meeting to discuss a particular issue, initially analysed their meeting as full of irrelevant digressions. On reflection and after further analysis they found that almost all the so-called 'digressions' had served a valuable purpose, though not necessarily in relation to the immediate problem they were currently discussing. The digressions had in fact provided invaluable background preparation for further larger meetings they were to attend at a later point. On the other hand, after analysing a rather unfocused problem-solving discussion, another group came to recognise that the ability to 'negotiate' and reach an agreed understanding of what needed to be done was crucial to achieving a successful outcome – as was reaching some sort of agreement as to how a meeting should be structured in different cases, as the comment in Interview excerpt 8.2 illustrates.

Interview excerpt 8.2

Context: Participant in practical workshop based on material collected in his workplace by the LWP team.

if you haven't got something structured + and you've got two people at each end of the spectrum, somebody who wants a very truncated let's get to the facts and get outta here meeting, and somebody else who wants to go there for a week + you're going to have some problems in terms of getting a resolution

The CED approach also has very obvious advantages when a communication problem is involved. Post-hoc reflection on the causes of a cross-cultural or interpersonal misunderstanding, for instance, can serve as a valuable first step in defusing tension and as useful preparation for avoiding a repetition of such miscommunication (cf Gumperz, Jupp and Roberts 1979; Littlewood 2001). Sometimes too, the insights gained from reflecting on habitual interaction patterns provide a way of addressing a wider personal or inter-group agenda in terms of power. Thus a worker who was concerned at the difficulties faced by Maori participants in official meetings commented as follows (Interview excerpt 8.3).

Interview excerpt 8.3

Context: Maori participant commenting on material collected in his workplace by the LWP team.

For an indigenous people, to have access to that type of knowledge and skills when we're in those type of forums so that we can actually get our messages across, so they are actually heard, would be a very powerful tool for us, because we are continually misheard, misrepresented, misinterpreted ... and from my experience, I just come home absolutely exhausted, I just feel like I've been sucked dry

Similarly, as suggested in the previous section, identifying the perennial topics of social talk and small talk in one's work group or the style of humour may be a useful first step in facilitating integration. Again the CED approach may be useful. A systematic period of observation followed by the analysis of specific instances, and reflection on why the pattern was not obvious initially – these are invaluable steps in the process of acquiring the relevant skills to fit into a new work team. A facilitator or mentor provides important support in this process (see Jones 1998), but it is managed primarily by the individual, or group, who identify the particular area of concern and work with the facilitator on improving their communicative skills in the specific context they have identified as problematic. The great advantage of this approach is its potential for sensitivity to the complex and specific contextual factors identified throughout this book as crucial in accounting for the dynamics of interaction. Developing the ability to observe, analyse and reflect on the communicative challenges in one's own particular work environment, and especially on the complex ways in which power and politeness are enacted in that environment, is empowering for any individual.

Conclusion

The detailed analyses of genuine workplace interactions presented in this book have illustrated a range of ways in which people signal and negotiate their working relationships with others in terms of both power and politeness. Managers frequently 'do power' overtly and in many contexts it is clearly regarded by participants in the interaction as unremarkable for them to do so. Many of the examples we have analysed illustrate that managers also have less direct, more linguistically polite strategies available to achieve their goals in a consensual way, while still marking status asymmetries, and thus maintaining their authority. In certain situations they may choose to dispense with enacting power altogether and choose to foreground interpersonal solidarity instead. Similarly, workers lower down the organisational hierarchy also make use of a wide communicative repertoire. They typically construct their relationships with those who have greater authority and influence and with their peers in rather different ways, using a range of facework strategies to accede to, cooperate with, contest or resist the enactment of power or to construct and maintain collegial relationships. We have also identified some interesting and contrasting patterns in the ways in which groups of people enact power and politeness discursively in different organisations, and have examined the extent to which these differences reflect and help construct and maintain distinctive communities of practice.

At a more general level, by combining a fine-grained qualitative analysis of naturally occurring interaction with close consideration of a range of contextual and ethnographic data, we have been able to explore the relationship between the interaction order of particular workplace situations and the wider social and institutional structures to which they contribute across a range of different workplace settings. The examples presented in each chapter were designed to illustrate how power and politeness are instantiated in a range of different discourse contexts, but at the same time they served to demonstrate the fundamentally dynamic and intersubjective nature of workplace talk, and the sequential effects of the constant realignment of participants' identities and goals as an interaction proceeds. We saw, for instance, how the same linguistic forms may be very differently motivated at different points in an interaction, and how particular discourse patterns may reflect quite different power dynamics and have varying pragmatic effects depending on the immediate and wider context. The richness of our data set has also made it possible to unravel the complexity of the ways in which shared understandings are built up through a series of related interactions, and the ways in which both transactional and social or affective meanings may be simultaneously constructed at a number of different levels in the course of an interaction.

From a theoretical perspective, examining a range of workplace data through the dual lenses of power and politeness has also made it possible to explore and evaluate alternative ways of modelling the same discourse structures and processes. For example, politeness theory may have the best explanatory power in interactions where both participants share the same transactional goals. But an approach which regards the workplace as a site for oppressive or repressive discourse (Pateman 1980; Fairclough 1989, 1992) may provide a better account in cases where, by virtue of their different positions in the organisation, or different attitudes to the management's objectives, participants' goals in an interaction conflict rather than coincide. Even at the level of a single interaction, a more satisfactory account of participants' motivations may be achieved by drawing on more than one analytical or theoretical model, as individuals shift from 'doing power' to 'doing collegiality' or even 'doing friendship' in the workplace. Alternatively, combining or comparing the insights gained from a number of different frameworks can make it possible to produce a richer and more compre- hensive analysis (cf Stubbe et al. 2000).

Finally, this multidimensional analysis of genuine workplace interaction has generated a number of practical implications and applications, as discussed in the first parts of this chapter. The workplace has always been a social context where status differences are especially salient, and one where people primarily interact with one another in pursuit of organisational imperatives rather than from personal choice. However, the modern workplace, with its typically flattened hierarchies and greater diversity than in the past, arguably places increased demands on the interpersonal communication skills of workers. Workplace roles and relationships have become less clearly defined and more open to negotiation, and with a greater emphasis on teamwork, talk itself increasingly *is* the work, not just a means to an end. In this kind of environment, the most effective communicators seem to be people who are flexible, responsive and reflective in relation to the way they interact with others.

The examples in this book highlight the interactive nature of interpersonal communication in the workplace, as well as the particular challenges involved in balancing the requirements of communicating about the task at hand (the 'work') with the relational demands inherent both in a particular interaction and in the workplace environment more generally. On the one hand, talk at work is especially focused on the achievement of concrete, task-related goals. Talk is a very important way of 'doing work' in most modern workplaces and this is the way it is most often viewed and explicitly valued – as a tool. However, as we have seen, talk is also the very stuff of workplace relationships and culture. Whether this is instantiated in identifiably social kinds of talk such as humour and small talk, or as part and parcel of the way in which core business or task-oriented talk is constructed, considerations of power and politeness inevitably constrain the way people talk at work.

In conclusion, as we have seen throughout this volume, verbal exchanges in the workplace perform important social and interpersonal functions, as well as the transactional meanings to which participants often overtly orient. The discourse strategies which characterise a particular interaction express not only the specific goals of the interaction and the relative roles of each participant in relation to those goals; they also actively construct the particular relationships between the people involved, in terms of social distance or solidarity – the politeness norms – as well as the participants' relative power in the organisation. The opening example in Chapter 1 illustrated these points very succinctly. The group's jointly produced humour served to defuse the tension created by Clara's very direct enforcing of her decision over the issue of the 'screendumps', while simultaneously subverting Clara's enactment of overt authority in the meeting. Our closing example similarly highlights the complex interrelationships between power and politeness in workplace discourse, although from a different perspective and in a very different context (Example 8.5).

Example 8.5
Context: Ginette, coordinator of a factory production team, is doing her 'rounds', and has stopped to talk to Lesia, one of the workers on the packing line. Lesia keeps on working throughout the interaction, moving back and forth between a stack of empty boxes and the bench where he is packing.

1 GIN: get up to anything funny over the weekend
2 LES: [shakes head]
3 GIN: did you go to church bro
4 LES: no no no no well we went to our game on Saturday afternoon + practice
5 GIN: you didn't go to church bro

 6 LES: no
 7 GIN: [smiling, mock serious tone] very sad bro
 8   [emphatically] how many times have I told you go to church every
 9   Sunday
10 LES: [smiling] oh yeah [turns away]
11 GIN: [teasingly] you just didn't want to put any money in the offering bowl
12   eh bro
13 LES: [smiles and keeps moving back and forth with boxes]
14 GIN: you're broke eh bro
15 LES: I've spent it all already
16 GIN: already bro? you did heaps of overtime last week bro +
17   you know how your church gives ten per cent + of your earnings +
18   I bet you only put in two point five per cent eh bro
19 LES: [chuckles]
20 GIN: the rest goes on your horses eh
21 LES: [smiles and mutters something under his breath as he turns away to get
       a box]
22 GIN: I'll tell your wife ++
23   look at Joe and what's his name [looks across at two other workers]
24   what kind of conversation could THEY be having d'you think
       [shakes her head, expression of mock disbelief on her face]
25   they're doing NO work WHATsoever

This brief excerpt provides a cameo view of the way Ginette skilfully enacts both power and solidarity as she performs her role as manager of this close-knit, multicultural factory team. While Ginette often adopts a very direct, almost authoritarian style (humorously alluded to here with her mock serious berating of Lesia (line 8, *how many times have I told you go to church every Sunday*), this is tempered and blended here with a range of both collaborative and contestive discourse strategies as she teases Lesia about the reasons for his supposed lack of generosity. In this way, Ginette works to build team solidarity and minimise the difference in status between Lesia and herself. She then neatly switches the conversation back to a business footing with her comment about the two workers who, unlike Lesia, are off-task while chatting (lines 24–25). This comment both subtly underlines her status as team manager and indirectly reinforces her expectations of how team members should conduct themselves. Ginette's skilful management of these multiple meanings allows her to assert control where required, while at the same time paying explicit attention to the face needs of her interlocutor, and accommodating and reinforcing the high solidarity culture characteristic of this particular community of practice. This closing example thus illustrates again the remarkable variation in the way people talk to one another in different workplace settings, while also underlining our theme – whatever particular discourse styles or strategies people choose to achieve their goals, power and politeness are inextricably intertwined dimensions of their workplace interaction.

Notes

1. See Holmes and Fillary (2000) and Fillary (1998) for more information on this process.
2. See Jones (1998) and Jones and Stubbe (fc) for further details of how this model may operate in practice.

Appendix

Transcription conventions

YES	Capitals indicate emphatic stress
[laughs]	Paralinguistic features in square brackets.
+	Pause of up to one second
(3)	Pause of specified number of seconds
... /......\ ... ... /.......\ ...	Simultaneous speech
(hello)	Transcriber's best guess at an unclear utterance
?	Rising or question intonation
-	Incomplete or cut-off utterance
. . .	Section of transcript omitted
XM/XF	Unidentified Male/Female

All names used in examples are pseudonyms.

References

Ackroyd, S. and P. Thompson 1999. Only joking? From subculture to counter-culture in organizational relations. In S. Ackroyd and P. Thompson, *Organizational Misbehaviour*. London: Sage. 99–120.

Ädelsward, V. and B.-M. Öberg 1998. The function of laughter and joking in negotiation activities, *Humor* 11, 4: 411–29.

Antonacopoulou, E. and L. FitzGerald 1996. Reframing competency in management development, *Human Resource Management Journal* 6, 1: 27–50.

Atkinson, M., E. Cuff and J. R. E. Lee 1978. Meeting talk. In J. Schenkein (ed.), *Studies in the Organization of Conversational Interaction*. New York: Academic Press. 133–54.

Austin, P. 1990. Politeness revisited – the dark side. In A. Bell and J. Holmes (eds), *New Zealand Ways of Speaking English*. Clevedon, Avon: Multilingual Matters. 277–93.

Barbato, C. A. 1994. The role of argumentativeness in the decision and communication outcomes of small decision-making groups. PhD dissertation, Kent State University.

Bargiela-Chiappini, F. and S. J. Harris 1997. *Managing Language: The Discourse of Corporate Meetings*. Amsterdam: John Benjamins.

Bellinger, D. 1979. Changes in the explicitness of mother's directives as children age, *Journal of Child Language* 6: 443–58.

Bergvall, V. L. and K. A. Remlinger 1996. Reproduction, resistance and gender in educational discourse: the role of critical discourse analysis, *Discourse and Society* 7, 4: 453–79.

Bernsten, J. 1998. Marked vs unmarked choices on the auto factory floor. In C. Myers-Scotton (ed.), *Codes and Consequences*. Oxford: Oxford University Press. 178–91.

Black, R. S. and J. Langone 1997. Social awareness and transition to employment for adolescents with mental retardation, *Remedial and Special Education* 18: 214–22.

Blau, P. 1955. *The Dynamics of Bureaucracy*. Chicago: University of Chicago Press.

Blum-Kulka, S. 1997. Indirectness and politeness in requests: same or different?, *Journal of Pragmatics* 11: 131–46.

Blum-Kulka, S., J. House and G. Kasper 1989. *Cross-cultural Pragmatics*. Norwood, NJ: Ablex.

Boden, D. 1994. *The Business of Talk: Organizations in Action*. Cambridge: Polity Press.

Brown, P. 2000. Might be worth getting it done then: realisations of directives in a New Zealand factory. MA thesis, Victoria University of Wellington, New Zealand.

Brown, P. and S. Levinson 1987. *Politeness: Some Universals in Language Usage*. Cambridge: Cambridge University Press.

Brown, P. and L. Robertson 2000. Contextual factors and factory directives. Paper presented at Language and Society Conference, University of Auckland. June.

Brown, R. B. and D. Keegan 1999. Humor in the hotel kitchen, *Humor* 12, 1: 47–70.

Butler, J. 1990. *Gender Trouble: Feminism and the Subversion of Identity*. New York: Routledge.

Cameron, D. 2000. *Good to Talk? Living and Working in a Communication Culture*. London: Sage.

Cameron, D., E. Frazer, P. Harvey, M. B. H. Rampton and K. Richardson 1992. *Researching Language. Issues of Power and Method*. London: Routledge.

Candlin, C. N. and S. Sarangi (eds) forthcoming. Special issue, *Journal of Applied Linguistics*.

Chadsey-Rusch, J. 1992. Toward defining and measuring social skill in employment settings, *American Journal of Mental Retardation* 96: 405–18.

Clark, H. and P. Lucy 1975. Understanding what is meant by what is said: a study in conversationally conveyed request, *Journal of Verbal Learning and Verbal Behaviour* 14: 56–72.

Clouse, R. W. and K. Spurgeon 1995. Corporate analysis of humor, *Psychology – A Quarterly Journal of Human Behaviour* 32, 3–4: 1–24.

Clyne, M. 1994. *Inter-cultural Communication at Work*. Cambridge: Cambridge University Press.

Coates, J. 1996. Women talk: conversation between women friends. Cambridge, MA: Blackwell.

Coates, J. 1997. One-at-a-time: the organization of men's talk. In S. Johnson and U. H. Meinhof (eds), *Language and Masculinity*. Oxford: Blackwell. 107–29.

Consalvo, C. M. 1989. Humor in management: no laughing matter, *Humor* 2–3: 285–97.

Cook-Gumperz, J. 2001. Cooperation, collaboration and pleasure in work. In A. di Luzio, S. Gunthner and F. Orletti (eds), *Culture in Communication: Analyses of Intercultural Situations*. Amsterdam: John Benjamins. 117–39.

Coser, R. L. 1960. Laughter among colleagues: a study of the functions of humor among the staff of a mental hospital, *Psychiatry* 23: 81–95.

Coupland, J. (ed.) 2000. *Small Talk*. London: Longman.

Coupland, J., N. Coupland and J. D. Robinson 1992. 'How are you?': negotiating phatic communion, *Language in Society* 21, 2: 207–30.

Coupland, N., S. Sarangi and C. N. Candlin (eds) 2001. *Sociolinguistics and Social Theory*. Harlow: Longman.

Craig, D. and M. K. Pitts 1990. The dynamics of dominance in tutorial discussions, *Linguistics* 28: 125–38.

Craig, R. T., K. Tracy and F. Spisak 1986. The discourse of requests: assessment of a politeness approach, *Human Communication Research* 12: 437–68.

Crawford, M. 1995. *Talking Difference: On Gender and Language*. London: Sage.

Cuff, E. C. and W. W. Sharrock 1985. Meetings. In T. A. van Dijk (ed.), *Handbook of Discourse Analysis*, Vol. 3. London: Academic Press. 149–59.

Davies, B. 1991. The concept of agency: a feminist poststructuralist analysis, *Social Analysis* 30: 42–53.

Drew, P. and J. Heritage (eds) 1992. *Talk at Work*. Cambridge: Cambridge University Press.

Dwyer, J. 1993 (3rd edn). *The Business Communication Handbook*. Sydney: Prentice Hall.

Eastman, M. 1936. *Enjoyment of Laughter*. London: Hamish Hamilton.

Eckert, P. 2000. *Language Variation as Social Practice*. Oxford: Blackwell.

Eckert, P. and S. McConnell-Ginet 1995. Constructing meaning, constructing selves: snapshots of language, gender, and class from Belten High. In K. Hall and M. Bucholtz (eds), *Gender Articulated: Language and the Socially Constructed Self*. London: Routledge. 469–507.

Edelsky, C. 1981. Who's got the floor? *Language in Society* 10: 383–421.

Eelen, G. 2001. *A Critique of Politeness Theories*. Manchester: St. Jerome's Press.

Ervin-Tripp, S. M. 1976. Is Sybil there? The structure of some American English directives, *Language in Society* 5: 25–66.

Ervin-Tripp, S., J. Guo and M. Lampert 1990. Politeness and persuasion in children's control acts, *Journal of Pragmatics* 14: 307–31.

Ervin-Tripp, S. and M. Lampert 1992. Gender differences in the construction of humorous talk. In K. Hall, M. Bucholtz and B. Moonwomon (eds), *Locating Power: Proceedings of the Second Berkeley Women and Language Conference April 4 and 5 1992, Vol. 1*. Berkeley Women and Language Group: University of California. 108–17.

Fairclough, N. L. 1989. *Language and Power*. Harlow: Longman.

Fairclough, N. L. (ed.) 1992. *Critical Language Awareness*. London: Longman.

Fairclough, N. L. 1995. *Critical Discourse Analysis: Papers in the Critical Study of Language*. London: Longman.

Fillary, R. 1998. Disability: research methodology issues, *Te Reo* 41: 203–7.

Firth, A. (ed.) 1995. *The Discourse of Negotiation: Studies of Language in the Workplace*. Oxford: Pergamon.

Fisher, S. 1982. The decision-making context: how doctors and patients communicate. In R. Pietro (ed.), *Linguistics and Professions*. Norwood, NJ: Ablex. 51–81.

Fletcher, J. K. 1999. *Disappearing Acts: Gender, Power, and Relational Practice at Work*. Cambridge, MA: MIT Press.

Gal, S. 1995. Language, gender, and power: an anthropological review. In K. Hall and M. Bucholtz (eds), *Gender Articulated: Language and the Socially Constructed Self*. London: Routledge. 169–82.

Gatenby, B. and D. Jones (eds) 1995. *Case Studies in Communication*. Auckland: Longman Paul.

Giles, H., N. Coupland and J. Coupland 1991. *Contexts of Accommodation*. Cambridge: Cambridge University Press.

Goffman, E. 1967. *Interaction Ritual: Essays on Face to Face Behaviour*. New York: Anchor Books.

Goffman, E. 1974. *Frame Analysis*. New York: Harper & Row.

Goffman, E. 1981. *Forms of Talk*. Philadelphia: University of Pennsylvania Press.

Graham, E. E., M. J. Papa and G. P. Brooks 1992. Functions of humor in conversation: conceptualization and measurement, *Western Journal of Communication* 56, 1: 161–83.

Greenspan, S. and B. Shoultz 1981. Why mentally retarded adults lose their jobs: social competence as a factor in work adjustment, *Applied Research in Mental Retardation* 2: 23–38.

Gumperz, J. J. 1982. *Discourse Strategies*. Cambridge: Cambridge University Press.

Gumperz, J. J. 1999. On interactional sociolinguistic method. In S. Sarangi and C. Roberts (eds), *Talk, Work and Institutional Order: Discourse in Medical, Mediation and Management Settings*. Berlin: Mouton de Gruyter. 453–71.

Gumperz, J. J., T. C. Jupp and C. Roberts 1979. *Crosstalk: A Study of Cross-cultural Communication*. Southall: National Centre for Industrial Language Training.

Hammond, S. A. 1996. *The Thin Book of Appreciative Inquiry*. Plano, TX: Thin Book.

Hampes, W. P. 1992. Relation between humour and intimacy, *Psychological Reports* 71: 127–30.

Hatch, M. J. and S. B. Ehrlich 1993. Spontaneous humour as an indicator of paradox and ambiguity in organizations, *Organizational Studies* 14, 4: 505–26.

Hatton, C. 1998. Pragmatic language skills in people with intellectual disabilities: a review. *Journal of Intellectual and Development Disability* 23: 79–100.

Hay, J. 1994. Jocular abuse patterns in mixed-group interaction, *Wellington Working Papers in Linguistics* 6: 26–55.

Hay, J. 1995. Gender and humour: beyond a joke. Unpublished Master's thesis, Victoria University of Wellington, Wellington, New Zealand.

Hernal, C. G., M. A. Fennell and C. Miller 1991. Understanding failures in organizational discourse: the accident at Three Mile Island and the Shuttle Challenger Disaster. In C. Bazerman and J. Paradis (eds), *Textual Dynamics of the Professions: Historical and Contemporary Studies of Writing in Professional Communities*. Madison, WI: University of Wisconsin Press. 279–305.

Holdaway, S. 1988. Blue jokes: humour in police work. In C. Powell and G. E. C. Paton (eds), *Humour in Society: Resistance and Control*. London: Macmillan. 106–22.

Holmes, J. 1982. Expressing doubt and certainty in English, *R. E. L. C. Journal* 13, 2: 9–28.

Holmes, J. 1983. The structure of teacher's directives: a sociolinguistic analysis. In J. C. Richards and R. W. Schmidt (eds), *Language and Communication*. London: Longman. 89–115.

Holmes, J. 1984. Modifying illocutionary force, *Journal of Pragmatics* 8, 3: 345–65.

Holmes, J. 1990a. Politeness strategies in New Zealand women's speech. In A. Bell and J. Holmes (eds), *New Zealand Ways of Speaking English*. Clevedon, Avon: Multilingual Matters. 252–76.

Holmes, J. 1990b. Hedges and boosters in women's and men's speech, *Language and Communication* 10, 3: 185–205.

Holmes, J. 1992. Women's talk in public contexts, *Discourse and Society* 3, 2: 131–50.

Holmes, J. 1995. *Women, Men and Politeness*. London: Longman.

Holmes, J. 1997. Women, language and identity, *Journal of Sociolinguistics* 2, 1: 195–223.

Holmes, J. 1999. Managing social talk at work: what does the NESB worker need to know?, *TESOLANZ Journal* 7: 7–19.

Holmes, J. 2000a. Victoria University of Wellington's Language in the Workplace Project: an overview, *Language in the Workplace Occasional Papers* 1.

Holmes, J. 2000b. Women at work: analysing women's talk in New Zealand workplaces, *Australian Review of Applied Linguistics (ARAL)* 22, 2: 1–17.

Holmes, J. 2000c. Doing collegiality and keeping control at work: small talk in government departments. In J. Coupland (ed.), *Small Talk*. London: Longman. 32–61.

Holmes, J. 2000d. Politeness, power and provocation: how humour functions in the workplace, *Discourse Studies* 2, 2: 159–85.

Holmes, J. forthcoming. Power and discourse at work: is gender relevant?

Holmes, J. and D. Brown 1976. Developing sociolinguistic competence in a second language, *TESOL Quarterly* 10, 4: 423–31.

Holmes, J. and R. Fillary 2000. Handling small talk at work: challenges for workers with intellectual disabilities, *International Journal of Disability, Development and Education* 47, 3: 273–91.

Holmes, J., R. Fillary, M. McLeod and M. Stubbe 2000. Developing skills for social interaction in the workplace. *New Zealand Journal of Disability Studies* 7: 70–86.

Holmes, J. and M. Marra 2002. Over the edge? Subversive humour between colleagues and friends, *Humor* 15, 1: 65–87.

Holmes, J. and M. Marra in press. Having a laugh at work: how humour contributes to workplace culture. (To appear in *Journal of Pragmatics*.)

Holmes, J., M. Marra and L. Burns 2001. Women's humour in the workplace: a quantitative analysis, *Australian Journal of Communication* 28, 1: 83–108.

Holmes, J. and M. Stubbe 2001. Managing conflict at work. Paper presented at AAAL, St Louis.

Holmes, J. and M. Stubbe 2003. 'Feminine' workplaces: stereotype and reality. (To appear in J. Holmes and M. Meyerhoff (eds), *Handbook of Language and Gender*. Oxford: Blackwell.)

Holmes, J., M. Stubbe and B. Vine 1999. Constructing professional identity: 'doing power' in policy units. In S. Sarangi and C. Roberts (eds), *Talk, Work and Institutional Order. Discourse in Medical, Mediation and Management Settings*. Berlin: Mouton de Gruyter. 351–85.

Hunston, S. (ed.) 1998. *Language at Work. Selected Papers from the Annual Meeting of the British Association of Applied Linguistics*, University of Birmingham, September 1997. Clevedon: British Association of Applied Linguistics in association with Multilingual Matters.

Hutchby, I. and R. Wooffitt 1998. *Conversation Analysis: Principles, Practices and Applications*. Cambridge: Polity Press.

Ianello, K. 1992. *Decisions Without Hierarchy: Feminist Interventions in Organisation Theory and Practice*. New York: Routledge.

Jefferson, G. 1972. Side sequences. In D. Sudnow (ed.), *Studies in Social Interaction*. New York: Free Press. 294–338.

Jones, D. 1998. Language in the workplace: towards a model for evaluation and development, *Te Reo* 41: 193–5.

Jones, D. and M. Stubbe forthcoming. Communication and the reflective practitioner: collaborations between sociolinguistics and organisational communication.

Jones, K. 1992. A question of context: directive use at a morris team meeting. *Language in Society* 21: 427–45.

Kiesling, S. 2001. 'Now I gotta watch what I say': shifting constructions of gender and dominance in discourse, *Journal of Linguistic Anthropology* 11, 2: 250–73.

Kingfisher, C. P. 1996. Women on welfare: conversational sites of acquiescence and dissent, *Discourse and Society* 7, 4: 531–57.

Kotthoff, H. 1996. Impoliteness and conversational joking: on relational politics, *Folia Linguistica* 30: 299–327.

Kotthoff, H. 1997. The interactional achievement of expert status: creating asymmetries by 'teaching conversational lecture' in TV discussion. In H. Kotthoff and R. Wodak (eds), *Communicating Gender in Context*. Amsterdam: John Benjamins. 139–78.

Kuiper, K. 1991. Sporting formulae in New Zealand English: two models of male solidarity. In J. Cheshire (ed.), *English Around the World*. Cambridge: Cambridge University Press. 200–9.

Laver, J. 1975. Communicative functions of phatic communion. In A. Kendon, R. M. Harris and M. R. Key (eds), *The Organization of Behaviour in Face-to-Face Interaction*. The Hague: Mouton. 215–38.

Laver, J. 1981. Linguistic routines and politeness in greeting and parting. In F. Coulmas (ed.), *Conversational Routine*. The Hague: Mouton. 289–304.

Lee, D. 1992. *Competing Discourses*. London: Longman.

Leech, G. 1983. *Principles of Pragmatics*. London: Longman.

Levine D. C. 1987. Small talk: a big communicative function in the organization? Paper presented at the Annual Meeting of the Eastern Communication Association. Syracuse. EDRS. ED283228.

Linde, C. 1988. The quantitative study of communicative success: politeness and accidents in aviation discourse, *Language in Society* 17, 3: 375–99.

Linell, P. 2001. Dynamics of discourse or stability of structure: sociolinguistics and the legacy from linguistics. In N. Coupland, S. Sarangi and C. N. Candlin (eds), *Sociolinguistics and Social Theory*. Harlow: Longman. 107–26.

Littlewood, W. 2001. Cultural awareness and the negotiation of meaning in intercultural communication, *Language Awareness* 10, 2–3: 189–99.

Malinowski, B. 1949. The problem of meaning in primitive languages. Supplement 1 in C. K. Ogden and I. Richards, *The Meaning of Meaning* (10th edn). London: Routledge & Kegan Paul. 269–336.

Marra, M. forthcoming. Decisions in New Zealand business meetings. Unpublished PhD thesis, Victoria University of Wellington, Wellington, New Zealand.

Martineau, W. H. 1972. A model of the social functions of humour. In J. H. Goldstein and P. E. McGhee (eds), *The Psychology of Humor*. New York: Academic Press. 101–25.

Mooney, M. 1980. The structure of directives in a New Zealand psychiatric clinic. Unpublished Linguistics Honours research project, Victoria University of Wellington, Wellington, New Zealand.

Morand, D. A. 1996a. Dominance, deference, and egalitarianism in organizational interaction: a sociolinguistic analysis of power and politeness, *Organization Science* 7, 5: 544–56.

Morand, D. A. 1996b. Politeness as a universal variable in cross-cultural managerial communication, *International Journal of Organizational Analysis* 4, 1: 52–74.

Morreall, J. 1991. Humor and work, *Humor* 4, 4: 359–73.

Mott, H. and H. Petrie 1995. Workplace interactions: women's linguistic behaviour, *Journal of Language and Social Psychology* 14, 3: 324–36.

Mumby, D. K. 1988. *Communication and Power in Organizations: Discourse, Ideology and Domination*. Norwood, NJ: Ablex.

Neill, D. M. 1996. *Cross-Cultural Communication: Collaboration in Intercultural Discourse: Examples from a Multicultural Workplace*. Frankfurt: Peter Language.

Ng, S. H. and J. J. Bradac 1993. *Power in Language: Verbal Communication and Social Influence*. Newbury Park, CA: Sage.

O'Quin, K. and J. Arnoff 1981. Humor as a technique of social influence, *Social Psychology Quarterly* 44: 349–57.

Pateman, T. 1980. *Language, Truth and Politics: Towards a Radical Theory for Communication*. London: Jean Stroud.

Pauwels, A. 1989. The role of language, language learning and linguistics in cross-cultural communication in the professions, Working Paper 1. National Centre for Community Languages in the Professions, Melbourne: Monash University.

Pearson, B. A. 1988. Power and politeness in conversation: encoding of face-threatening acts at church business meetings, *Anthropological Linguistics* 30: 68–93.

Pilkington, J. 1998. 'Don't try to make out that I'm nice!': the different strategies women and men use when gossiping. In J. Coates (ed.), *Language and Gender: A Reader*. Oxford: Blackwell. 254–69.

Pizzini, F. 1991. Communication hierarchies in humour: gender differences in the obstetrical/gynaecological setting, *Discourse in Society* 2, 4: 477–88.

Pomerantz, A. M. and B. J. Fehr 1997. Conversation analysis: an approach to the study of social action as sense-making practice. In T. van Dijk (ed.), *Discourse as Social Interaction*. Sage: Thousand Oaks. 64–91.

Psathas, G. 1995. *Conversation Analysis: The Study of Talk-in-Interaction*. Thousand Oaks: Sage.

Pschaid, P. 1992. *Language and Power in the Office*. Tübingen: Gunter Narr.

Pufahl Bax, I. 1986. How to assign work in an office: a comparison of spoken and written directives in American English, *Journal of Pragmatics* 10: 673–92.

Roberts, C., E. Davies and T. Jupp 1992. *Language and Discrimination: A Study of Communication in Multi-Ethnic Workplaces*. London: Longman.

Rodrigues, S. B. and D. L. Collinson, 1995. 'Having fun'?: Humour as resistance in Brazil, *Organization Studies* 16, 5: 739–68.

Sarangi, S. and C. Roberts (eds) 1999. *Talk, Work and Institutional Order Discourse in Medical, Mediation and Management Settings*. Berlin: Mouton de Gruyter.

Sarangi, S. and S. Slembrouck 1996. *Language, Bureaucracy and Social Control*. London: Longman.

Scheerhorn, D. R. 1989. Minding your P's and Q's in interpersonal decision-making: the politeness of messages as a consequent of decisional and relational goals. Unpublished PhD thesis, University of Iowa.

Scheeres, H. 1998. New workplaces: talk and teamwork. Paper presented at Sociolinguistics Symposium 12, London.

Sinclair, J. McH. and R. M. Coulthard 1975. *Towards an Analysis of Discourse*. London: Arnold.

Sligo, F., S. Olsson and C. Wallace (eds) 1997. *Perspectives in Business Communication: Theory and Practice*. Palmerston North: Software Technology New Zealand.

Sollitt-Morris, L. 1996. Language, gender and power relationships: the enactment of repressive discourse in staff meetings of two subject departments in a New Zealand secondary school. PhD thesis, Victoria University of Wellington, Wellington, New Zealand.

Sollitt-Morris, L. 1997. Taking a break: humour as a means of enacting power in asymmetrical discourse, *Language, Gender and Sexism* 7, 2: 81–103.

Spencer-Oatey, H. 1992. Pragmatic competence and cross-cultural communication: an analysis of communication between speakers of English and Chinese. Unpublished PhD thesis, Lancaster University, Lancaster, UK.

Spencer-Oatey, H. 2000. Rapport management: a framework for analysis. In H. Spencer-Oatey (ed.), *Culturally Speaking*. London: Continuum.

Stenstrom, A.-B. 1994. *An Introduction to Spoken Interaction*. London: Longman.

Stubbe, M. 1998a. Researching language in the workplace: a participatory model. *Proceedings of the Australian Linguistics Society Conference*. Brisbane, University of Queensland, July. www.english.uq.edu.au/linguistics/als/als98/

Stubbe, M. 1998b. Striking a balance: language, gender and professional identity. *Proceedings of the Fifth Berkeley Women and Language Conference*. Berkeley Women and Language Group: University of California. 545–56.

Stubbe, M. 1999a. 'Just do it . . . !' Discourse strategies for 'getting the message across' in a factory production team. In J. Henderson (ed.), *Proceedings of the 1999 Conference of the Australian Linguistic Society*. www.arts.uwa.edu.au/LingWWW/als99/proceedings

Stubbe, M. 1999b. Just joking and playing silly buggers: humour and teambuilding on a factory production line. Paper presented at NZ Linguistics Society Conference, Massey, 24–26 November.

Stubbe, M. 2000. Talk that works: evaluating communication in a factory production team, *New Zealand English Journal* 14: 55–65.

Stubbe, M. 2001. From office to production line: collecting data for the Wellington Language in the Workplace Project, *Language in the Workplace Occasional Papers* 2.

Stubbe, M. 2003. 'I've got a little problem!' The discourse organisation of task-oriented discussions in professional workplaces. (*Language in the Workplace Occasional Papers 6.*)

Stubbe, M. forthcoming. What *is* miscommunication anyway? Analysing problematic discourse in workplace interactions.

Stubbe, M. and J. Holmes 2000. Talking Maori or Pakeha in English: signalling identity in discourse. In A. Bell and K. Kuiper (eds), *New Zealand English*. Amsterdam: John Benjamins/Wellington: Victoria University Press. 249–78.

Stubbe, M., C. Lane, J. Hilder, E. Vine, B. Vine, J. Holmes, M. Marra and A. Weatherall 2000. Multiple discourse analyses of a workplace interaction. *Wellington Working Papers in Linguistics* 11: 39–85.

Stubbe, M., J. Holmes, B. Vine and M. Marra 2000. Forget Mars and Venus, let's get back to earth!: challenging gender stereotypes in the workplace. In J. Holmes (ed), *Gendered Speech in Social Context*. Wellington: Victoria University Press.

Sultanoff, S. 2002. Taking humor seriously in the workplace. www.humormatters.com/articles/workplac.htm

Swacker, M. 1979. Women's verbal behaviour at learned and professional conferences. In B. Dubois and I. Creuch (eds), *The Sociology of the Languages of American Women*. San Antonio: Trinity University. 155–9.

Talbot, M. M. 1998. *Language and Gender: An Introduction*. Oxford: Polity Press.

Tannen, D. 1990. *You Just Don't Understand: Women and Men in Conversation*. New York: Morrow.

Tannen, D. 1994. *Talking from 9 to 5*. London: Virago Press.

Tannen, D. 1995. The power of talk: who gets heard and why, *Harvard Business Review* 73, 5: 138–48.

Thomas, J. 1995. *Meaning in Interaction*. London: Longman.

Tracy, K. and N. Coupland 1990. Multiple goals in discourse: an overview of issues. In K. Tracy and N. Coupland (eds), *Multiple Goals in Discourse*. Clevedon: Multilingual Matters.

Unger, R. K. (ed.) 1989. *Representations: Social Constructions of Gender*. Amityville, NY: Baywood.

van Dijk, T. A. 1998. Principles of critical discourse analysis. In J. Cheshire and P. Trudgill (eds), *The Sociolinguistics Reader. Vol. 2. Gender and Discourse*. London: Arnold. 367–93.

van Dijk, T. A. 1999. Editorial: critical discourse analysis and conversation analysis, *Discourse and Society* 10, 4: 459–60.

Vine, B. 2001. Workplace language and power: directives, requests and advice. PhD thesis, Victoria University of Wellington, Wellington, New Zealand.

Watts, R. 1992. Relevance and relational work: linguistic politeness as politic behaviour, *Multilingua* 8: 131–66.

Weber, M. 1947. *Max Weber: The Theory of Social and Economic Organization*. Trans. A. M. Henderson and T. Parsons. New York: Free Press.

Weedon, C. 1987. *Feminist Practice and Poststructuralist Theory*. Oxford: Blackwell.

Weigel, M. M. and R. M. Weigel 1985. Directive use in a migrant agricultural community. *Language in Society* 14, 1: 63–79.

Wenger, E. 1998. *Communities of Practice: Learning, Meaning, and Identity*. Cambridge: Cambridge University Press.

Wenger, E. and W. M. Snyder 2000. Communities of practice: the organizational frontier, *Harvard Business Review* January–February: 139–45.

West, C. 1990. Not just 'doctors' orders': directive-response sequences in patients' visits to women and men physicians, *Discourse and Society* 1, 1: 85–112.

Williams, M. 1988. Language taught for meetings and language used in meetings: is there anything in common?, *Applied Linguistics* 9, 1: 45–58.

Willing, K. 1992. *Talking it Through: Clarification and Problem-solving in Professional Work*. NCELTR Research Series. Sydney: Macquarie University.

Winick, C. 1976. The social context of humour, *Journal of Communication* 26: 124–8.

Wolfson, N. 1983. Rules of speaking. In J. C. Richards and R. W. Schmidt (eds), *Language and Communication*. London: Longman. 61–87.

Woods, N. 1989. Talking shop: sex and status as determinants of floor apportionment in a work setting. In J. Coates and D. Cameron (eds), *Women in their Speech Communities: New Perspectives on Language and Sex*. London: Longman. 141–57.

Ziv, A. 1984. *Personality and Sense of Humor*. New York: Springer.

Index

action learning 173
action research 20
advice 54, 70, 150
agendas 72–3
appreciative inquiry 173
attenuation 6, 36, 46, 47–8, 146
Austin, P. 135 n4
authority
   challenges to 7, 58, 119–21
   in problematic talk 148–53
avoidance strategies 159–60

background knowledge 9–10, 13, 23, 25
Bargiela-Chiappini, F. 59
Bergvall, V. L. 104
Bernsten, J. 33
Bradac, J. J. 6, 100
Brown, P. 17 n2, 17 n5, 17 n10, 31, 34, 51, 55 n9, 114

Cameron, D. et al. 20
Case Studies
   humour and workplace culture 1
      123–6
   humour and workplace culture 2
      126–30
   humour and workplace culture 3
      130–3
   meetings 1 78–81
   meetings 2 81–5
CDA *see* Critical Discourse Analysis
CED (Communication Evaluation
   Development) model 173–6

Chadsey-Rusch, J. 171
Cleese, John 169
Clouse, R. W. 135 n6
Clyne, M. 54 n2
Coates, J. 125, 133, 159
coercive discourse 5
collegiality
   amongst men 127
   amongst women 125
   'doing collegiality' 15, 53, 97–100,
      160–1, 168
   humour in 111–14, 125
   see also interpersonal relationships
communication
   emphasis on 172–3
   between ethnic groups 158
   skills and training 169, 171–2,
      173–6
   social constructionist approach
      11–12
Communication Accommodation theory
   6
Communication Evaluation
   Development (CED) model
   173–6
communities of practice 2, 12, 130,
   168
   humour in 15–16, 122–33, 169–70
contestive discourse 8
context 1–3, 8–12
   background knowledge 9–10, 13, 23,
     25
   and dynamics 37–40

context (*continued*)
  immediate discourse 8–9
  institutional/wider context 10–11
  interpersonal relationships 9, 89
  physical setting 9
  workplace culture 2
  see also communities of practice
control acts 54, 54 n2
  see also directives
Cook-Gumperz, J. 12
Coupland, J. et al. 96
Critical Discourse Analysis (CDA) 5
  challenges to authority 7
  coercive discourse 5
  contestive discourse 8
  discourse and inequality 150
  oppressive discourse strategies 100
  repressive discourse strategies 100,
    104
Cuff, E. C. 59
culture 108 n6
  see also communities of practice

decision making 75–7
declaratives 32, 33, 34
deference 6–7, 17 n5, 44–7, 50
directives 31–3, 53–4, 54 n2
  'bald-on-record' 3, 33, 55 n4
  context and dynamics 37–40
  between equals 40–2, 115–16
  in factories 31, 33, 34–7
  imperatives 33–4, 44
  indirect strategies 39–40
  intensifying devices 34–6, 55 n6
  intent structures 32
  'marked choices' 33
  mitigation devices 32, 36–7, 38,
    42–3, 114–15, 116–17, 124
  negotiation 32
  office workers 33–4, 37–40
  to subordinates 33–40
  to superiors *see* requests
  task-oriented 44–6
  '*want*'/'*need*' declaratives 33, 34
  see also hints; requests
directness 7, 49, 146
disability, intellectual 166–7, 168,
  170–1

discourse
  coercive discourse 5
  contestive discourse 8
  formality in public discourse 100
  gender style 136 n9, 159
  institutional discourse 18–19
  reproducing inequality 150
  see also Critical Discourse Analysis
    (CDA); discourse strategies
discourse markers 101, 102, 105
discourse particles 77, 79
discourse strategies
  avoidance 159–60
  directness 7, 49, 146
  discourse markers 101, 102, 105
  discourse particles 77, 79
  echoing devices 43
  hedging *see* hedging devices
  hesitation 7, 32, 46, 48
  imperatives 32, 33–4, 44
  intensifiers 34
  modal verbs 34, 35, 38, 41, 46
  oppression 100
  pragmatic particles 6, 32, 43
  pronouns 35, 38, 41, 46
  qualifiers 46
  repetition 35, 43
  repression 5, 100, 104
  self-deprecation 84, 113–14, 127
  summarising 37, 73, 77, 79–80
  swearing 35
  tags 41, 46
  vagueness 49, 146
Dwyer, J. 63, 64

Eastman, M. 109
echoing devices 43
Ervin-Tripp, S. M. 52, 55 n14
ethnographic information 9, 12, 13, 23,
  108 n6
  see also Maori

face 3, 17 n2
  face attack acts 117, 119, 135 n4
  face needs 3, 77, 80–1, 146–7, 150,
    153, 179
  'off record' acts 51–2
  positive facework 15, 17 n10

factories
    data collection 25–8
    database 13
    directives 31, 33, 34–7
    humour: Case Study 126–30
    jocular abuse 94, 117–18, 128
    meetings 10
    miscommunication 140–4
    participant observation 26
    power and politeness 178–9
    recording talk 26–8
    requests 44
    research feedback 28, 29–30, 30 n5
    small talk 91, 93–4
Fairclough, N. L. 5, 100
Fletcher, J. K. 64, 85, 89, 108 n5, 112
'footing' 38
formality
    in meetings 59–61, 60f, 131
    in public discourse 100
form(s) 17, 31–4, 36–40, 44, 51, 53,
    69, 77, 95, 118–19, 128, 177
function(s) 38, 56, 78, 80, 89–92, 94,
    96–9, 106–7, 109–10, 114, 116,
    119, 146, 165
    multifunctional(ity) 46, 89, 109, 110

gender
    collegiality 125, 127
    in database 12
    discourse style 136 n9, 159
    humour 136 n9
    in meetings 61
goals see meetings: goals; workplace goals
Goffman, E. 12, 17 n2, 38
government departments
    data collection 21
    database 12–13
    interview excerpts 18, 22
    meetings: Case Study 78–81
    negotiating 'downwards' 151–3
    negotiating with the boss 145–6
    small talk 167
    see also meetings; office workers
Greenspan, S. 171

Harris, S. J. 59
Hatton, C. 166

Hay, J. 111, 119, 135 n3, 135 n5
hedging devices
    agreement 42
    hesitation 7
    humour 114, 116
    for mitigation 6, 36, 38, 161
    in negotiation 146
    uses 55 n6
hesitation 7, 32, 46, 48
hints 50–3
    continuum 50–1
    and face 51–2
    humour 52
    routine inferences 52
Holmes, J. 50, 55 n6, 89, 135 n1, 135
    n4, 147
humour 134–5
    amusing workmates 110–14
    Case Study 1 123–6
    Case Study 2 126–30
    Case Study 3 130–3
    challenging authority 119–21
    criticism and 112–13, 116–17
    definition 135 n1
    fantasy sequences 111
    functions in the workplace 109–22,
        135 n2
    gender and 136 n9
    as hedging device 114, 116
    hints 52
    and intellectual disability 170–1
    irony 52, 118, 124
    jocular abuse 94, 117–22, 128,
        132–3, 135 n4, 135 n5
    licensing professional challenge
        117–21
    maintaining good relations 114–17
    in meetings 71, 77, 83–5, 109
    new employees 122, 169–71, 175–6
    nurturing harmonious relationships
        15, 110–17
    as politeness strategy 7–8, 15
    repartee 111, 112
    sarcasm 118, 120, 121, 124, 131–2
    self-deprecation 84, 113–14, 127
    seminars and training 169
    and workplace culture 15–16,
        122–33, 169–70

identity
  social 9, 11, 54
  professional 54
imperatives 32, 33–4, 44
institutional discourse 18–19
insults *see* jocular abuse
intensifiers 34
interaction order 12
interpersonal relationships
  context 9, 89
  cultural specificity 108 n6
  humour and 15, 110–17
  new employees 165–72, 175–6
  relational practice 108 n5, 112
  skills and training 169, 171–2, 173,
    175–6
  see also collegiality
irony 52, 118, 124

Jefferson, G. 69
jocular abuse
  challenging authority 119–22
  between equals 94, 117–19, 132–3,
    135 n4
  in factories 94, 117–18, 128
  office workers 118–19
  towards subordinates 135 n5
Jones, D. viii, ix, 172, 176
Jones, K. 38

Kingfisher, C. P. 104
Kotthoff, H. 119
Kuiper, K. 135 n4

Language in the Workplace Project
    (LWP) 12–14, 17 n7
  data collection 20–9, 107–8 n2;
    (factories and small businesses
    25–8; larger meetings 24–5; office
    workers 21–3)
  database 12–14, 13*f*
  ethnographic information 13, 23, 25
  feedback 19–20, 23, 28, 29–30,
    30 n5
  methodology 13–14, 19–20
  objectives 12
Laver, J. 96, 99, 108 n4
Levine, D. C. 102–3

Levinson, S. 17 n2, 17 n5, 17 n10, 34,
    51, 114
Linde, C. 108 n4
Linell, P. 11
LWP *see* Language in the Workplace
    Project

management between equals
  directives 40–2, 115–16
  humour 115–16
  mitigation 42–3, 161
  off-record resistance 156–62
  on-record disagreement 154–6
  power and politeness 40–3
  see also hints
Maori 12, 17 n9
  power and inequality 156–60, 175
  solidarity 160–1
Marra vii, ix, 24, 71, 77
meetings
  agendas 72–3
  Case Study 1 78–81
  Case Study 2 81–5
  chairing 57–8, 64–5, 70, 71, 73,
    79–80, 82–3
  data collection 24–5
  decision making 75–7
  defining 59
  directives 32
  experts 76, 77
  factory 10
  formality 59–61, 60*f*, 131
  gender in 61
  goals 61–5, 64*f*
  humour 71, 77, 83–5, 109
  interpersonal dimensions 80–1, 83–5
  keeping on track 73–5
  linear structure 68–71, 68*f*, 78–9
  management strategies 71–8
  participants 61, 71, 77–8
  power and politeness 5–6, 56, 57–8,
    64–5, 71, 85–6
  purposes 61–5, 64*f*
  recording talk 24–5
  research studies 56, 57
  small talk before 87–8, 90–1, 107–8
    n2
  social objectives 64–5

meetings (*continued*)
  spiral/cyclical pattern 68, 68f,
    69–71, 81–2
  structure 65–71, 78–9, 81–2
  subversion 58
  summarising progress 73, 77, 79–80
  three-phase structure 65–7
method/methodology/methodological
    vii, viii, 13–14, 18–30, 51, 151
minimisers 47
miscommunication 137–44
  on factory floor 140–4
  office workers 137–8, 139–40
  see also problematic talk
mitigation
  between equals 42–3, 161
  strategies *see* mitigation devices
  to subordinates 35–6, 38
mitigation devices 32, 36, 42–3
  attenuators 6, 36, 46, 47–8
  echoing devices 43
  'familial' terms 124
  hedging 6, 36, 38, 161
  hesitation 46, 48
  I suggest 38
  minimisers 47
  mitigated declaratives 32
  modal verbs 38, 41, 46
  positive reinforcement 36
  pragmatic particles 6, 43
  praise 36
  qualifiers 46
  repetition 43
  summarising 37
  tag questions 41
  tags 46
  we/you 38, 41, 46
  see also humour
modal verbs 34, 35, 38, 41, 46
Mooney, M. 51
Morreall, J. 169
Mumby, D. K. 56

narrative 84, 125
negotiation
  with the boss 144–8
  in directives 32
  hedging 146

  with subordinates 148–53
  see also requests
New Zealand 12, 31, 33, 138
Ng, S. H. 6, 100

office workers
  contextual information 23
  data collection 21–3
  database 13
  directives 33–4, 37–40
  hints 51–3
  humour: Case Studies 123–6, 130–3
  jocular abuse 118–19
  making contact 21–2
  management between equals 40–3
  miscommunication 137–8, 139–40
  negotiating 'downwards' 148–53
  negotiating with the boss 144–8
  recording talk 22
  requests 44–50
  research feedback 23, 29–30
  see also meetings; small talk and social
    chat

participant observation 26
Pateman, T. 15
politeness
  for conflict avoidance 160, 161–2
  deference 6–7, 17 n5, 46
  between equals 40–3
  humour 7–8, 15
  negative 17 n5
  towards subordinate 5–6, 58, 153
  see also face
power
  coercive 6
  collaborative 6
  covert strategies 100–1
  and deference 7
  definitions 3–5
  'doing power' 2, 58, 73, 100–6
  'expert' power 4, 76, 156
  formality 100
  hedging 161
  oppressive discourse 100
  'power to' vs 'power over' 6
  relative power 4–5
  repressive discourse 100, 104

power (*continued*)
  resistance to 104
  societal issues 156–60, 175
  see also Critical Discourse Analysis
    (CDA)
pragmatic particles 6, 32, 43
problematic talk 138–9, 162–3
  attenuation 146
  between equals 154–62
  face needs 146–7, 150, 153
  hedging 146
  institutional authority 148–51, 153
  negotiating 'downwards' 148–53
  negotiating with the boss 144–8
  off-record resistance 156–62
  on-record disagreement 154–6
  politeness 153, 160, 161–2
  see also miscommunication
pronouns 35, 38, 41, 46

qualifiers 46

rapport management 56
recording talk
  factories and small businesses
    26–8
  meetings 24–5
  office workers 22
  video recording 24–5
reflection as learning strategy 172–6
relational practice 108 n5, 112
Remlinger, K. A. 104
repetition 35, 43
requests 44–50
  deference 44–7, 50
  in factories 44
  objectives 44, 46–8
  strategies 44, 46, 47–50
  task-oriented directives 44–6
  see also negotiation
research feedback 19–20, 23, 28, 29–30,
    30 n5
Roberts, C. 22, 172
Robertson, L. 55 n9

Sarangi, S. 22, 172
sarcasm 118, 120, 121, 124, 131–2
self-deprecation 84, 113–14, 127

sequence 61, 69, 84, 92, 110–12, 115,
    123, 133–4
Sharrock, W. W. 59
Shoultz, B. 171
small businesses
  data collection 25–8
  database 13
  meetings: Case Study 81–5
  miscommunication 140
  research feedback 28
  see also office workers
small talk and social chat 15, 88–9,
    106–7
  as boundary marker 90–3
  data collection 107–8 n2
  distribution in the workplace 89–96
  doing collegiality 97–100, 168
  doing power 100–6
  inside work talk 93–6, 108 n4,
    166–7
  and intellectual disability 166–7, 168,
    170–1
  and job loss 171
  before meetings 87–8, 90–1, 107–8
    n2
  new employees 166–9, 175–6
  relational practice 108 n5, 112
  skills and training 171–2
  social functions of 96–106, 166–9
Snyder, W. M. 130
social chat *see* small talk and social chat
social constructionism 11–12, 89
social identity 9
social integration
  and intellectual disability 166–7, 168,
    170–1
  interpersonal skills 169, 171–2, 173,
    175–6
  managing humour 122, 169–71,
    175–6
  small talk 166–9, 175–6
social reality 3
sociolinguistic research 18–19
  see also Language in the Workplace
    Project (LWP)
Sollitt-Morris, L. 100
speech act(s) 15, 31, 110, 114, 120
Spencer-Oatey, H. 56, 156

Spurgeon, K. 135 n6
Stubbe ix, 172, 177
subversion 58
Sultanoff, S. 171
summarising 37, 73, 77, 79–80
swearing 35

tags 41, 46
Tannen, D. 159
team-building 14, 64
'thick' description 22

vagueness 49, 146
van Dijk, T. A. 150
video recording 24–5
Vine, B. 54, 54 n2, 55 n7, 55 n8, 70

'want'/'need' declaratives 33, 34
Wenger, E. 2, 123, 130
Winick, C. 120
workplace culture *see* communities of
    practice
workplace goals 14, 53